CH SPURGEON'S FORGOTTEN COLLEGE ADDRESSES

Forgotten annual conference, college and communion addresses

A Sequel to 'Forgotten Prayer Meeting Addresses.'
Compiled from The Sword And The Trowel
by Terence Peter Crosby

Day One

© Day One Publications 2016
First printed 2016

ISBN 978–1–84625–543–4

British Library Cataloguing in Publication Data available

Unless otherwise indicated, Scripture quotations in this publication are from the
Authorized (King James) Version (AV), Crown copyright

Published by Day One Publications
Ryelands Road, Leominster, HR6 8NZ
☎ 01568 613 740 FAX 01568 611 473
email—sales@dayone.co.uk
web site—www.dayone.co.uk
North American—e-mail—sales@dayonebookstore.com
North American—web site—www.dayonebookstore.com

Cover design by Wayne McMaster
Printed by TJ International

Contents

Contents

An All-Round Ministry

S purgeon's magazine, *The Sword and the Trowel*, provided the material for various collections of his addresses and writings compiled after his death in 1892. Among these was *An All-Round Ministry*, published in 1900 and containing twelve of his Presidential addresses at the Annual Conference of the Pastors' College, namely those delivered in 1872, 1874, 1875, 1877, 1880 to 1882 and 1886 to 1890. The 1876 address, *The Holy Spirit in connection with our ministry*, had already reappeared in the second series of *Lectures to my Students*, published in 1881; in 1883 Spurgeon was for the first time absent due to illness. The 1891 address, *The greatest fight in the world* (1 Timothy 6:12, delivered on 21 April 1891), was published separately in 1891. Of the other addresses the following also appeared later in *The Sword and the Trowel* and are here reproduced.

Annual Conference addresses in this volume showing original years of publication in *The Sword and the Trowel*

1892

1. p. 389 The great shield of faith (Ephesians 6:16, delivered at Upton Chapel, Lambeth, on Monday 20 April 1891)

1896

2. p. 353 The reality of religion (delivered at Dalston Junction Chapel on Monday 6 May 1889)

1909

3. pp. 445 & 493 (2 parts) Stand fast (delivered on Tuesday 22 April 1884)

1910

4. pp. 1, 49 & 105 (3 parts) Taking stock (Mark 16:15–16—a note in *The Sword and the Trowel*, May 1878, indicates that this was the address given on the morning of Tuesday 9 April 1878)

Details of 8th to 27th Inaugural Conference addresses
1872–1891 (* = apparently unpublished)

Year	Date	Subject
1872	Tuesday 16 April	Faith
1873	Tuesday 1 April	Encouragements in pastoral work*
1874	Tuesday 14 April	'Forward!'
1875	Tuesday 13 April	Individuality and its opposite
1876	Tuesday 4 April	The Holy Spirit in connection with our ministry
1877	Tuesday 10 April	How to meet the evils of the age
1878	Tuesday 9 April	Taking stock
1879	Tuesday 6 May	'To the discouraged'*
1880	Tuesday 20 April	'A new departure'
1881	Tuesday 3 May	Light, fire, faith, life, love
1882	Tuesday 18 April	Strength in weakness
1883	ABSENT DUE TO SICKNESS	
1884	Tuesday 22 April	Stand fast
1885	Tuesday 5 May	The glory of God the preacher's one aim*
1886	Wednesday 5 May	What we would be
1887	Tuesday 19 April	Stewards
1888	Tuesday 17 April	The evils of the present time, and our object, necessities, and encouragements
1889	Tuesday 7 May	The preacher's power, and the conditions of obtaining it
1890	Tuesday 22 April	The minister in these times
1891	Tuesday 21 April	The greatest fight in the world

Some Friday morning addresses delivered at the annual Pastors' College Conferences appeared in *The Metropolitan Tabernacle Pulpit* (nos. 2213, 2879, 3211 and, probably, 2185). The 1887 inaugural address, *Stewards*, included in *An All-Round Ministry*, was later repeated as *Metropolitan Tabernacle Pulpit* no. 3350.

Lectures to my Students

Some of the lectures in the four volumes of Spurgeon's *Lectures to my Students* had also appeared first in *The Sword and the Trowel*, while some others which were not included can be found in the volumes of Spurgeon's contributions to the periodical reprinted by Pilgrim Publications, namely 'Preach Christ in a Christly manner' (March 1881), 'How to attract a congregation' (August 1883), 'A thump from a "down-caster"' (October 1884), 'Long sermons' (February 1886) and 'Alexander on Bucephalus' (August 1886). A few others reappeared in the first section of *The Soul Winner*, published in 1895 (see below). But there are several other lectures which have appeared only in *The Sword and the Trowel* in later years, mostly after Spurgeon's death, and these are here reproduced as a sequel to *Lectures to my Students*.

Lectures to Spurgeon's students in this volume showing original years of publication in *The Sword and the Trowel*

1888

5. p. 569 What we aim at (September 1888)

1891

6. p. 545 A reminiscence and a warning (Jeremiah 45:5)

1892

7. p. 685 Beaten oil for the light (Exodus 27:20)

1893

8. pp. 357 & 421 (2 parts) Gifts neglected and gifts stirred up (1 Timothy 4:14 & 2 Timothy 1:6)

1894

9. pp. 481 & 529 (2 parts) The first Baptist minister (Mark 6:20; John 5:33, 35; 10:41; Acts 13:25)

1895

10. pp. 157 & 205 (2 parts) Young preachers not to be despised (1 Timothy 4:12–16—delivered in 1887)

The following lectures have been omitted from this volume:—
In *The Soul-Winner* (1895):
    What is it to win a soul?
    Qualifications for soul-winning—Godward
    Obstacles to soul-winning
In *C. H. Spurgeon's Sermons preached on unusual occasions* (Pilgrim Publications, 1978):
    Ministerial joys (an address to the students of the Pastors' College, on one of their visits to 'Westwood'—*The Sword and the Trowel*, September 1896).

Also included:

Till He Come

The Sword and the Trowel also provided all the material for this posthumous collection of twenty-one communion meditations and addresses, published in 1896. Nine of these items also reappeared in the posthumous volumes of *The Metropolitan Tabernacle Pulpit* (nos. 2982, 2990, 3107, 3124, 3249, 3267, 3295, 3307 & 3319). The final address in *Till He Come* (Revelation 1:17–18) was delivered at the close of one of the Pastors' College Conferences and can be dated to Friday 21 April 1882.

Some of the addresses were delivered to congregations of thousands at the Metropolitan Tabernacle and others to small gatherings in Spurgeon's sitting-room at Mentone in the South of France, his usual winter retreat for almost the last twenty years of his life. The following addresses fall into the same categories.

Communion addresses in this volume showing original years of publication in *The Sword and the Trowel*

1896

17. p. 585 Christ's superlative loveliness (Song of Solomon 5:9–16—Communion meditation)

1903

18. p. 497 He shall see his seed (Isaiah 53:10—Communion address at Mentone, Lord's Day afternoon, 4 December 1887)

19. p. 545 Signs of the Saviour (Matthew 12:39–42—Communion address at Mentone, Lord's Day afternoon, 15 December 1889)

20. p. 593 Grace for grace (John 1:16—Communion address at Mentone, Lord's Day afternoon, 8 December 1889)

1904

21. p. 441 Separation from the world (2 Corinthians 6:15–18—United Communion Service, The Metropolitan Tabernacle, probably on Monday evening, 15 November 1880)

1910

22. p. 573 At the Lord's Table (before Communion Service at the Metropolitan Tabernacle, Monday evening, 12 February 1866)

Also included: more Mentone messages

1893

23. p. 1 The Sabbatic year in the olive garden (Exodus 23:10–11)

1894

24. p. 1 The gleanings of the olives (Deuteronomy 24:20)
25. p. 349 A land of olive oil (Deuteronomy 8:8)

This volume is completed by an expanded version of the chronological index to Spurgeon's sermons which originally appeared in the fourth volume of *365 Days with Spurgeon*. In the years since its publication it has been possible to date several more undated sermons; in addition relevant items which appeared in *The Sword and the Trowel* have been included, together with several known Bible references of sermons of which there appears to be no trace.

Acknowledgements

As with previous volumes in this series I am grateful to those whose assistance has been invaluable: to Judy Powles, Librarian of Spurgeon's College, for granting access to the original materials; to Dr Digby James, for his photographic and computing skills; and to Mrs Trudy Kinloch, for her editorial work.

Terence Peter Crosby

East Grinstead

'We must have him'*

I AM glad, dear friends, to see so many of you coming here spontaneously this evening. I cannot but believe, seeing this, that God did bless the Word yesterday to many of you. The best news I have heard for many a day was when I was seeing enquirers after last Sabbath evening's sermon; a brother said to me, 'Ah! sir, you should have been up in the top gallery to see how many people were weeping and how many there seemed to be impressed.' As I looked round I could myself tell, by the sight of pocket-handkerchiefs, that something was going on. You know I was not talking to you about your mother's death, or about funerals, and all that kind of thing, making an appeal to your feelings. I was just quietly talking about judgment to come, speaking God's own Word as best I could, and feeling that God was speaking to you, and I was so glad. I do feel, my fellow-members of this church, that we cannot exist as a church without being all of us fully in earnest. The fact is, the colossal size of this church requires that we should always be at a burning-heat to be kept together as a mass. We must dissolve and melt away, we must cease to be, if we cease to live with the life, and power, and energy of the Holy Ghost within us. Nothing will do but that we must have a momentum equal to our bulk. There must be a motion forward, a velocity equal to our bulk, or else we shall surely rot above ground. As for my own personal piety, I do feel that when I am not warmed to glorify God my religion yields to me no comfort, and I could almost give up were it not for the grace of God. When I cannot feel my heart warm, cold religion is the worst dish on the table. Cold religion gives no comfort to the soul that receives it, and is consequently of little or no benefit to those who are round about. I never feel afraid of your getting too earnest. If you had not a solid groundwork of doctrine, if you did not receive the doctrines of grace, I might fear that you would run into the wildest excesses; but being grounded and founded upon the covenant truth and the eternal purposes of God in our salvation, the more fire we can have the better. It is here that we are more likely to be deficient than in any other point. When we get warm with the love of Christ, we do not know how much comfort we give ourselves, nor how much good we do to others. Unless we are all active, do you not know that we shall soon all be mischief-makers? If we are not all of us earnest about souls we shall be worse than useless, for we shall begin to do mischief in the Church of God. In every agency we have at work, if God does not own it, what a waste of effort there is, but if God only blesses it, what must the result be? See, dear friends, we have several agencies in which we rejoice, and for which we thank God every time we bow the knee. I am sure when I looked at the class that I addressed last Sunday, I could only praise God that there was such an one. Then I remembered that there was a much larger class downstairs, and there are our young brethren in the College, scores of whom go forth to preach the Word every Sabbath day; and, oh! what must the result be if we get a blessing upon it all! But if we do not get a blessing, the whole thing is a mockery; we have a name to live, but it is a spiritual death upon a large scale. If it must come to this, I implore the Lord to let me die before your spiritual life is thus diminished. I would sooner be banished from the earth, I would sooner be banished utterly from the world, than I would see this church merely existing, as some churches do, without any life, or energy, or power. To us the Holy Spirit is absolutely indispensable. We cannot do without him at all. *We must have him,* and it is only by his power that we are kept together, and only by his energy can we by any possibility remain. Yes, WE MUST HAVE HIM.

And what a joy it is to hear the cries of converts, and what sweet music to hear them say, 'What must I do to be saved?' What holy mirthfulness it excites in every Christian's breast to know that sinners are saved. What is the joy of the Christian man who becomes a father in God of souls born again! What is the holy exhilaration of the spirit of the Christian matron who becomes a mother in Israel! You young and you old, you who have known the Lord for years, and you who found him but yesterday, do seek, as you may be able, to find out the lost sheep of the house of Israel. Oh! that we might see the blessing of God resting upon all our churches! We do not want it upon our own church alone, but we want to see *every* church blessed. We do not want the rain to come only upon our garden, while every other plot is dry, but we want the whole sky to be covered with the cloud of divine mercy, so that the drops may descend upon every hill of Zion.

Foreword

Note

*   A prayer meeting address, published in *The Sword and the Trowel* 1905, p. 280.

The great shield of faith

Address at the conference public meeting at Upton Chapel, Lambeth, on Monday 20 April 1891*

'Above all, taking the shield of faith, wherewith ye shall be able to quench all the fiery darts of the wicked.'—Ephesians 6:16.

DEAR FRIENDS,—These brethren have come home from the war, and they are going out again very soon. They will be returning to hard fighting, bleeding wounds, a great deal of suffering, and very little of earthly honour and glory; for they are good soldiers of Jesus Christ, called to endure hardness for his name's sake.

I think I can say of the brethren I see before me, that they have brought their shields home with them. You recollect the terse admonition of the brave Spartan mother to her son, when he was going forth to fight for his country: 'Either come back *with* your shield, or *on* it;' that is to say, 'Either bring back your shield when you return as a conqueror, or if you are killed on the battlefield, let it be your bier, and be brought back dead upon it; but on no account be parted from your shield.' There are some of our brethren who have not come back from the war; over them we sorrow, and yet rejoice; for they have received the victor's crown of glory; but most of our company have come home, bringing their shields with them; they have not cast away their confidence, 'which hath great recompence of reward.'

This shield, mentioned by the Apostle, was a large one; it was not the small round shield that was worn on the arm, useful as that was when men were fighting at close quarters; but this was a very large shield, as large as a door, and the soldier who stood behind it was covered by it from head to foot. Our brother Johnson, when he came back from Africa, told us that he always knew when there was going to be a fight amongst the natives, for they took the doors from their huts, and used them as shields; battle-doors, I suppose they might be called. The shield here mentioned was this kind of battle-door, a great all-covering defence, behind which the Christian warrior was preserved from all the fiery darts of the wicked. The gospel which we believe, the faith which we hold, covers us from head to foot, and we can hide behind it, secure against every enemy of our souls.

What is this faith, which is like a shield? Well, first of all, it is faith in God. Dear brethren, *we believe in God;* we believe in him up to the hilt, do we not? We believe that there is a God; he is a real factor in our lives;—

'A living, bright reality.'

We trust in God whatever happens to us. I think you must have heard of that remarkable utterance of our beloved brother, Dr Saphir. His wife lay dead, and he himself was very ill—he has since 'gone home'—but when our good friend, Dr Sinclair Paterson, went to see him, he quoted this text, 'God is light, and in him is no darkness at all.' We believe in God; there is nothing wrong in him. Let him teach us what he will, we believe in him. Let him do with us what he will; we believe in him. Let him give us what he will; let him take from us what he will; we will not quarrel with God, for we believe in him, we trust him implicitly. By faith we plunge into this blessed sea of the eternal Godhead, and find 'waters to swim in.' Yes, we believe in God.

And *we believe in his son, Jesus Christ.* O my brethren, what a joy it is to know the Mediator, and his precious blood! We cannot do without the Christ of God; God in our nature, the ever-blessed One, our Substitute, and so our Redeemer. We believe in him. Yes, we believe in the Christ of Calvary: 'the gospel of the shambles', as blasphemous mouths have dared to call it, is our gospel. Many saints have gone to the shambles for it, being 'accounted as sheep for the slaughter'; and so would we, right cheerfully, rather than give up this glorious truth. This is our great shield, that covers us from head to foot, even the blood and righteousness of our Lord Jesus Christ.

'Midst flaming worlds, in these array'd,
With joy shall I lift up my head.'

We believe in the Word of God; we are old-fashioned enough to stand firm in our belief in our mother's Bible, our father's Bible. The 'higher critics' would tear this precious Book to pieces if they could; I do not know what they would not do with it if they could have their way. I was informed, this afternoon, that a tutor of a college had been teaching the students under his care that Matthew, Mark, Luke, and John did not write the four Gospels that bear their names. I can quite believe that he said it; and I should have believed my informant if he had told me that the man declared that there never were any Gospels at all. Nothing surprises me now; I am quite prepared to hear, not only that Moses did not write the Book of Genesis, but that nobody else wrote it, and that there is not such a Book in existence. My powers of belief have become very large with regard to the 'broad school' of the present day; I believe that, 'because they received not the love of the truth, that they might be saved,' for this cause God has sent them 'strong delusion, that they should believe a lie' (2 Thessalonians 2:10–11); and it is my firm conviction that any lie is more likely to be believed by them than the truth of God. A spirit of falsehood has taken possession of many who set themselves up as leaders and teachers of others.

But *we* believe in this Book; and, amongst other precious things in it, we believe in its promises. Oh, how often has our heart been lifted up when some choice word of promise has been laid home to our soul by the Holy Ghost! I stand behind the promises of God as a Roman soldier stood behind his great shield; and I defy the devil himself to get at me there. I hope that none of you have come to the point of criticizing God's promises instead of believing them. Nay, nay, nay; when a man is hard up, he never criticizes a cheque, but he goes to the bank, and gets the cash for it; and when we are in great and growing need, we do not criticize the promises of God; but we take them to the Bank of Faith, and God turns them into current coin of the kingdom of heaven.

Then, next, *we believe in God's Covenant.* That is a strange, uncouth word, to some people's ears. We have friends about who have never heard it; and if their pastors were asked why they never preached about the covenant, they would reply, 'Covenant! That is a Scotch thing, is it not? Something to do with the Puritans, and men of that ilk? They are all dead now; at least, nearly all; there are just a few of them left, like fossils of the olden time; they cling to this obsolete form of religion, but there are so few of them that they will soon be quite extinct!' *So they say,* brethren; but we shall see; and meanwhile, we poor fossils *do* believe in the covenant;

we are almost as absurd as David, who said, 'He hath made with me an everlasting covenant, ordered in all things, and sure.' He who understands the covenant has reached the very core and marrow of the gospel; but how few do care about it nowadays! Yet behind that glorious truth you and I can hide in safety, like warriors behind their great shields, protected from every foe.

Once more, dear friends, *we believe in the Spirit of God*. 'I believe in the Holy Ghost,' is not with us a mere formal expression; but the utterance of our heartfelt conviction. I have heard of a Church school, in which the children were taught the Apostles' Creed, and each child had to say a sentence. One day the clergyman came in, and asked them to repeat it to him. They managed all right for a time, but all of a sudden there was an awkward silence. The clergyman said, 'Why don't you go on?' One trembling little voice replied, 'Please, sir, the boy that believes in the Holy Ghost isn't here today.' I fear that is true of many churches and many pulpits; those who believe in the Holy Ghost are not there! His very name is scarcely heard in some places of worship; and all ascription of glory and honour to him is lost in the mention of an 'influence.' The glorious Third Person of the Sacred Trinity is now generally concealed under the neuter pronoun 'it', as though the modern school cared for him no more than anything else that they might call 'it.' Brethren, he is much more than an 'it' to us; we believe in the Holy Ghost, and behind him we hide ourselves and our teaching; and we feel that there we are secure against all the assaults of our adversaries.

There is one aspect of our great shield in which many brethren are increasingly rejoicing. *We believe in the second coming of Christ.* Some of our friends have no idea of the force and joy that come to the man who, by faith, has this thought constantly before his mind, 'Christ is coming; Christ is coming.' Our Lord's words are, not merely, 'I come quickly,' but, 'I am coming quickly.' He is already on the road, the axles of his chariot-wheels are red hot, the heavenly coursers are hastening onwards with all speed. He is coming quickly; it is a long way he has to come; he has had many things to do while he has been away; he had to go to heaven to prepare a place for his people, and when he has done that, he will come again. He will be here soon; let us cry to him, 'Come, Lord Jesus, come quickly, before thy truth utterly perishes out of the earth!'

'Lift your heads, ye friends of Jesus,
  Partners of his sufferings here;
Christ to all believers precious,
  Lord of lords shall soon appear:
    Mark the tokens
Of his heavenly kingdom near!'

We hide behind this faith in him that cometh quickly, and we feel perfectly secure and content, blessed be his holy name!

Paul says that, with this great shield of faith, we 'shall be able to quench all the fiery darts of the wicked.' Does the devil ever attack ministers? Brother Williams, I expect you find, as I and all our brethren do, that he singles out ministers for his fiercest assaults. His tactics are like those of the king of Syria, when he said to his captains, 'Fight neither with small nor great, save only with the king of Israel.' So Satan says to his followers, 'Pick out the man who leads the way, and give him the hardest blows you can strike, shoot at him the most fiery arrows you have in your quivers.' Yes, dear friends, you who are in business, and are troubled by bad debts, competition in trade, and so on, need not imagine that you are the only persons who have trials and temptations. I do not know that I would change temptations with you, I had rather bear the ills I have than fly to others that I know not of; but yet I would not advise any man to desire to endure the temptations that fall to my lot; and I expect my brethren here would all say the same. If they could hold up their shields, and you could see them, you would perceive that they bear many marks of the fray. They are honourable marks, for the shield that is like glass, and has never been in battle, is no credit to a warrior. You would see black spots, as though fire had touched the shields; and so it has, for the fiery arrows from Satan's bow were quenched there. If those shields had been made of wood or tow, they would have been all ablaze long ago; but having come from the heavenly armoury, the fiery darts could not set them on fire, although they left the mark where they struck the shield. Some of our shields are all dinted and bruised by the blows received on many a hard-fought field; but they have always quenched the enemy's fiery darts, and made them fall powerless to the ground.

I will mention some of the fiery darts that Satan hurls at us. Here is a very common one: '*If you preach that doctrine, you will lose some of your best friends.*' The minister, who casts away his great shield of faith, says to himself, 'I believe that truth; but if I preach it, I shall offend Mr So-and-So. He is a good subscriber, and very kind to me, and I cannot afford to lose his help. I do not feel called to take that text next Sunday.' That fiery dart has wounded him, and he will not easily recover from its effects. Perhaps some of you know what it is to have a deacon rush into the vestry, just as you are going to preach, to tell you that Mrs So-and-So has given up her sittings, and will never come to the chapel again, because of some observation you made the previous Sabbath-day, which was so dreadfully personal. You had no intention of saying anything of the kind, you only delivered the message that your Master gave you. That is one of the 'fiery darts of the wicked.' How shall you meet it? Get behind your great shield, have faith in God, believe that he will bear you through unscathed; and down will go that fiery arrow to the earth, quenched.

Here is another of Satan's suggestions: '*You will not have anything to preach about soon; you will be quite spun out.*' That fiery dart may not come near some of you; but it has been aimed at me many a time. Some of our brethren are very hard-headed, and are therefore not affected by temptations that are very trying to others. I have heard of a brother, who was travelling by railway, and he would put his head out of the carriage window; so the guard said to him, 'You must not put your head out, for there is some ironwork under one of the bridges, that might get damaged if your head struck it.' All ministers are not hard-headed enough to injure ironwork; and there are times when our poor, suffering brains are sorely perplexed as to what we shall say to the people. Then is the time to hide behind our great shield, and trust in God to give us the message he wants us to speak in his name.

Some brethren have another fiery dart shot at them: '*How will you get shoes for the children? Where is the money coming from to meet that grocery bill, and the rent and taxes?*' The man who has not faith in his God, and faith in his call to the ministry, will give up the work, and run away from it. If God has not called him to the work, he had better give it up; but if the Lord has counted him faithful, putting him into the ministry, he hides himself behind his shield, and trusts in God for the shoes, and the money, and everything else.

One of the most fiery of all Satan's arrows is this: '*You have not had any conversions for ever so long; you are no use in the ministry.*' It may happen, even to a most useful brother, that there may come a lull in his work: the good people, who were converted under his ministry, have left the town or village, and others are slow to fill their places, and he does not see the church flourishing as it once did. I am very apt to get depressed, so I can sympathize with our brethren when they are 'down in the dumps'; and if we do not see the fruit of our labours, we ought to be troubled, and we ought to look carefully into our own hearts to see if there is anything there to hinder the blessing from coming. If we have to ask, with Isaiah, 'Who hath believed our report?' let us cry mightily to the Lord, whose 'remembrancers' we are, and 'take no rest, and give him no rest, till he establish, and till he make Jerusalem a praise in the earth.' (Isaiah 62:7. R.V.) So shall this fiery dart be quenched.

If all these arrows fail, the devil will try another shaft: '*Perhaps there is no truth in the gospel, after all; possibly it is all a delusion.*' What man, who really thinks for himself, has not sometimes been assailed with doubts concerning even the fundamentals of our holy faith? If he is a reader of modern religious literature, and is brought into contact with ministers of the broad school, he will have a plentiful crop of doubts very speedily. I might not have had such an intense loathing of the new theology if I had not seen so much of its evil effects. I could tell you of a preacher of unbelief, whom I have seen, in my own vestry, utterly broken down, driven almost to despair, and having no rest for the sole of his foot until he came back to simple trust in the atoning sacrifice. If he were speaking to you, he would say, 'Cling to your faith, brethren; if you once throw away your shield, you will lay yourself open to imminent dangers and countless wounds; for nothing can protect you but the shield of faith.'

The last fiery dart of the devil may be this: '*The gospel is true; but have* YOU *any part or lot in the matter?*' 'Do ministers ever have to ask that question?' enquired one. I am sorry that we ever should have to ask it; but remember—

'He that never doubted of his state,
He may, perhaps he may, too late.'

It is not altogether an evil thing to be obliged once more to 'examine yourselves, whether ye be in the faith;' on the contrary, it is what we are bidden to do. Still, after years of communion with Christ, the suggestion that we have no saving interest in his death is a fiery dart, and nothing but the shield of faith can quench it. God help us all to hide behind that great shield!

Now, in closing, I want just to say two or three things about this shield. If any of you here have not believed in the Word of God, and in the Christ of God, you will never get rest until you do believe. There is no rest for the soul anywhere else except in the finished work of the Lord Jesus Christ. The man who has Christ, has rest; but no other man has it. There is no rest for the intellect, for the heart, for desire, for hope, for faith, for love, but on the pierced hand of Christ, and in his wounded side. Get there, and you shall find rest unto your souls.

If you have faith, get more faith. You will not err in believing too much, if you believe all that there is in the Scriptures, and all that is conceivable concerning Christ. As the hymn puts it,—

'Believe, and keep right on believing.'

Keep on believing; more and more make thyself sure that these things are eternal verities; and whereas thou couldst have questioned once, seek to attain that assurance that is past all questioning, so that thou canst say, 'I know whom I have believed, and am persuaded that he is able to keep that which I have committed unto him against that day.' It is a good thing to get to that point of definite belief from which even Satan cannot drive you with all his fiery darts.

Then, *hide behind your shield.* The ancient warriors hid themselves so completely behind their great shields that they were not visible to their foes, and therefore were not exposed to their darts. It is a grand thing when even the devil cannot get at us because we are covered by the great shield of faith. It is well when our people do not remember anything about *how* we preached because they are so taken up with *what* we preached. Let it be our delight to be hidden behind the faith that we proclaim to others.

But *if we do not let the enemy see us, we must let him see our shield.* Whenever Satan comes to our places of worship—and he will be among the sons of God as often he can—take care that, if he speaks the truth concerning you, he will be obliged to say, 'That man is certainly a believer; he has faith in God, he believes in Christ, and he does preach the gospel.'

As for yourselves, *you must see the inside of your shield;* the outside of the shield is for the enemy, but the inside is for you. What a blessed, comfortable inside the gospel has! Get inside the gospel, dear friends; have it all round you; get into the very centre of the doctrines of grace, those glorious truths of electing love, redemption from among men, regeneration by the Holy Ghost, and final preservation unto eternal glory. These doctrines will be to you like the inside of a warm, downy nest, to the little birds that have no other home.

Finally, brethren, *cast not away your shield* of faith, 'which hath great recompence of reward.' It has recompensed you up till now; it will recompense you to the last; so may you find it, and God bless you all! Amen.

Note

* This speech was the prelude to the Presidential Address, delivered on the following morning, and afterwards published under the title of *The Greatest Fight in the World.*

The reality of religion

An address delivered at the conference public meeting at Dalston Junction Chapel, on Monday evening, 6 May 1889

MANY years ago, dear friends, there was founded a Pastors' College, of which I was and still am the President. The Institution has grown until, today, I think I may say that we have sent out into the ministry exactly eight hundred men,—not a small number to have gone forth from our midst to preach the gospel of Jesus Christ. These brethren have been greatly blessed in winning souls. Since the year 1865, when our statistics were first collected, 83,037 persons have been baptized, and there has been a clear increase of 68,784 church-members. That is a result for which we have great cause to praise the Lord.

I am very thankful that so many of our brethren who were educated in the Pastors' College still remain with me in our new Association, but I hope that none of them are with me merely because of their attachment to myself, but because of their attachment to the great truths which we hold in common. I have had to pass through sore trials, as you know; they have not been by any means small ones; but had I foreknown and foreseen everything that has happened, I would have done exactly as I did. Indeed, like Luther, I could 'do no other;' I am not able to make a compromise concerning the truth of God. I am so constituted that I can only believe that 'twice two are four,' and I have not sufficient genius, or whatever other quality may be needful, to admit that it may be four and a quarter, or perhaps only three and a half. It may have been very easy, very comfortable, and possibly very clever for others to have acted otherwise than I have done; but I could not do it, nor shall I begin to try to do it.

With just that preface, I wish to say a few words to you about—

The reality of religion

Many people in the world seem to be under the impression that religion is a kind of invention, or fancy, or myth, a thing without any stern reality. The making of money is regarded as the main chance, earning their daily bread is looked upon as a reality; but hearing sermons, believing certain truths, and professing to be converted by them,—all this is regarded as a kind of mirage, real enough to the good people who are able to believe in it, but having no true reality in itself. You and I, dear friends, do not think so; we believe in the reality of those things which we have received by revelation from God, but do you not think that the world may have come to the conclusion that religion is merely a profession because we have ourselves acted in a measure as if it were so? If these things are not real to us, they are not likely to be real to the outsiders; many of them do not read the Bible, but they do read us. Many of them do not care what John, or James, or Peter, or even the Lord Jesus Christ did; but they notice what John Smith, who is a deacon at the Baptist Chapel, does, and they take note of what James Brown, who is a minister of the gospel, does. The world will pay attention to the men and women living in their midst, and it will very often judge the Bible by them. I heard, the other day, of a man who was speaking of his mother; he is not, I think, a Christian, but his mother was an old-fashioned Calvinist of the real old school. He said, 'Those people who went to such-and-such a chapel were terribly narrow, but my mother and those who were round about her believed in God; God was very real to her, she could see God's hand in everything, and she used to speak of God as a real person with whom she was very closely acquainted; I do not find people talk like that now.' I wish that every mother would leave the impression upon her son that God was wonderfully real to her. A sensible man may say to himself, 'My mother was no fool, and if God was so real to her it will be wisdom on my part to seek to make him just as real to me.'

In order that we may try to make religion real to others, there is something that the preacher will have to do, and a great deal that the people will have to do.

First, dear brethren, WE WHO ARE PREACHERS OF THE WORD, MUST BELIEVE WHAT WE PREACH.

I do not know how to trust myself to speak of *the men who have two creeds,* and I am sorry that I know many who have. One is for private consumption, for their own personal belief, or to be introduced at 'fraternal' meetings, and other gatherings where brethren of their own way of thinking meet together; but they have a very different creed when they come into the pulpit. If this gets to be a very general thing, ministers will become a by-word and a proverb, and they will make religion to be utterly contemptible among honest men and women. Let it never be so with us, brethren; as for myself, I believe nothing that I do not preach, and so far as I know, I am prepared to preach everything that I believe; if I acted otherwise, I should count myself worthy to be shut up in a prison cell for life as a rogue and a vagabond. The honest minister, the man who can say, 'I believed, therefore have I spoken,' is the one who will make his hearers believe religion to be real.

Such a man, too, is *happy in his preaching*. Have you noticed how many of the old preachers, such as Rowland Hill and Whitefield, seemed to show by their very faces how greatly they enjoyed the truths they were preaching? Their people came together enthusiastically, to hear something that was worth hearing; and the preacher himself appeared to be getting as much good out of the sermon as his hearers were; he looked like a man at a banquet, who, while he was helping others, was also having a feast himself. Those who hear such a man say to one another, 'That minister himself enjoys what he preaches to others,' and they go away with the conviction that there is something real and delightful in it.

Beside that, brethren, we must be *earnest in our preaching*. I have heard of people going to sleep during the sermon,—I do not mean at Dalston; my dear Brother Burton will take care that you do not do that. One divine said, 'Our people do not sleep much during my sermon, for I have instructed the sexton to wake them up;' but the person to whom he was speaking very wisely replied, 'You should instruct the sexton to wake *you* up, because, if you were thoroughly awake, your congregation would be wide awake, too.' People do not usually go to sleep while they are listening to a minister who is really earnest; they cannot do it. If you wish people to attend to you, brethren, give them something worth attending to; feed them well with knowledge and discretion, and as they are fed, and you are earnest, they will see that there is something real in the religion you profess.

I think also that the man who will convince the world of the reality of true religion is one who is seen to be *truly obedient to God's Word*. When I go into the pulpit to preach, I profess that I am about to speak in God's Name; not to utter my own words, but the Word of the Lord, which liveth and abideth for ever. Our good friend, David Davies, told us a good story, the other day, about a boy who would not do anything that his mother commanded him, and someone said that he was showing the strength of his mind, but she replied, 'I think he shows great strength of *don't mind.*' That is what many men are doing, nowadays, with the Word of God; if anything in the Bible does not quite suit them, they 'show great strength of don't mind,' and refuse to obey it; or perhaps they say that they take the general sense of the Scripture, but as the words are not inspired, they do not feel that they are binding upon them. I think that our reverence for the Scripture ought to be supreme, I do not believe that it can be carried too far; and, personally, I would go the length of saying that I accept every word of it from the beginning of Genesis to the end of Revelation, as it was given by God in the original documents. I believe that the Bible teaches the truth about natural history, or about any sort of history, or about philosophy or anything else; and that, although there have been historical statements in it which have been questioned for a while, some old stone has been turned up at Nineveh, or somewhere else, containing an ancient record showing that the Bible was right all the time. Anyhow, I will sink or swim with it; and I am firmly convinced that, unless we do truly believe in the Word of God, and loyally bow to its authority, we shall not persuade the people of the reality of the truths we teach. If we give them an inch, they will take an ell. If you admit that there is even one error in the Word of God, you have got rid of the Infallible Author; if he can err on one point, if he is mistaken on some minor matter, depend upon it he is not to be trusted in the more important points. No, brethren, we dare not talk like that; this Word of God is our Master, we are not the masters of it; we believe it, we seek to obey it, and as the Lord liveth, before whom we stand, whatsoever he saith unto us by his Word, that will we preach in his Name.

I think that I hardly need say to any minister of the gospel that *we must be very honest and true ourselves*. I should recommend you to be very honest in everything,—in the payment of accounts and in making out statistics. If you have been losing members from your church, do not try to make it out that you have had an increase; do not any of you ever give proof of the truth of the accusation that 'religious statistics are a pious way of lying.' Never adopt the dodges and tricks that are popular with so many. Let us have the truth at all costs; if it is good news, let us rejoice in it; if it is not, let us ask the Lord to give us more grace, so that the next year's record may be a better one. A little error in a preacher's conduct or conversation may make his hearers think that there is no reality in his religion.

Brethren, let me say one thing more to you; I think that the man who will convince the world of the reality of religion is *the man who is, as we say, 'all there,'* especially when he has any opportunity of serving Christ. There are men who are 'all there' in a sense I do not mean, in their white cravats and other paraphernalia; but when there is a soul needing to be pointed to the Saviour, they are not 'all there,' but 'all at sea.' I wish that all ministers were like one whom I knew right well; I spoke to one of his hearers, and he said to me, 'Ah! sir, he is a man of men; if he comes to pay you a visit, you know that he has been in the house, and you remember that you have met with him, for he leaves such a gracious influence behind him.' You remember that part of the blessing upon Asher was, 'Let him dip his foot in oil,' and that should be the minister's portion also; wherever he goes, he should leave the unction of his gracious influence behind him.

Now, in the second place, I want to show you how THE REALITY OF RELIGION CAN BE SEEN IN THE PEOPLE, as well as in the preacher.

This part of my subject is as important as the former portion, for *religion, to some people, is a mere name.* It is not every member of the church who recommends religion, it is not every church-member who gives even his own family an idea that there is anything in his religion. There are others who have hardly the name of religion. I remember a man saying to me, 'I don't go and shut myself up in a stuffy church or chapel, I stay at home, and worship the god of nature.' 'Ah!' I replied, 'your god is made of wood; is he not?' for I had heard the man playing skittles on the Sunday morning. There are some people who have no more religion than that man had; and it is a pity, when that is the case, to try to retain even the name of it.

In the case of others, *religion is only a side issue,* like an off-hand farm to a farmer. They carry it on as a sort of additional shop to provide for contingencies that may possibly arise; but it is not their meat and their drink, their very life and soul. Now, brethren, if you do not really live your religion, religion is not going to give you either life or joy. If it is not everything to you, it is really nothing to you.

Some I know, alas! to whom *religion is an occasional fit.* It comes upon them all of a sudden, and they go in for it very vigorously, but they do not keep it up. They are like the man concerning whom it was asked of his child, 'Is your father a Christian?' and the answer was, 'Yes, sir; but he hasn't worked at it much lately.' Suppose you were to die between these fits, dear friend, where would your soul be?

To some, I am afraid that *religion is a means of securing a position,* and, therefore, they are attracted by it. They get to be thought something of in the little community, perhaps they are made officers of the church; and though there is no very wonderful honour in that, yet there are some people who will covet it, and profess to be religious in order to attain to it. Now, if we get many such in our churches, we shall be very apt to make the world judge that there is no reality in our holy religion.

Dear friends, members of this or any other Christian church, I pray you to keep clear of all shams; especially fight shy of *sham doctrines.* Nowadays, there is even a sham doctrine of election; and there are numbers of gentlemen who are great adepts at using the old phrases, but giving to them altogether new meanings. You Dalston people are happy in being able to hear a man who says what he means, and means what he says; but there are many congregations where it is not so. I read, the other day, of a man who spelt the word psalm,—'salm,' and he said he dropped the letter 'p' out because it meant nothing to him; and I am afraid that many, in the same way, drop the doctrines because they mean nothing to them. I believe in a real election of grace, and a real redemption,—a redemption that redeems,—I believe in the real, eternal, unchanging love of God, and in a real Heaven, and, alas! in a real hell.

Beware also, dear friends, of a *sham experience.* It is very easy to pray or to preach somebody else's experience as if it were your own; but I beg you never to go in this matter an inch beyond the ground on which you have yourself travelled. Never tell either the Lord or his people about something that you say happened to yourself when, all the while, you only read it in a book. A sham religious experience is a horrible thing.

Avoid also everything like *sham living,* dishonest transactions of every kind. I heard, the other day, of a man who had paid his creditors only a shilling in the pound, and who had said to a friend, 'I have not lost quite all my means, for I transferred a good deal of my property to my wife before my bankruptcy.' That is very shocking.

But, oh, how many there are who have only *sham religion!* These people are not usually to be found at prayer-meetings. If there is to be a comic or dramatic entertainment, they can manage to be present; but if it is 'only a prayer-meeting!' they will make up some excuse for stopping away; it is wet, or they fancy they have the stomach-ache, or something else the matter with them. Ah! it is not the stomach that is wrong, it is the heart that needs to be renewed. Someone who spoke of the friends who were at home 'on beds of illness' was told that he might also have mentioned those who were 'on sofas of wellness.' I must not ask questions, but I hope you are not acquainted with many of that sort in this region.

I come back to my main point, let us have everything real and true throughout; if there are any shams that must be used up, let them be used somewhere else, and not upon religion; there, let us be real and sincere right through, even to the core. We have made distinct progress in many respects, but we do not seem to have so many elderly Christian people as we used to have, ever ready for a profitable chat upon Christian experience. What times some of us have had, and still have, bless the Lord! We have talked of the leadings of God's providence, and of answers to prayer; and then we have got on to the doctrines of grace, and the covenant ordered in all things and sure, and we have gone home greatly refreshed and strengthened. I wish we had more of such fellowship, and more prayer together. To pray in the morning, before you go forth to your daily duties, is well; and to pray at night, when the day's toil is over, is also well; but, brothers and sisters, not only do that, and come to all the meetings for prayer, but try to make other occasions of joining in supplication and thanksgiving. When a friend drops in to see you, do not let him go till you have had a word of prayer together. Those little seasons of communion will be very sweet and very helpful, and will tend to make prayer very real to you. Saturate your whole life with prayer; and let not your religion be like veneer upon the surface, but a real vital force which enters into your inmost soul, and influences your whole life to the glory of God and the good of men. The Lord grant it, for Christ's sake! Amen.

Stand fast

Inaugural address at the twentieth annual conference of the Pastors' College Association, on Tuesday 22 April 1884

IT was rather more than one hundred years ago that a certain Mr Harris, of whom I know nothing more than his name, had a very long visaged, melancholy friend sitting in his study with him. He had been speaking about the horrible condition of the times in which they lived with great unction and great gloom, when Mr Harris, taking down a book from the library shelf, read to his friend as follows:—'In our time it may be spoken more truly than of old that virtue is gone, the truth is trampled under foot, the clergy are in deadly error, and the devil reigneth;' whereupon the melancholy doctor said, 'That author has exactly expressed the truth, those are my views. I never saw a more accurate description of the times than that.' 'What times,' said Mr Harris, 'do you allude to?' 'Why, of course,' he said, 'I allude to the present times, there could not be a fitter description of the present times.' Mr Harris replied, 'I was reading from a book by Sir John Mandeville, dated 1371.' It is a very remarkable circumstance that in all ages the worst times have occurred. During the little period in which I have lived there has been a crisis at least every six weeks. I have lived to see the prosperity of England altogether destroyed; I have lived to see truth fallen in the streets, and blasphemy abounding; I have lived to see Calvinism dead and buried in an unutterable abyss whence it can never rise. I believe a great many persons saw the same thing long ago. There is a theology that teaches us there can be two deaths, two annihilations; so it has occurred to many even in my time, I have seen them die, and then die again, and then I have seen them once more utterly destroyed, and uprooted, and blasted, and passed away, and forgotten, and then forgotten, and blasted, and withered again. I did not intend to commence with anything like a joke, but with something that should be by way of good cheer to us to remember that if the days are dark there have been dark days before and they have come to an end; and if there be storms of thunder and lightning now, there have been other storms before these, and out of these clouds the precious crystal drops have fallen to bless the earth. So we may hope that these dark and stormy times will be followed by the clear shining after the rain after a little while, and we may pluck up heart, remembering what was written by Sir John Mandeville, and not talk as though it was something altogether unique that we had to endure.

Well, there are several matters which at this time may no doubt cause us great disquietude. Our friends who have come from the country, a numerous and worthy band, naturally lament the depletion of our villages, and so do I. I believe that our yeomen were among the strength of our denomination, and of the Christian Church; but alas! in many places they have almost ceased to be. If there should come hard times for landlords I should not much regret that the *lex talionis* had been fulfilled upon them; they have made it hard enough for the poor farmer, they have refused him the means of toiling on the earth on which he was born, and if they have to suffer for it by-and-by I shall not marvel, because there is a Judge that ruleth in heaven, and who somehow or other bringeth about vengeance upon the oppressors. Yet while this is passing on, and the supporters of our village churches are migrating, and all the young men of promise are coming up to the great towns and cities, the village pastor is left to look on the fold which contains a greatly diminished flock.

But if you think that there is anything better in London you are greatly mistaken. Let Mr Brown stand up for but two or three minutes, and there are many who will speak in the same sad strain as he would, and they will tell you of the horrible huddling together of the people, of the sort of semi-starvation which enables people not to live, but yet scarcely to have the felicity to die, if to them it can be a felicity to die at all; ah me, if you want a hard post it is amongst the multitudes of this infidel city; for now the mass of the people do not come to hear the Gospel, and considering that three-fourths of the preachers of the Gospel cannot be 'understanded of the people,' as the old phrase has it, if they did come, I do not particularly marvel, but I do deplore it with all my heart. These are bad things. You village people send us up the main body of the people that come to hear us at all. When I ask a 'candidate,' 'Are you a born Londoner?' it is very seldom that he says 'I was born in London,' but the major part tell me they learned their habits of church-going and chapel-going in the country, and they come up here and they help to keep religion alive among us. It was not so once, the sound of the church-going bell was attended to. There are still a few villages where everybody goes to a place of worship, but there are no quarters of London where that is the case now, and we have to deplore that the very habit of coming to hear the Word seems to be dying out.

Then, in addition to these matters, we have our own personal trials and temptations. Some are troubled with a dire poverty, and it is hard for them to bear that as well as to sustain the burdens of their pastorate. I would it were not so, yet may I glory that there is never found a lack of men who prefer to enter our ministry with its poverty; though there is no hope of having a cathedral and a palace, there is always a man ready for a little village chapel even though there is no manse attached to it. We have enough to bear since we have the common trials of other men, and in addition we have these special trials which are sure to be ours.

Perhaps some will tell me that the greatest difficulty we have now is the constant worldliness of Christian professors. A great many ministers have educated their people up to this point. They brought the theatre to their schoolroom, and now the people go to the theatre themselves. They had amusements, as they called them, which could not possibly conduce to the prosperity of anybody's soul. I am sad to say that I have heard of amusements and entertainments in which there has been no mention of God, or Christ, or of anything to the advantage of ordinary morality, they seem only intended to waste time; and when the people learn to be worldly, who wonders, if we become their educators? We see wealth taking away the very life of godliness out of some of our churches. 'Where shall we go to find society with which our children may associate?' is the question that is asked by many parents, instead of saying, 'Where can I find true servants of Jesus Christ who will help us, and whom we can help?' We can see the same worldiness amongst the working classes. Many have to ask, 'What shall we eat, and what shall we drink, and wherewithal shall we be clothed?' and that dire necessity drives all higher and better and more spiritual questions out of their mind.

But if I had to put my choice on the blackest devil of all the devils that are abroad, I should certainly select this—the tendency that there is at this time to lay aside every truth which is established and received, on the very ground that it is established and received, and to take up with any novelty; no, they are not novelties, I do not know of a single doctrine which appears to be novel which has not been taught long ago, and exposed long ago, and proved by its evil effects to be no doctrine of God and of his grace, but a doctrine of mischief. But there are nowadays multitudes of spirits who are for ever learning and never coming to the knowledge of the truth, they certainly prove all things after a way, but do not hold fast that which is good, though they cling tenaciously to everything that is mischievous and evil. Now, my subject today will easily be learned when I give you the watchword of the Conference, which will be the watchword for the year; it is this, STAND FAST. I think if ever there was a time for that word it is now. 'Hold fast that which thou hast.' 'Having done all, stand.' 'Be ye steadfast, unmovable, always abounding in the work of the Lord.'

THERE IS GREAT NEED OF STEADFASTNESS IN THESE TIMES. Sometimes the chief word to be spoken is this: 'Speak unto the children of Israel that they go forward;' and there have often been times when the Church has had to weep as the people did at Bochim, and they have had to go backward, and seek for Christ where they lost him, and seek for truth where they missed it, and seek for their first love where it departed from them; but just now I shall not say anything about retreating or advancing, I shall only speak about standing fast. And, first of all, *the very existence of innumerable opinions, and a very general belief that there is some advance to be made in theology,* ought to make us stand fast. According to some there is a spirit of the times of which we are to keep abreast. I have heard that expression very often, I do not know what it means, and I suppose there is some sense in the expression, 'Keeping abreast of the times.' What sense I make out of it is detestable; I have nothing to do with the times, I have to do with eternity; but as far as I can understand what is meant by this cry, it is that there was a theology for the Apostles, and there was another for their immediate successors, and gradually the change of the times has moulded Christianity into different forms and shapes during the last eighteen hundred years. I cannot say how often the doctrine alters, in my time it has altered many times. In eighteen hundred and ten one form of truth was believed, then the gospel of culture underwent a change, and in eighteen hundred and twenty you might have got another gospel, eighteen hundred and thirty wanted another, eighteen hundred and forty another, and eighteen hundred and fifty, sixty, seventy have not been at all satisfied with the theology that commenced the century. There has been a brand new gospel coming out every decade of history; at least, that seems to be the notion of some. Of course, we do not profess to be inspired with new revelations, but somehow we excogitate a gospel out of ourselves; like the German artist, I suppose, who excogitated a camel out of his inner consciousness. It is said to have been very difficult to decide whether his camel was not a cat or any other kind of four-footed animal. These men go on making their own gospels, until every man is his own Bible, every man his own revelation, every man his own teacher. I am afraid it is coming to the same pass as when every man is his own lawyer, and then you know what kind of client he has. As for ourselves, I do not suppose any of us are such fools, yet when these things are everywhere scattered abroad, it becomes us, who do not believe in anything of the sort, to stand fast. We believe, that once for all, the everlasting Gospel sprang from the mind of God, as Minerva is said to have sprung from the head of Jupiter, full grown and fully armed, never to be improved upon. We have got one Gospel, and if any man preach any other Gospel than that which has been given by God, let him be accursed. We have not any fellowship with him; I will have fellowship with him as far as he keeps to that, but no further. As to the top and bottom of it all, there is one only revealed Gospel to be taken as it is given, and to be held most firmly, and we make no kind of charitable pretence of a compromise about it. We stand to that faith which we have received, whatever others may do or say.

Another reason why we need to be steadfast is *the abundant pretentiousness of those who are advancing new views*. You are aware, dear brethren, that all of us who hold to the old truths are ignorant, uneducated people, and of course we only preach to the ignorant; in fact, we are a company of fools. Well, it is something to know that, if we have not been aware of it before. We have been so often told it that we ought to have some kind of confidence in the fact. And who are these gentlemen who know all these fresh things? Men of culture! Men of thought! I used to think they might be. I had a kind of reverence and awe for them at one time; I felt like the fox when he first saw a lion, my heart sank within me. But I have seen them several times, and now I must confess that I feel as if I were the lion, and they were the fox. I have heard men talk of culture whom I supposed were cultured; why, I would eat them by the score for breakfast. Here I do not speak in my own proper personality, but as the representative of the men whom they despise, taking for a pattern of them the old Puritans. They send me their books sometimes, and they say to me, 'This has got something in it, here is some thinking here;' and if you put it under a microscope you cannot discover, even with all the power that you can bring to bear upon it, the smallest particle of thought; and yet within one page of my old John Owen or Thomas Manton I will find as much learning as would last ten thousand of them for a century. I should like to condense an immeasurable quantity of sarcasm, and hurl back with righteous indignation the everlasting sneer about our ignorance. We will accept their definition of our ignorance, but tell them there are persons other than ourselves who are ignorant and uncultured, and the trade-mark of the uncultured is that they sneer at others, and that they call themselves cultured. I only for a moment wave their trade-mark in their face. We do not profess that we are cultured, or that we are learned, or that we are clever; we only say that as compared with them we are so. Yet I can very well imagine some dear brethren in the country who have met with such a man. At the fraternal meeting he takes the lead not because he knows any Latin or Greek, or because he understands philosophy, but he talks as if he did, and he knows a few big words, and flings them about until our poor brethren think that really there is something very wonderful in it. Well, do not feel so any more. Put these brethren in their proper place; if they are idols do not you be silly enough to worship them, for some have done so very much to their detriment.

We need to stand fast, again, *because there is in some minds an evident love of change*. I do know some brethren who are apt to catch any disease that may be in the air. Some healthy men can go into a poisoned atmosphere, and escape without injury; but these people, if there were a disease within fifty miles of them; would be certain to take it. There are many such about, very receptive brethren. They follow the light, as Hodge did, when he found himself in a pool through following an *ignis fatuus*. Their great love of light leads them to make a rush after every light that nobody else has seen. As for those that bless us, such as Orion, the Pleiades, or the sun, and the moon, and the stars, they do not care for them, but an *ignis fatuus* now! they never saw such a thing as that before! How glorious it is to have that spirit of chivalry that enables you to run after a Jack-o'-lantern! These brethren have got it, and off they go. Some brethren are born with Germanic heads, and therefore they cannot help criticising everything. The Germans themselves sometimes have a laugh at such people. You may have heard the story of Hans Priam, who was a man that always pried into everything, and found fault and criticised. He was told that he should go to heaven if he would not criticise what he saw. Hans got along all right till he saw some angels carrying a big beam. He wanted to laugh, but he would not do so for fear of being expelled from Paradise. Presently he saw other angels trying to fill a tub with holes in the bottom of it, and he felt very much inclined to say how inexpedient and unwise it was. At last he saw a chariot that had a horse yoked to each side of it. Now Hans had been used to horses, so he felt sure of his ground, and he broke out at once, 'What are you doing? It cannot go in that fashion.' The story says that Hans was summarily ejected, and that he had just time to turn his head and see that the chariot was mounting upwards, for the horses had wings. Then said he to himself, 'I dare say that there was an explanation to the other things I could not understand, and I should have let those things alone.' There is a Hans Priam about still, and the genius of Hans Priam remains in many men. Though a doctrine be from God himself these people fancy that they can improve upon it. If they had been present at the creation they could have suggested many excellent alterations to the Creator. This spirit leads them to be everything by turns and nothing long. They find difficulties everywhere, of course they do, and I am glad of it, I would not desire to have a creed that I could understand from top to bottom. How could it have come from God? How could it have been an expression of his thought if it was not in some points above man's understanding. Some people want everything squared like a dice piece, so that they can measure, and calculate, and understand everything, and if they cannot do that they are off to another theory, when suddenly they find that there are difficulties there, and before long they have been to every point of the compass, and spend their whole life in the intense delight that is to be found in a fool's paradise. There is no creed, nor non-creed but has its crux. You cannot fly into unbelief itself, and go to the uttermost depths of knownothingism without meeting with difficulties. I may say of the infinite in truth, whither shall we flee from its presence? Were we to ascend into heaven, or descend into hell, we cannot get away from it. Until we get faith we shall never find a resting-place.

No doubt in these times there are some that have much need of steadfastness, *because of the apparent non-success of the Gospel in their hands*. Oh, dear friend, would anything ever succeed in your hands? I do think that question never did occur to some, and that if it were suggested to some whom I know it would be the nearest possible approach to the truth. Whenever a question of such a sort does come, and you hate the man that puts it to you, I hope you will think that very likely you ought to put it to yourself. Sometimes it is said, 'Well, I have not seen sinners saved, and churches built up; I find I do not get on where I am, and therefore I think I will change.' Perhaps you had better change, it will be a benefit to the Gospel itself, the Gospel may do better in being preached by someone else, and you may do less hurt by going away than you will do as you are now as an inefficient and useless servant of Christ. Still do not imagine that a change of sphere is all that you want. A man went out to see a friend, and it was while a horrible north-east wind was blowing. When he came back to his wife, he said: 'Let me do whatever I will, this north-east wind will trouble me. When I was going it blew in my face, and when I came back, then the wind turned round on me, and it blew on my back.' I knew a brother that did not get on at all, so he changed his place, but the wind blew on him still; he became a Plymouth Brother, but still the wind blew on him; he joined the Church of England, and still it was the same; and so it will be until he leaves the ministry alone; until he gets out of it the wind always will blow on him. Remember that it does not prove that the Gospel is a failure because you are.

Then, again, we have need to stand fast *because the devil is constantly tempting us*. Whoever he does not tempt, he will tempt a true minister of God. If there is one man in all the world who never shall rest or be quiet from his temptations, it is the man whom God makes useful. I am sometimes reminded of a queer Irish story which illustrates this point. A gentleman said to a man whom he met, 'Pat, if the devil were to come now and take one of us, which would he take?' 'He would take me,' at once replied the witty fellow, 'because he is sure he could have your honour any day.' The story is laughable, but it contains a very great truth. There are other men who will go wrong enough without being much troubled by Satan, but if you are firm in the truth of God, you will be tempted and tried. Therefore, 'Put on the whole armour of God, that ye may be able to stand against the wiles of the devil.' If you turn your back there is no protection for you, and his deadly shafts will pierce you. 'Whom resist, steadfast in the faith.'

There is no other way of overcoming that arch enemy than by just standing where God has put you on his own eternal truth, and holding your own, and God's own, against all his assaults.

I do not know whether any of you find a special need of steadfastness *from the lapse of years*. You have been so long preaching the Gospel, so many years in the same place, so long bearing trials for the truth, and what is worse bearing the contradiction of sinners against it. Do not be weary; and faint in your mind. You will do well to be weary of everything else, for if you cannot rest in the monotony of the Gospel, I am quite sure that you cannot rest in the discords of unbelief; for, after all, within that monotony all harmonies are concentrated. Only ask God to give you a better, and a more musical ear, tuned more to the harmonies of the universe, and you will find wondrous symphonies within the Gospel which you preach. Oh, I have preached it here these thirty years, and more, and it is a deal newer to me now than when I began. I find much more in it that gives variety to my mind than I did when first I commenced my ministry. If you can press through that little period of trial which does come to most minds, you shall find it to be the same with you. Have you thought that you have pretty well gone through all that the Bible teaches? there is a lot more that you do not know, and if you will try to know some more of it, you shall get into the charming varieties that there are in the revelation which God has given. So much, then, upon our need of steadfastness in these times.

But now what shall I say upon the question, WHAT IS THIS STEADFASTNESS? How can I describe it? Well, *it does not consist in just standing still, and being at ease*. I do not call that steadfastness. There are some people that never move simply because they are sound asleep. Steadfastness is something more than that. I have seen churches in this condition. Though they have had a creed they have never done any active service for the Master. They have put the creed into a case somewhat like those in which we have preserved meat; there it is hermetically sealed, having no influence upon them. If any one were to touch it, and try in the least degree to revise it, to alter a word or even a syllable of their human creed, they would be in a great passion, yet they have never looked into it. I believe a creed is to a man what a trust deed often is to a chapel, nobody has ever seen it, and very often nobody knows what the trust is, and the trustees themselves do not know; but it is a dreadful thing when a trustee of the Gospel does not know what he is put in trust with. We are put in trust with the Gospel, and our first duty is to know clearly what that Gospel is, and then intelligently to hold it, and to let it exercise all its benign influence upon our hearts.

I do not think that standing fast means *shutting your eyes to the faults of your own denomination, or to the faults of your creed*. You may have errors in your creed which you ought to see. A man who was asked how it was that he did not see any faults in his wife said, 'Whenever I look at her I shut my eyes to her faults.' That may be a good rule with regard to your wife, but it will not do to deal with truth in that fashion. Be willing to see all that you ought to see, be anxious to see all that you ought to see, and what you do see that is of God, mind that you hold fast to it.

Steadfastness, it seems to me, *begins with knowing the truth*. You cannot be steadfast in a thing you do not know. The thing is to get the truth into yourself, not adopting it professionally, and preaching it professionally, but getting it to be part and parcel of yourself so that you and the truth cannot be separated. We have heard of a clergyman who attended balls, who was asked by his Bishop why he went there, and he said he never went to such places when he was on duty. The Bishop very wisely asked him, 'When do you think a clergyman is off duty?' When a Christian man is off duty, when a minister is off duty, he is just the same as when on duty, for it has become a part of his nature to be always on duty. I saw in the streets of a foreign town some performing dogs walking, dancing, and acting as though they were almost semi-human. A few hours afterwards, I happened to go and sit down in an olive grove for a quiet rest, when lo! my friends whom I had seen wearing coats and hats as though they had been men or boys came into the same grove where I was, about a dozen of them, and there was not one of them on two legs, or wearing a hat or a coat, they scampered all about the place. The dogs were dogs still. Now I have known men who have been wonderfully sound and orthodox in the pulpit, but they have gone out on a trip, and have set aside their scruples and convictions. Now of all things in the world there is nothing that I hate more than a performing dog of a minister. I would not use these homely similes if I knew how to put my meaning better, but I do not. I think it is a loathsome thing when a man becomes the pastor of a church as per order. You send to the College for a man to be sent to a church. The man is sent down as though he were a bale of goods ordered and invoiced, and he goes although he does not care a single atom for the truth he has to preach. May God drum such men out of the regiment. No, brethren, if you are steadfast, you must have got the truth, and must believe that you have got it.

Steadfastness, it seems to me, consists *in a deepening conviction of the truth,* believing it more firmly every day, every experience ought to make you strong. Every victory, even every defeat ought to make the truth more true to you; every sense of weakness, every manifestation of strength ought to bring you more into harmony with the mind of God, the Spirit himself bearing witness with your spirit, not only as to you yourself being born again, but also as to the truth suiting itself and adapting itself to all the varied experiences of your life. The heavier the hand presses on the stamp the better is the impression on the wax, and the more likely is it to remain. You must ask the Lord to put a heavy hand on you sometimes that you may have a deepened impression of what it is you have got to do for him. Somebody has said that a surgical operation would be necessary to get a new doctrine into my head. It would require a surgical operation, and such a surgical operation as they cannot perform. He that put what I know into my brain alone can take it out, and no one else can do so. A motto that is put upon John Calvin's portrait is this, 'He took fast hold;' and I like a man of whom that can be said. I begin now to rejoice whenever I find a bigot; there is so much loose thinking in the world that it is a treat to me to see a strong hyper-Calvinistic-strict-communion brother. I feel right glad to meet with him although I am not one myself, but I say to him, 'You and I are very nearly alike, we do believe *something,* and what we believe we believe firmly and strongly.' There will be nothing accomplished, there can be nothing accomplished by the feebleness of doubt, all deeds worth anything have been done by men of faith. There is a triumphal arch erected to the memory of the heroes of faith in the eleventh chapter of the Epistle to the Hebrews, but the tiniest cairn that was ever made with the refuse of a rubbish heap would be more than sufficient to celebrate the accomplishments of unbelief, for it has achieved nothing but mischief.

I think that steadfastness includes also *a joyful confidence of success.* I like to see a brother so fully believing that the Word he has to preach is that which will save sinners and gladden the hearts of God's people, that the brother goes to his work in such a spirit that sinners are saved and saints are gladdened. He has confidence when he goes forth in the morning, so he makes the bells ring in his own soul, and he goes to his work ringing the bells of heaven for there is to be joy today. That is the kind of brother that the Lord does use in converting souls. I sometimes bless a man for letting me have a look at his face, it is as good as a day's holiday; there are some of you of whom I can say that, there are some of whom I could not. The man that is fully confident, that man that is joyfully persuaded that even Bow Common goes to be converted, that is the man who is likely to be steadfast. The man who is sure that little Slocum-in-the-Marsh will be revived despite the squire and the parson, he is confident because he has got the wonderful message which will work effects that will be more than magical, *he* is the sort of man to make hell tremble and heaven rejoice, he is God's chosen instrument for blessing the world and gathering in his own. That man deserved a monumental column who in the darkest days in France never despaired of the Republic; so let it be with us, let us be men who in the darkest days never despair, but believe right up to the hilt. Be not satisfied with just enough faith to save you, but believe right up to the hilt in solid confidence that God's word cannot return unto him void, but must prosper in the thing whereto he has sent it.

The preacher who is confident of success will also find *great personal enjoyment in his work*. I think the stable-minded man will often say, 'These doctrines are my meat and my drink.' If one says to him, 'Why do you preach these doctrines?' He replies, 'I cannot help it, for the last time I was down in the dumps, and ready to die, this truth came to me and it made me laugh for joy, and I cannot give it up.' 'Why,' says a brother, 'do you really believe in that substitution of Christ that you preach about?' If ever you hear me quibbling about the blessed doctrine, put me into Bethlehem Hospital at once, for I shall have gone mad. I will tell you why I am sure of this. I was once in despair, as few have been; I was driven to my wit's end, and almost to my life's end, with a horrible sense of sin, and I did attend a ministry where I believe the atonement was believed in some such sense as this, that Jesus Christ did something or other, which in some way or other, is connected with the pardon of men. Well, that never gave me any comfort, but when I learned that he suffered in my stead, I got a ray of light, and following that ray of light I came to the cross, and—

'E'er since by faith I saw the stream,

Thy flowing wounds supply,
Redeeming love has been my theme,
  And shall be till I die.'

If you get behind the door, and suck the marrow from the bone of the doctrine, if alone in secret you drink of the wines on the lees well refined, oh, you will be positive and awfully dogmatic about the truths you hold. Men that burn well, or that can suffer for the truth, are the men who have enjoyed the truth; and I believe in proportion to the intensity of your enjoyment of the truth will often be the tenacity with which you will hold it.

Steadfastness will include *a very brave testimony to the truth*. I do believe, brethren, that if we are steadfast ourselves we shall never be afraid to preach the truth that we believe, whoever may come in. Is not there a brother here who was dreadfully frightened at the sight of a white cravat worn by a gentleman the other day in the chapel where he was preaching? He thought to himself, 'That surely is the President of the Baptist Union;' or he said to himself, 'That is one of those wonderful men from London.' Of course, all London men are wonderful men. You have only to put on the bill 'from London,' and you are sure of a congregation. Now, at the end of the service it turned out that he was only a waiter from the inn. You have been afraid a great many times of that brother who has imbibed some heretical notions, and you drew it very mild when you were preaching because you were a little afraid of him. Do not be afraid of anybody; if you are, you have great reason to be afraid. Be afraid to be afraid. Have so much fear of God that the fear of man has gone. Do you know what undenominational Christianity is? It is good water with all the flavour boiled out of it. I met with some water in Italy, and I was told that it was so pure that nothing was so good except that which fell directly from the skies. I never want to have any more of it, there was no taste in it. When I get to hear a sermon I like one that has a flavour. It used to be said of some of our old people, 'they have got a sweet tooth;' well, so have some of us, and we like a bit of sugar, something tasty and sweet. It is said that if we leave out this and leave out that we shall attract more people. Now you must have noticed that the more rigid, and the more intolerant, a sect seems to be in its belief, the more will it find favour with real manly men. It is an odd thing but I am sure it is so. You shall see, High-Churchism—well, we all ran it down, as it deserved to be in some aspects of it; but those who taught it believed something or other; they believed some very stupid things, and the men preached them, and they did not hesitate to preach them boldly, and the people learned something. Now, here is a man stands up, and says, 'Now, my dear friends, I want to be abreast of the times, and therefore I hope I shall not use any expression which might seem direspectful to the various forms of intellectual development, I have so much respect for culture that in the catholicity of my spirit and the largeness of my mind I mean, well, whatever you think I mean.'

Brethren, I have had the felicity to read so much sarcasm upon the orthodox that I feel that some kind of reparation is due to the other side, hence I diverge a little with a view to them. The intense gratitude that I feel to them for holding up a mirror in which I can see myself makes me feel that I must do a little of the same kind of thing for them. May it be blest to them. What is there in all the world that ought to make you afraid? 'I had as lief not be as live to be in awe of such a thing as I myself.' What can there be to frighten you if you are speaking the truth? If you are telling lies, be afraid; but if it is God's truth, in God's name speak, fear nothing, but go ahead. But you may be poor, and there may be grave reasons why you should not speak out. There have been better men than you who have been poor, but who have not been ashamed of the Gospel of Christ. But you may lose your pulpit. Well, suppose you do; there is one great cathedral always open to you, where there is a canopy beneath which angels delight to carol the praises of God. Do not be afraid of anybody. God made the world for you, and he will find a place for you in it. Remember the promise, 'The meek shall inherit the earth,' and in due time they shall, though sometimes they have to fight to get that peace.

Another point of steadfastness, if I do not weary you, is this, when a man is steadfast he comes *to rest in the Lord*. When he is in a great fidget, and a hurry, and a worry, he is not steadfast. You know how one of the great fathers spoke when Julian, the apostate, had come in, and everything seemed to be going to the bad, and many were losing heart. He said, 'Well, with regard to the Emperor, that little cloud will blow over very soon.' The man believed, and therefore was not afraid, but rested in the Lord. That hand of Uzzah, what a deal of mischief it has done in the world! If it had been lifted up in prayer instead of being put up to steady the ark it would have been much better. The ark of God is all right; it is much more right because just now it seems so wrong. Here is what should make us quite confident about it, it is God's ark, it is not yours. If it were yours it would soon go to pieces, but it is God's. Did he stop half-way in making the world; did the Creator leave part undone in his great work? No, he went on till it was all complete, and when he had finished the house he brought out his child, and put him in it. The ark of God is super-human, and as for all the difficulties, God foresaw them long ago, and the enemies of the truth too. Sometimes when they think, 'Now we have done it, now we have crushed the Gospel,' if you listened you would hear a laugh. 'He that sitteth in the heavens doth laugh, the Lord doth have them in derision,' and as for their blasphemous talk, he ordains to bring his glory thereby. All parts of the plan are under destiny. I do not know, brethren, how it is with you, but when I am ill I always have to fall back on predestination. I believe in the free will of man as far as any man believes it, but I believe in the free will of God, and in the grand tussle that is going on I am sure that victory will be his who is first and last and midst, without whom there is no breath even in the blasphemer's nostrils. Therefore let us be calm amid the bewildering cry, for God is with us.

Another thing that will always help us to be steadfast is *the sight of the results*. I have come down several times lately from the death-beds of my church-members. I have never seen, during these thirty years, a trace of fear in any one of them whenever they come to die. My brother has heard many testimonies that I have not. Do they not die well, brother? (Mr J.A.S., 'They do.') They have been so joyful that I have longed to go with them, they have died so full of life that I have felt that it was like the ocean beating back the river, and filling it full of its own force. Here is a dear brother who was with us last year, who is now suffering from cancer. He is filled with pain, but he writes me a letter full of joy every week, and whoever goes in he tells them about how soon he will be with his Lord, and I believe his only trouble is that he has got to leave the Tabernacle, and the Pastor, and all the dear friends there. He is glad in the Lord, and as I think of him I say to myself, 'This will do, this truth that I have preached. I shall go on preaching it for it helps saints to die well.' Then you may see also the steadfastness of those who live. There is a great 'modern-thought' man, not a hundred miles from here, with a very small following, and he attributes it to this.

He says, 'The neighbourhood is impregnated with the sentiments of a certain notorious preacher, and it would not so much matter that his views have spread in the district, but for the fact that, when once those views are received, they seem to shut out every other view of truth, and I have never known a person who has once imbibed them who has ever given them up.' I thanked him for that word, and I thought I would go on saying the same things if that was the effect they produced. I wonder how people die who have nothing to live on except their own thoughts, who have hardly faith enough to believe in their own being. Do not lead a gipsy life, and pitch your tent wherever you please. I am not much in love with that sort of thing, for I have known and I have heard of enough of its evil effects to loathe it. A man was once observed, in Canada or Australia, fencing in some very poor land, and a friend said to him, 'I should not fence that in if I were you. Why it would starve a lark, and a herd of cattle must perish on it.' He replied, 'That is why I am enclosing it, to keep them out.' That is why I am paying no particular attention to this barren plot of modern thought; if anyone tried to feed there he would starve, I am quite sure. But oh, let us see souls converted, that is the grand point, not only saints dying well and living well, but sinners saved. We cannot give up that which wins a soul from death. You get into the atmosphere where the old Gospel is preached and loved, you will be warmed and cheered, but go where it is not the fashion of the preacher, but where all sorts of novelties are taught—here bring my great coat, wrap me up, I am chilled to the bone, there is a cold blast from the pulpit that freezes everything. How does the prayer-meeting get on? 'Well, we have given that up.' How many come to the week-night service? 'Oh, we have a prayer-meeting and a sermon together, because there are not enough to make two services, so we rolled it into one.' And how many do you get to that one? 'There is a very nice number.' How many? 'Why sometimes there are twenty.' And you notice the way in which they do not love one another, and that little is done towards reclaiming the harlot, or looking after the drunkard. That is the atmosphere these things beget. But if you keep knowing what you do know, and especially if you keep to the grand doctrines of the Cross, and to the atonement by blood, and to the deity of Christ, being very precious in your esteem; if all the great cardinal truths that God has revealed are exhibited as things, not for discussion, but for enjoyment, you will find that there is an atmosphere all around you which will be your soul's joy and help.

A word or two by way of COMMENDATION OF STEADFASTNESS, AND REBUKE OF THE REVERSE.

He who stands fast grows. I might have said he that does not move makes progress. This world stands fast enough, and yet it is continually progressing. 'He has fixed it so that it cannot be moved,' is a great truth, yet it is always revolving round the sun. The man that is planted will grow, but he who is constantly transplanted will never come to perfection.

Again, there is this advantage, that *he gains on other people.* People somehow come to respect a man when they know where to find him. At the first they may differ from him, and even be angry with him, but when they find that he will not alter they think that they had better try to ascertain what it is about him that is different from themselves, and by-and-by they will come to this that they half think that he is right, and that they had better agree with him, and by-and-by he altogether converts them, and draws them to himself.

Then, also, when a man is steadfast, *his work lasts.* If you do not preach something solid, which you believe, and ought to believe, you may build very fast, but all will come down. What a miserable sight it is to see a fine edifice all wrapped in flames, and burned to the ground. If it had been never so small, and had been gold, silver and precious stones, when the fire was raging, it would have stood the test. I believe that those who are fixed in their views, and have received the truth, because the truth has received them into its embrace, are fittest for the Lord's use. They are not the wreckers' lanterns, hung on the rocks, to lure the ship to its destruction, they are the fixed lighthouse on the Eddystone, from which the light gleams forth, preventing the vessels from being dashed to pieces.

THESE ARGUMENTS I WOULD THROW IN TO MOVE YOU TO STEADFASTNESS. First, *truth must be fixed.* Truth cannot be a vanishing quantity. What was true a hundred years ago must be true now. What was true once is true for ever. Some people say that Whitefield's and Wesley's views were very well for their age, but they would not do now; but they are as true today as far as they were true then, for truth is for all time, and for all eternity.

Remember this, too, that *your Lord and Master was no doubter.* Can you find a trace of a doubt in his whole history? 'But he was God,' you say. And he was a man, too. If to doubt be a duty, then Christ omitted it. Did he ever extol doubt as containing more in it than half the creeds? He never hesitated, he never doubted, and that not simply because he was God, but because he dwelt with God. He was sure of the truth by actual fellowship with the God of truth, why should he doubt? And if we get into the same region, according to our capacity, we shall not be doubters. When did Jesus say, 'These are my views at the present time, but I take the liberty to advance'? Let the doubters find another Master, he marches not in the same regiment as the doubter who spiritually destroys himself, and doubts the very word which the Lord has given. He does not believe anything, and thinks it wrong to be sure of any point, makes his creed up every Saturday morning as he prepares or reads his sermon for the last time. That is not the way that Christ walks. He never goes into the slush, and mire, and bog holes of eternal doubt; he speaks what he does know, and testifies what he has seen. I only ask you to be confident about what the Master has said; I do not ask you to be dogmatic about what you think; very likely your thoughts will perish with you; but with regard to what is said by Christ, and what is taught in his holy Word, hold to that as with hooks of steel, take it to your very heart, and never part with it, come what may. 'Twere infinitely better that you were buried than that you should ever deny the things that you have preached by the power of the Holy Spirit.

Again, I remind you that *God is no changeling*. If he had changed in anything I should have thought that we should have altered with him; but we live not under the governance of the changing moon, but under that of the sun which has neither parallax nor tropic. Let us be the unchanging children of the unchanging Father, and believing that light is today what it was when the Creator said, 'Let light be,' let us, as children of the light, walk in the light.

Remember also, *the recompense of reward*. I believe it shall be given to steadfastness and faithfulness. Well believing is a part of well doing. Our intellect is to be under the government of God as our King and Lord, and we are to submit in everything to his rule. Who is he that gave liberty to one province of our nature to rebel against God? He who talks of free thought means usually rebellious thought, and in effect he says, 'Let us break his bands asunder, and cast his cords from us.' I am bound to believe whatever God tells me, and I must and I do bow my intellect before the majesty of his supremacy. If I do not know, and I cannot measure, and I cannot comprehend it, my faith delights in the incomprehensible, and rejoices in the infinite. She waded once up to her ankles, and she shivered in the cold; but now has she plunged beneath the waters to swim in, and there is no chill there, and she has often found a calm that cannot be described. She may dive, and as she dives deep into this sea, deeper, and deeper, and deeper still, she finds that the lower she descends the more she feels that she is in her element, for the life that God has given us is of that kind that it makes us at home in the truth of God. Wherefore, again I say, be steadfast.

It is time that I had done, but I will just say this, before I close, *to assist you to be steadfast*. And first, *by way of advice*. You want to be steadfast, I am sure you do, then *follow the truth for its own sake*. Do not be a minister of the Baptist denomination because you have got a living, even though it be not a very fat one. Do not do as some do, go to another denomination because there seem more openings there. If the truth goes through the mire, down the Cut-throat Lane, and even into the Valley of the Shadow of Death, cling to her skirts, and forsake her not; for as God liveth, the truth must live, and he that clings to the skirts of it shall not be put to shame.

Then, *let God be your God,* and do not be your own God. Augustine says, 'When I was following my own devices, I made a God of my intellect, and I felt much more troubled to establish my own opinions than I did to find out what was divine teaching.' And it is so. Do not be your own God, or you will be a devil; let God be God, and bow yourself before him.

Take care that you keep up your joy in the Lord. There is nothing like this joy if a man wants to keep the devil or men from troubling him. I was walking once on the beach at Mentone, when a man met me who was carrying a bundle of sticks, perhaps one hundred. Do you know what I said to him when he wanted me to buy one? I said nothing, but just held up my own stick. You see, I had got a better one than he had, so I did not want his. Oh, there are a number of men who will come with their sticks, and want you to have one of them. If they do, just show them the one you have got. It will put you out of harm's way if you have such enjoyment in the Lord that you do not want anything else. I think in the olden time, in the State of Massachusetts, it was decided by the people that they would be governed by the laws of God until they had time to make some better ones. That resolution I have passed in my own mind, that I will be under the rule of divine truth till I have got the time to think out something better.

I should advise you to *study* so that you may be steadfast. Do not be content with the outside of things, do not be satisfied with the surface of things. You will find that there is a hard part on the outside of the truth, look into the soul of it, get at the juice. You say, 'Bones, bones, bones,' yes, but break them, and then you may sing, 'My soul shall be satisfied as with marrow and fatness.' Get at the marrow of the truth, experimentally realise it in your own heart, by the power of the Holy Ghost, and I am not afraid about your being steadfast.

And often, I bear this *testimony,* and I think I can bear this testimony without any boasting, if my whole surroundings do not permit me to speak, I do not know who can. You shall find that in keeping to the old truth shall be your spiritual advantage as a servant of Jesus Christ. You will not find anyone getting on better than you are. The new machine does not work any better than the old one does. What have those done who have adopted the new views? Will they find us a church like ours? Will they find us continued conversions under anything else? They cannot; nor can they find a happier man, more satisfied and content with the work he has to do, nor one who with a thousand infirmities, and cares, and pains, and aches, would change places with Gabriel if he had the opportunity. No, I love you too well to lie to you: and if I were mistaken I would tell you. But I have gone on now for thirty years, I have gone on for thirty years in one place, and I do not believe that I should have been thirty months in one place if it had not been for my keeping to the Gospel. When our American friends have been to the Tabernacle, they try with infinite wisdom to tell the secret of Mr Spurgeon's power, and, as a rule, they say they do not know what it is, most of them say they cannot make it out. They say, 'He has no presence, he is a very ordinary person, though he has a loud voice yet there is nothing original in his preaching, nor anything very remarkable or rhetorical.' They give a description of my nose, and eyes, and beard, and moustache, that is all very nice and interesting. One person wrote in a paper, 'I heard So-and-so; he was a great orator, and what he said was very good, but I do not know where he got it from. I heard another noted preacher, but I did not care for his sermon; there was nothing about the Gospel in it. I went to hear Mr Spurgeon, and he preached just as an ordinary Methodist would do, and it was just Jesus Christ and him crucified, and somehow I felt I did not want anything else.' Yes, and that is just it, brethren. I believe that sheep will keep to that fold where there is something for them to eat, and they have after all a pretty good discernment, and they do not mind very much whether the gate is painted blue or yellow so long as there is good food within. You shepherds, mind that you tie them up by their teeth. Give them plenty to feed upon, and let that food be the Gospel of Jesus Christ.

But somebody says, 'Well, I do not know, the Gospel does not seem to operate upon me in that way, it does not seem to fire my spirit, and bless me.' No, perhaps not; but why is that? There was a gentleman once lecturing upon mechanics, and he said to the young men, 'Now suppose that you had made a pump, and suppose you had put every piece together in its proper place, and that when you began to pump, the water did not come, what would you say?' Several very admirable answers were given, but there was one young man who was not so philosophical as the rest, and he said, 'I should say that there was not any water there.' So when the Gospel does not affect your inner life, and move your soul as it ought to be moved, I should say that there is not much inner life to be affected, and there is not anything in you to be stirred. This machine does not fail except when it is tried upon those who are not in the right condition for its operations upon them. My testimony, brethren, and I give it for what it is worth, is that it is well to hold not only to evangelical truth, but even to the sterner portion of it, the Calvinistic. Thomas Jackson, I mean Dr Jackson, and I were one day dining together at Dr Campbell's, and he said to me, 'I am always glad to think that you are a Calvinist.' Now considering that Dr Jackson was a Wesleyan that was a remarkable statement; but he went on to explain what he meant, for he said, 'We Wesleyans are the only Arminians that remain evangelical as a body.' It is so with Arminianism, if it is not linked with great earnestness it is apt to go off into Socinianism. I do know this that whatever Calvinism is or is not, it is certainly a very great hold-fast. Now I am not a young man and to you who are young men I give this testimony. Sometimes I am asked, 'Why do you cling to that Calvinism that is dead?' Is it? Perhaps it is. I was reading the story of the battle of Waterloo, it will illustrate what I mean to do. A Scotch regiment had got into difficulties during the battle, and in the thick of the fight a colour-sergeant was struck down and killed, but he gave the standard such a death grip that another sergeant who wished to carry the colours on failed to remove it from his hand. He pushed back the dead man's hand as far as he could, but it could not be stirred, and though the French were close to him he took the dead man up, and carried him away, standard and all. And because somehow I cannot dis-sever the Evangelicalism from the Calvinism, if it be a dead man, I will carry that and all. Yet if a man thinks it dead he may have to think again. During the great plague of London, there was in the city a Scotch piper, who had tired himself out, and fell asleep in Smithfield, and there he lay upon a settle, and when the men with the dead-cart came by, picking up persons who had died of the plague, they took our piper up, and they put him in the dead-cart, bag-pipes and all. By-and-by Alexander awoke, and not knowing wherever he might be his first instinct was to play the pipes. He had not played the pipes more than half a minute before there was not anybody to drive the cart, for they said the devil was in it. They have picked our Calvinism up for dead, and they have put it in the cart, down among the dead men. Give them a turn at the pipes, brethren. Blow a shrill blast on the pipes, and there will not be a man left to drive the cart.

Taking stock

A conference address on Mark 16:15–16*

I AM anxious that we should stand still awhile and consider whereabouts we are, and what we are, and what we have been doing and what we propose to do. I want that we pass ourselves in review, and form some estimate on all these matters, take stock as they do in business, and cast up our accounts, and see how things stand with us. My dear brethren in Christ, ours is a very high calling, and we have entered upon a very daring ambition—to speak for God, to be shepherds of the blood-bought flock, to be successors not only of apostles, but of Christ himself, in the work of winning souls. Some men who have soared high have had a terrible fall, and unless we succeed in our mission it will have been a fall, it will have been weakness ever to have had the ambition and to have entered upon the enterprise. I cannot bear to think of a gallant ship that seems destined to plough the sea for many a year sinking on a sudden, and I cannot endure to hear, as we sometimes do, of great mechanical skill having been employed to produce a machine that will not work, so it is sad when in other ways we see wasted energy ending in nothing but failure. I am sure we do desire beyond all things that we who are ministers of Christ should make full proof of our ministry, that when it comes to a close we may have fulfilled it to the utmost and proved ourselves to be good ministers of Jesus Christ. It will be a terrible thing at the end of life to feel that the battle has been fought and lost for ever, that we have made a mistake, having got into a calling for which we were unfitted, and have kept in it unworthily. Everything that we do must be tried as with fire. There is no hope of our being able to build somewhere on the sly—the flames will reach to the villages as well as to the large towns, and to the little works done in Sabbath Schools as well as to the great works done in large congregations, for every man's work must be tried as with fire; and though, I trust, we ourselves shall be saved, it will be a sad thing at the last part of life to see all our life's work blazing away, and to have nothing left at our death-bed but a handful of ashes. We sowed a great mass of wheat, sowed as we thought good seed, but we have got no harvest and no sheaves to take with us into the presence of our Lord. Now if we have been trusting to fallacies, it will be well to know it; if we have been, up to the present time, on the wrong tack it will be well to put about now, before we get—and perhaps we have already got—on the margin of the grave. It will be well solemnly to consider our ways, and to see how far we are short of the mark of our high calling in Christ Jesus, and may God help me to direct your thoughts to that end. It will be a great pity to have lost our own life-work, but it will have been a greater pity to have deceived other people, preaching falsehoods, industriously leading them in paths of error. It will be a poor result after having tugged and toiled with brain, and, as we thought, with heart too, after labouring with all our ability, to find that we have only set before men a mere mirage instead of bringing them into the green pastures. It will wring a man with anguish, it will sting him as doth an adder, if he has to reflect that he has caused the loss of others, and that through him those that did run well have been hindered, and if those that sought the wicket gate have been turned aside, and the kingdom of Satan strengthened instead of weakened. It will go hard with such a man when he comes to his last moments. God grant us to die in a ditch, or to fall by the hands of savages, sooner than we should ever lie upon the downiest couch with the reflection that we have caused the souls of men to wander from the commands of God. Worst of all will be the consciousness of having dishonoured God—I speak not to ungodly men, but to you who are of a happier type, after the pattern of faithful Abraham, for the God of Abraham is our God. Multitudes of professing Christians have done things which seem to imply that God's commands are pure mistakes in their eyes, but I trust, brethren, that we feel that the worst thing we can do is to dishonour him who calls us his servants. Even the salvation of souls must ever be to us as nothing compared to the glory of the Most High. Let him be clothed with majesty; let him be true though all men be liars, though all things else should perish he is the first and he the last to us. And if on reflection we should have to say, 'I have done much that has not honoured him, I have kept back truth that might have made him glorious in the hearts of men, I have not commended his great name as I should have done,' how shall we dread to stand before him, and fear to approach him, whom, even in our pulpits, we have put to an open shame. Brethren, it must never be so, it must not be so with one of us, we must not miss our way. We need to be in an agony of earnest supplication so that we may not fail as to our own lifework, or in bringing souls to Christ, or glory to God.

There are some matters which do not require much judgment in order to discern that they are wrong. Verily we may put many things to the ground at once by applying the rule which our Saviour has given us, 'By their fruits shall ye know them.' Before, then, we act upon any principle, or proceed to inculcate any dogma which we ask men to receive upon authority, it will be well to look as to the results which are likely to follow from their wider application. Now, brethren, I think it does not need that you should bring forth your vigorous logic to prove that the current teaching now become so general has any tendency to make men strong of faith, and to deepen them in their belief in the Lord Jesus Christ. Many sermons are admirable if the Gospel be 'Doubt and you shall be saved.' If their intention be not to create doubt their result will be so most assuredly. I believe that more becomes known by our people concerning the different forms of scepticism through the teaching of ministers than in all other ways; we are the advertisers for the devil in our sermons. Some preachers seem always to be going about, paste brush in hand, sticking up notices concerning the ridiculous absurdities of 'modern thought.'

Certain sermons cannot possibly help our people to faith in Christ. They resemble the process which is repeated upon a poor dog at the Grotto at Cannes. When the performance begins he knows pretty well what is going to happen to him. He is dipped into the gas which rises about up to your knees, then he is thrown into the water, and he revives, and goes back again ready for the next exhibition. But that dog is not likely to be one of the most efficient hunters or watchers, and when our hearers are taken Sunday after Sunday, and plunged into a bath of doubt and sceptical thought, they are not very likely to become strong in the faith.

Those who have criticised us freely on other points give us credit for a good share of common sense. I have common sense enough to know that to go and talk about my doubts is a poor way of working for Christ. Taking stock of myself this morning, if I have ever done so I would regret it. Suppose we have to deal with careless souls, with men who will not think. What shall we do with them? What shall we present to them as the truth of God? Suppose we go to them and begin to speculate about the future, looking beyond the river, and declaring that we cannot see what is there, but we really do think that somehow or other there is a larger hope than many have preached; it is true it is not revealed in Scripture, but our large-hearted charity makes us believe it is so—can you imagine any being led to Christ by such teaching? How many would be caused to cry out, 'What must we do to be saved?' How many would be made upon bended knees to weep before the Lord because of the terrible result of sin? Will they not far rather continue in sin, and abide where they are, indulging still this wondrous 'larger hope,' and going into further iniquity.

I will put this matter in its true light by one question. If you have a brother or sister, if you had grown-up sons and daughters, or if, being yourselves sons, you have a father still unsaved, would you stand by your father's bedside and say to him, 'Dear old father, trust in God that though you die without repentance you will still meet me in another world'? Can you say to your brother, about whom you are under concern, 'Dear brother, confide in the "larger hope" that you will not be for ever cast away from God, go into eternity and run the risk of annihilation, or of restoration'? Would you persuade him to such senseless folly? I am sure that you would not. No, by the grace of God, the souls we love shall never be commended to a risk like that, for even if it were true we are on the safer side, even if there be a mistake, if there were no hell—and I am persuaded that there is—yet still it were better far to warn men of a danger greater than exists than that we salved their consciences, and administered to them a soporific, instead of arousing them with all our might, and bidding them escape for their lives. No, Sirs, you send me into the world to win souls, to warn the careless, to lead men to decision, you must not first of all take from me one of the most powerful arguments I can use; you must not withhold from me one of the best weapons I can wield if you expect me to do exploits in the name of God. It does seem to me to argue a want of judgment, and a lack of sense to deal thus with what God has revealed. Put it into practice, and see what will come of it; mark how it works—it eats as doth a canker, its fruit is corruption, and evil, and only evil, and the farther it goes the worse the result will be seen to be.

The result of this present modern thought, dear brethren, is not a thing of question, for it has been tried so many times over, again and again and again. Wherever you see the rise of unbelief, you may always know what to expect as the natural effect. Point me to the spots where faith has been shaken, where speculation has been rife, and you point me to the spots where spiritual life has been almost extinct, and where such a thing as conversion has been almost unknown. Only look at the state of our own country in the days of Doddridge, just before Whitefield and Wesley were raised up by God. Dr Watts and other eminent divines of that age were perfectly sound in themselves, but not very deep, and sometimes not very strong; they got to be very genteel, and they were exceedingly thoughtful, it was rather their own thought than God's thought. Then they became more and more philosophical until the bulk of our churches had swung round to within a little of Socinianism. Never was religion at a lower ebb, nor morals either; it was a plague and curse upon the whole kingdom—was that 'advanced thought.' Then came up again the old rough Scriptural style of speech, men heard once again the old, old story, 'Repent ye, and believe the Gospel.' Wesley and Whitefield went forth preaching salvation by the Blood, and regeneration by the Holy Spirit, and these wise men began to preach it down, but it is a thing that does not go to be preached down, and ere long it triumphed to the praise of God. In the history of Christ's church this has recurred so often that the whole thing ought to be looked upon like the idolatry of the children of Israel. It came out in the wilderness, it came out as a fever after they reached the land of Canaan, the calf of Bethel was but the counterpart of Aaron's golden calf. This abomination must be utterly destroyed; like the temple, there must not be one stone left upon another. I would treat is as the Romans treated everything that reminded them of the Emperor Caligula, whom they hated so bitterly that they broke every statue of him that could be found, and I believe there is not to be found anywhere one statue of the man of whom his subjects said, 'Let him be accursed.' They utterly broke in pieces every memorial of him. This thing has been, in the churches, such a curse so many times over—it has brought us to the very verge of destruction—that it is to be looked upon as an evil that must be removed at any cost.

Now try this teaching upon yourselves. A good test of certain teaching is its effect upon ourselves. I remember trying once upon myself that splendid doctrine of perfection. You smile brethren; it was a very amiable delusion, and pleased a good many people for a time. I thought I would try the Lord in prayer in the spirit which I felt was suggested in books I had read. I had been very familiar at the mercy seat for many years; and I had often been astonished to find how readily the door was opened when I knocked, but this time I came in a new fashion. I came once that way, I tried it to see how I should fare. In answer to the question, 'Who's there?' I replied, 'One who is perfectly consecrated to God,' which I think I could say truly, 'one who believes himself to be sanctified, body, soul and spirit wholly the Lord's.' The good messenger at the gate shut the little door so that I blessed him for it afterwards. I knocked again. They said they did not know me, they never heard of such a person saved by the name that I had given. It was an imposition. I did it really and truly and honestly and heartily, but I never got any comfortable sense of acceptance in prayer when I tried it. I knocked once more and told them that I was Charles Spurgeon, a poor sinner saved by grace who was looking up to God alone for mercy and felt himself wonderfully unsanctified, full of corruption and iniquity. The door flew open, out they came crying, 'We know you, you have been here before so often. Come in thou blessed of the Lord, wherefore standest thou without?' It is for me a matter of simple necessity. I never tried that style again, it does not pay. I do not mean to glory in myself any more, I did once, I felt that I was sanctified, and that I could not any longer say, 'O wretched man that I am! who shall deliver me from the body of this death?' But it did not answer. I will never do it again. So it is with these other teachings which are infinitely worse; if you will try them, brethren, you will soon prove what effect they will have. Get away from believing and get into speculating, and see how you will pray; see how you delight in the Lord; see how you can preach. Have you by this kind of teaching been brought into full sympathy with Christ? I am persuaded you will feel that its influence is altogether deadly to you, and a thing to be escaped from. We see what evils come of this thing; I notice that when men cannot believe the simple Gospel they always believe some folly directly. There shall be week after week attacks upon the orthodox faith; what will come next? Articles upon spiritualism, as sure as you live; it cannot be helped. If the pendulum swings with too much force one way, it must go back just as far the other way. Men will not believe in the Everlasting God, but they will believe in any devil or ghost of which they are told. It is the nature of this evil spirit that it cannot keep itself clear from its own accusation, that while it cries out against the credulity of the orthodox, it leads its disciples into a credulity infinitely more astonishing, and vastly less excusable. Brethren, we shall not I trust run any risk of becoming victims of superstition as others have been before us, but when I look upon this mysterious thing of the present day I am reminded of a story that I read in a book of travels in India. The writer said that he had seen some wonderful things in that country, amongst others one day he saw two conjurers with a chain 50 cubits long. They flung one end of it up in the air and there it remained—a dog walked up the chain and disappeared, then a goat came forward and did the same, then a lion, and afterwards a tiger walked up and vanished. Verily, I do not believe that such a thing could have occurred, but our 'deep thinkers' are showing us something remarkably like it. They have flung a great chain up in the air; where it is fixed nobody knows, but we can see some of its links. They have sent the doctrine of the atonement up this chain, and the doctrine of the immortality of the soul, and the doctrine of the deity of Christ, and I am told that even the resurrection, and the death of Christ, and the personality of God are to be regarded as moot points in the association of intelligent men that will be formed soon. They are all going up the chain one after another, until I have wondered what is going to be left. What is the conclusion at which they will arrive? At present the conclusion is one in which nothing is concluded at all.

The effect of this upon one's mind would be perfectly horrible—every hope, every consolation, every expectation, every resting place of our soul gone, and there is given us in return certain books which pretend to great knowledge, but which have very little indeed in them. The whole thing seems to me to be a taking away from us of that walking by faith which is the very essence of the Christian life. Rather take us away from the speculation of men like ourselves, to the teaching of revelation, the invaluable and infallible instructor in all things. The devil likes to see us getting our gold and making our own golden calf and saying, 'These be thy gods O Israel'; but may we be saved from the very tinge and touch of this thing, for its very shadow is baleful to the soul.

Our way, it seems to me, is to live in the realities of Christian service. Get into the back streets if you have any inclination towards the new doctrines, see how many of the people living there you will reclaim from drunkenness and open profanity by teaching the would-be popular heresies. Try them also upon yourselves, see how much nearer they will bring you to Christ, and if they do not deepen your spiritual life, fling the whole thing away, do not be for ever bothered by it, answer it once for all, have done with it, and go on with your own work.

And now let us come to this examination of our own work. Let us do it, brethren, as if death were close to us. A good accountant keeps his books so that you may call upon him at any moment, they are always in such a state that they are fit to be seen by anybody, all straight and clear, and a Christian man should so keep his whole life that it would make a good finish at any minute. If the angel of death should come down this morning while I am speaking to you here, how would he find your life work? Would it make a good finish, brother; is it complete? It ought to be always. I like Bengel's thought of dying—he did not believe in Christian men making a fuss about dying, they ought to live so as to be ready to die at any minute. 'As if,' he said, 'I were in company, and a friend came to the door, and I answered the enquiry, and finding that he wanted me just looked in and said, "Dear friends, I am going," being always ready to go.' I wish I could bring something of the kind before you now—the caresses of weeping friends, the still room, the audible tick of the clock, and the failing eyes—making each one feel as if he might at this moment be called away, or the Lord himself might suddenly come into his temple. Try, dear brethren, to think of that last tremendous day when we shall surely take our place, we must be there, and we shall have to give an account of the things done in the body whether they have been good or whether they have been evil.

I. It will help us to form our judgments under the influence of death and resurrection and judgment if I ask you to THINK OF YOUR WORK, FIRST, IN THE LIGHT OF YOUR COMMISSION, 'Go ye into all the world, and preach the Gospel to every creature. He that believeth and is baptized shall be saved, but he that believeth not shall be damned.' The first question that we shall raise is, 'Have we preached *the Gospel*?' Are we sure that it is the Gospel, not a, but *the* Gospel, that we have preached? Has it been good news to sinners? Have we preached Christ Jesus, for it was concerning him that the angel sang, 'I bring you glad tidings,' that is to say the Gospel, he himself being the Gospel? How many of us will have to say in our dying moments, 'I wish I had preached Christ more'? You are to go and preach Christ and him crucified, the death and resurrection of Jesus. How often in the Acts and Epistles we read of preaching Jesus, but how much is included in that expression! Have we preached faith, and justification by faith, insisting very clearly upon the believing, and salvation not of the works of the law, but of grace through faith? Probably we have done this, but have we preached side by side with it, regeneration? Have we been as clear as we should be about 'Ye must be born again'? There are many people who know nothing whatever of this, they believe they are saved because Christ died for them, so they say; and yet they are living such lives that we are sure they are still living in sin. It is true that men are saved if they really believe in Christ, but that other truth must be brought very prominently forward, otherwise certain revival teaching will do almost as much evil as good—'Repent, and be converted,' 'Repent, and be baptized.' John came preaching, 'Repent ye, for the kingdom of heaven is at hand,' and we must put before our hearers the necessity for the work of repentance graciously wrought in us by the Holy Spirit. I should be afraid when I came to die that I had not made sound work of my ministry if I continually cried out, 'Believe, and live,' if I had not also preached, 'Repent, and be converted,' and if I had not made distinctions between the faith which is the faith of devils and the faith of God's elect. We are to preach the Gospel, the whole of it. There are some truths that are called high doctrines; well, they are so, but there is a utility in everything in the Bible. There is no herb but has some use, no bird or tiny insect that dances in the summer's air is useless, nor is there one truth of God's Word without its special mission. Our ministry should be all round, complete, harmonious, according to the large-heartedness which the Spirit of God will give to us, preaching in its proper season every part of the truth of God. Do not leave out the eternal choice that God has made, nor the effectual redemption that Christ has offered, preach these doctrines again and again, let the atonement and substitution and the like be your theme continually. Do not leave out the work of the Holy Ghost, lest you should grieve him and lose all power.

'Go ye into all the world and preach the Gospel.' Preach *the* Gospel. I have never to ask myself, 'What Gospel have I to give the people next Sunday, for I am advancing continually, and must consult the new books so as to be abreast of the times?' In these days you must buy a book at least every week, and you ought to get a new one every day, in order to learn the last version of theology that has come out. You must put away the old capes and muffs of your grandfather's time, and get the best new expensive dress that can be bought in Bond Street or Regent Street. We have got to cut out the old truth in the same way, instead of keeping to the same truth evermore. It really seems to me we shall have to get the old god-makers back again; like one I saw in Pompeii before the image of a goddess. He did not know what she was to be called, whether she would be worshipped as Venus, or Vesta, or Juno; the face, the real expression of individuality, was left to be supplied according to his customer's taste. And the modern thought gentlemen have an outward form and visage that in some respects resemble evangelical Christianity, but they are quite ready to be fashioned into the likeness of Venus, or Diana, or Vesta, or anything else that may be taught by the last great apostle of heresy, and to put on a new face to please their patrons.

This is what we cannot do—our statue is carved and cut and fixed, yes, carved in adamant! The truth remains unaltered and unalterable, since God did not send a Gospel into the world that was to be developed (which is the favourite word used now), with liberty for it to be manipulated just as men chose, and melted like wax into any form they pleased. The truth, *the* Gospel, is a rock, and I hope you can all rise up and say, 'As far as we know it, we have stuck fast to the everlasting Gospel of the blessed God. We can do no other, so help us God.'

Our next enquiry upon our commission is—have we *preached* the Gospel? 'Go ye into all the world, and preach the Gospel.' I do not call all that I hear from a pulpit preaching, I really think that the word means something rather more than some preaching would seem to imply: it is to go as a herald, then it cannot signify doing it in the very quiet, mild, lady-like manner of some preachers who give their hearers large quantities of poetry and other adornments of oratory as if that was all that they had to say, nor is it my idea of preaching to put before the people multitudes of figures more or less incongruous. I must confess that my idea of preaching hardly reconciles me to the thought of reading every word. If we are really to preach to the fullest extent and prophesy in the name of the Lord, there must be an earnest, intensified speaking out of the truth, and not a mere going through it. There are some preachers about whom you might wonder as you do when you see a fly in amber. You marvel how it got into the amber, and so you wonder how such a creature as that got into a pulpit, that is the only curiosity you have about him. I have known some preachers who seemed to be under the impression that pulpits were made for them, and churches formed for them rather than they for the churches, they have not any practical purpose to serve, the time has come for the sermon and they make it or they borrow it. They are exceedingly well versed in the 'Handbook,' and their one great anxiety is how they can get introduced to the vacant churches so that they may get into a better position. Their use is very much like what the primitive tribesman's idea of the telegraphic wires was. 'Man,' says he, 'what are dem wires for?' 'Why, to keep up de posts.' 'Well, den, what are de posts for?' 'Why, to keep up de wires, of course.' So it seems as if churches were to maintain ministers, and ministers were to maintain churches, as the one great end of their existence. I need scarcely say that, to our mind, preaching is something very different from this; it is to go first as a herald, to go before the King and announce his approach, to say, 'The King cometh.' I think we have not preached at all unless we preach with the sound of our Master's feet behind us. The preacher is not a herald unless he precedes his King and goes forward at his command and proclaims, 'The King himself is coming.' Have you preached, brethren, or have you merely filled a pulpit, or belonged to the association? I like to hear it said of a man, 'He did preach; he was a preacher; he never read a book about German theology, the very sound of German is strange to him; but oh! the fellow could preach. He was no hand at the Penny Reading, he might have made a very poor show at the Young Men's Mutual Improvement Society, but he did preach; he would not have made a Secretary, he was not a good Committee man, but *he could preach.*' I want that to be true of us all.

We are to preach the Gospel, but according to our commission, we are to preach the Gospel *to every creature.* Come, brethren, there is a little sifting to be done here. Have you preached the Gospel to every creature? Have you preached to the young? Dear young people, it is hard to keep them quiet. One reason is because our sermons are not what they ought to be, otherwise there would be a little bit for the boys and girls. You know boys and girls can be made to listen; I have seen a congregation of them listening as attentively as older people ever did. You know how they listened to the Lord Jesus Christ, the most admiring of his auditors were the children, they delighted to hear him preach. Do not many preachers go on from year to year without uttering a single sentence that a child could carry home and understand?

'To every creature.' Have you tried to meet each case of experience? Have you looked after God's aged people, have you looked after the tried, the desponding, the despairing? Have you tried to go after the odd cases? Have you sometimes rambled in your sermons? The sheep will wander, and you have had to ramble in order to find them. Have you ruined your sermons sometimes in the judgment of your methodical hearers so that you might wander after poor old Mary, or say something that would meet the case of a young enquirer, as you have tried to get on his track? That is the thing to do, to preach the Gospel to every creature. Oh! let us endeavour more and more after this. We must not have a favourite run of subjects, and neglect all the rest: the gardener must water all the plants in the garden, he must not be so fond of the fuchsias as to let the geraniums die; and he must adapt his watering to the plants under his care: so our preaching must be adapted to each person in our congregations.

Then there is another word, 'Go ye into *all the world*,' not that one man is to do this, but the whole body of Christians. Now, have we had a fair proportion of this work? Do you not think that we have among us today some brother who ought to be transplanted to do work for God on a foreign shore? It is not, gentlemen, the brother who cannot succeed here, he probably will not do there; the best man to go abroad is the man who can do well either at home or out, and our churches should be ready to send out these men. Many a brother might put to himself the question, 'Am I where I ought to be? Have I a special call from God to go further with his Gospel?' We cannot go before God as a Conference, and answer to this commission, unless we have a far larger proportion than we have now of men who go abroad to tell of the love of Christ. Blessed above many shall he be that shall not build upon another man's foundation, but that shall go forth to lay in foreign lands his foundation for the temple of the living God. 'Go ye therefore, and teach all nations, *baptizing them* in the name of the Father, and of the Son, and of the Holy Ghost.' I shall not want to question you as to whether you have attended to that part of the commission. Do not be ashamed of it; if you do not think your Master commanded it, drop it; but if you believe it is his order, let it very distinctly occupy the place Christ assigned to it. Perhaps you may not be personally to blame in this matter; well then, go on with it, teach the baptism, insist upon the baptism, deliver it out of the hand of the Philistines who would transform it into a regenerating rite, save it from being considered a 'seal of the covenant,' preach it as the burial with Christ which belongs to the dead in Christ, as the type of the resurrection with Christ which belongs to those who are truly begotten again in him from the dead. By putting it in its rightful place you will be answering error and teaching truth in all its fair proportions at the same time. I do not believe there is a Baptist living who is ever likely to make too much of baptism; most of us keep it too far back. Do not make too much of it, and do not make too little of it.

'*Teaching them* to observe all things whatsoever I have commanded you.' There is to be teaching after baptism. Some say that this text evidently proves that we are to baptize all the nations, and not merely the believers; then why do they not do it? Why do they not go and baptize a nation of heathens? Their own senses teach them better. When they go to the heathen and preach Christ as their only Saviour, and some of them believe, they must baptize the converts, so they baptize believers. 'Well,' we say to them, 'do it here as well as there.' After the converts are baptized and received into the church, they must be taught to observe all things which Christ has commanded. Remember when you come to the end of your ministry you will have to question yourself about the teaching you have given your people. If you do the work of an evangelist, do so; but the pastor has to feed, and the feeding is by teaching. I think I once read that a comet is made of a substance so attenuated that many thousands of miles of it could be contained in a very small space. I almost fancy that some of the material of the last comet was obtained by certain of our brethren, and has been used in their sermons ever since. I know of no other substance so thin and attenuated as that which is employed by some preachers. Put something into your discourses, brethren, something solid, something weighty, something good, and something instructive, something for your hearers to feed upon. And then we are to teach them to observe *all things that Christ has commanded*. Seek to know all that he commands, do not let anything be omitted, even the simplest of his precepts. Teach them what he says about moral conduct as well as about church matters, the duty of parents to children, children to parents, husbands to wives, and wives to husbands, teach them to observe every command and precept of Christ. Can you read your commission through and say, 'I have fulfilled every part of it'? or must you this morning say, 'Lord, I have come short here, I have come short there'? Now whatever the point is in which you have been wanting, confess the failure, and ask for grace that it may not be so again.

II. Now I ask you a second question, not what has been your commission, but WHAT HAS BEEN YOUR AUTHORITY? If you look at Matthew's account you will see that, 'Go ye therefore' immediately follows, 'All power is given unto me in heaven and in earth.' The *'therefore'* carries us back to our authority, and hence, beloved brother, you are always to *preach in Jesus Christ's name.* If you say to your people, 'I tell you this' they may ask, 'Who are you to make such statements?' But saying it in the name of Jesus you may say, 'I,' not 'I or my own authority,' but, 'I, because Christ has said it, I, being a mouth for him, say this to you.' We cannot assume, and never wish to assume, any priestly authority; but we ought to gird ourselves with the authority of Christ when we are proclaiming his Gospel. If I am about to tell a tale, men may listen or not; but if I am speaking in the name of Jesus, they are bound to listen and to believe. They will sin against Christ if they do not, they will be casting his cords from them. I feel sometimes when I am preaching that I must command the people in the name of God there and then to believe in Jesus Christ; and I believe that when that is done in faith, it will generally and constantly be the voice of the Holy Ghost to the sinner so that he speaking by our lips shall say as when of old Paul said, 'The times of this ignorance God winked at; but now commandeth all men everywhere to repent.' It is not 'If you will or not,' but it is God's own message as truly as if it thundered from Sinai, though it sweetly comes in melting accents from Calvary. Deliver it, not with bated breath, nor yet with suspicion lurking in your heart, but believing it, knowing it to be God's message to mankind. Let us wrap about us the prophetic mantle, and speak in the name of God.

'All power is given unto me in heaven and in earth. Go ye therefore, and teach all nations, baptizing them, etc.' Brethren, have we spoken *in Christ's power?* That is the point, it is not enough to say, 'I will do it,' have you done it? Have there been times when we know, and our people know, and none could question it, that there has been a power of undoubted force? If we had sought it more, and believed in it more, and endeavoured to retain it when we had it, we should have had more of it. I tell you sometimes what I like to read about myself, 'This man is certainly no great preacher, he is not at all comparable to so and so, he is not a great thinker, he is not a great orator, but when you come away from hearing him you feel that he has done you good, and brought you nearer to God.' I had rather they should put me down as nothing at all, and yet have to say, 'God evidently does speak to men's hearts through that man.' I had rather have that than any honour I can imagine; that is the power, the power, the power divine that will go with a very simple ministry. Oh! have I not known men who have made me weep? They have been my masters, I would willingly sit at their feet; and yet as preachers they have been very poor things, they did not know much about books, they were almost illiterate, but ah! well, they knew their mission, and their Master knew them, and his power was upon them. You know if I receive a letter brought by a powdered footman with a lace coat and fine silver buttons, and I open it and it contains nothing at all but a card, I do not think much of it; but if a poor countryman comes to my door, and does not even bring a well-written note, but bluntly says, 'My master from the country told me to call here and bring you a hundred pounds for the College,' I feel that I should be profited by his ministry, not that I think any better of the countryman than the gent in buttons, but the difference was in the masters of the two people. So, when your Master gives you some glorious message to deliver, it will not matter much about you, if your Master has been with you, and clothed you with power.

Brethren, have we, still thinking upon this matter of divine authority— have we spoken *with faith in that authority?* Do we really believe that Christ is Lord to the glory of God the Father? Do we believe that he sitteth now in glory enthroned at his Father's right hand, and that no matter what men and devils do and say, yet shall his kingdom stand? Are we sure about his teachings, confident about every jot and tittle of them, and so do speak with faith in him? We may well do so, for the grand old cause is safe enough; we need not fear, for our Master's crown does not rock upon his head. You may well speak with authority and not as the scribes, for the Lord is with you when you are with him by faith. Our work is to be regarded every hour as one might have looked upon the Colossus at Rhodes. The man who made it was ordered to engrave upon it the name of Ptolemy, but he engraved it in the cement which did not last much longer than Ptolemy himself; while he cut his own name in the solid stone, and there it stood till the Colossus was taken down. There are some men that are trying to cover the Gospel with their patent worldly Christian cement, on which they inscribe their own names, but it will not stand, death which doth all things else impair will impair that also, but the name of Jesus of Nazareth will be found written upon his own glorious Gospel. Did you notice one word which I must mention in connection with our commission—'Lo, I am with you alway.' Come, brethren, have you preached having Christ with you? Would you have preached as you have done at times if you had been sure that Christ was present? Would you not have preached very differently if you had seen him come walking into your chapel? I fancy you would have said to yourself, 'I must get on to something else, this is not a sermon fit for him to hear, I must preach what the Master loves, for *there he is.*'

'Lo, I am with you alway.' What bravery it gives a man in speaking to know that Christ is there to witness that he speaks the truth; and how earnestly and yet how modestly and how self-depreciatingly he would preach in the presence of that Lord compared with whom he is less than nothing. In your building for God you take a trowel and spread the mortar, but there is another eye that is watching your work; you lay stone upon stone, and the building rises, but there is another hand at work upon it; and what you are doing, *you* are not doing after all, for it is he that doeth the whole of it. Never think of going without him; be like the old Welsh preacher, who had not come to the chapel one day when he was to preach. A boy was sent to fetch him, and on returning he said, 'I went to his chamber, and I heard him talking. I do not believe he will come, for I heard him saying to someone else in the room he would not *go* unless he would go with him, and the other party did not say a word.' 'Ah,' said one of the hearers, 'he was saying to the Lord, "I will not go except thou bless me," they will both come,' and so they did. That is the style in which we must go to our work, and not go without him, and then we shall be able to look back upon our life's mission with joy whenever we come to the end of it.

III. I must hurry on to ask a few QUESTIONS ABOUT OUR SPIRIT IN PREACHING, because if we are to go in his name, we ought not only to regard the commission and authority, but we should also regard the spirit which becomes us. We cannot go in the name of Christ to preach the Gospel *anyhow;* our King must be served in the best spirit possible. Have you always been as *intense* as you might have been? You have been at a white heat sometimes, have you been so always? Have you done all that ever you could every time that you have preached? It was a capital testimony borne to Howe before he was an admiral that while the other captains would ask how they were to accomplish what they were commanded, Howe always did it without asking how it was to be done. Have you done your Master's orders, followed out his bidding, without questioning till the very life within you has been in harmony with his?

Have you been *loving* in spirit? Have you been like the Master in this respect? 'He is a fine man,' was said of a preacher once, 'a John the Baptist, only he would appear not to have eaten much wild honey.' We want brethren that love people to Christ; it is the way to save them, keep on loving them till they cannot hold out any longer. Love begets love; and God's Spirit through the begetting of love begets love in our hearers. And have we been *faithful?* We feel when we get to be loving to the highest degree, how important it is to be faithful. Sometimes when you are rebuking sin in a man you deal very gently with him, you hope he will fish out what you mean by what you have said, you tolerate evil in a brother, and you encourage where you ought to condemn. We must mourn before God if this has been our case. May there not be a failure in our consistency? During the past year have we kept faithful, has the first love been upon us, have we been going on and on and on, not rapidly perhaps, but constantly and patiently? If so, unto God be the glory; if not, a reform must take place at once.

IV. It may help us to GO OVER OUR ACTIONS, as well as our spirit. How about the *study?* Have you studied, brethren? I hope you have; I trust you will never be amongst those who can discourse nonsense in any quantity; there are sufficient persons who are gifted in that line already, or who are entering upon it. I hope you do study the Word of God, and other books that will help you to understand that. Your Biblical studies—are they as earnest as they should be? No, brethren, we must not let any going out to tea parties or sweethearting interfere with our studies; everything must be done in its own place; no domestic cares, no attention to the little garden, no going out on the pretence of making calls, must be allowed to take the place of study. Then about *our daily lives*—how about them? Has your life really supported the Gospel you preach? Someone said to me concerning one of our brethren, 'Oh, sir, he lives what he preaches; everybody can see that he lives it.' It is such a terrible thing to have a minister who differs in his life from his teaching. Then, again, *the visitation of your church*, are there no errors and failures there? How often pastoral visits will degenerate into little silly gossip by which there is more hurt done than good! I cannot say if it has been so, I can only suggest the enquiry; if it has let us be humbled, and amend for the future.

V. The last thing should be about OUR RESULTS. We cannot always estimate our success by the effects which we can see, but sometimes out of results you will really be able to judge, because there is some relation between the results that can be seen and the effects which are really produced by our preaching. How about your *congregations?* Full to the doors! Very well, keep it so; it is easy to scatter a congregation; I know some gentlemen who are good hands at that work. Your place is half empty—someone says, 'I wish I could see ours half full.' It is very wonderful how the people do come to hear the Gospel; I often say to myself, 'How is it that they can sit and listen to such a poor tool as I am?' We feel that when we think of our own preaching. When we go and hear some of our brethren preach, then we think we do very fairly. Well, brother, if I may suggest the enquiry, if you have an empty place, just ask yourself, 'Have I done everything that I could to fill those empty seats; I cannot be the means of saving souls that are not here; have I done all I might in stirring up my people to do what they can to bring others under the sound of the Gospel?' Thus should it be. Resolve that you will get the Gospel to the people somehow, and get a congregation from somewhere or other. Well, now about *the conversions;* we cannot convert people; regeneration is not in our power. Quite so; but suppose I have preached for twelve months and have not had any conversions. I think I must not put that down to divine sovereignty; I must begin to say, 'What is the reason that I get no harvest? This seed that I sow is good seed, surely all of it does not fall on bad or stony ground, there must be a good bit of soil somewhere. I have feared if this Gospel be as powerful as it once was, for after preaching it all this time I can only get somewhere about fifty people to hear me. Perhaps, however, after all, I may not be doing the work in the right way; perhaps I do not ask the people to call at my house; perhaps if I were to give out that I should be happy to meet enquirers, a good many might come; perhaps they want me to visit them—at any rate, I cannot be doing all that I might be doing, or I should surely have more results to the preaching of the Gospel.' Who must be blamed? If any of you have children that are unruly and disobedient, whose fault is it? The person who ought to be blamed is yourself; you ought to have made them obedient. So it is with your people; if they are not what they ought to be, you must be a better preacher, make your preaching so that they cannot help being profited by it. You say they are like stones, then go and ask the masons how they work in stone the will of their master; but your hearers are worse than stones, they are adamant, well then go and ask the diamond-cutters how they do their work; but they are harder than diamonds, then go and ask the Lord to give you that strength which cuts those that are harder than diamonds. You must have conversions, you must be ready to say, 'There, I will die for these souls rather than they should die.' It must become a matter of anguish and agony to you if your hearers are not saved. Suppose you were to pick out about half-a-dozen of the best brethren you have in your church, and say to them, 'I cannot go on as things are going; if you three or four will just meet me here privately that we may pray God to send down his Spirit, if you will agree to it we will join hands and pledge ourselves together that we will not give the Lord any rest until he sends us a blessing.' I believe that would be a glorious way of making a commencement. After a little while go into the pulpit and say to the people, 'I am your minister, called by you to this position, I am not going to mince matters in the least; I feel that God is not with us, and I am miserable; shall I go away and labour where God will bless me, or stopping here will you join me now earnestly to beseech the Lord to be with us?' It looks like business when you come to that, and it would soon prove how many were in earnest for a blessing. Just see to that brethren, if there is no conversion work in your midst. Then you may judge yourselves by *the growth of your churches,* I do not mean in size, but in grace. There ought to be a grand host rising up from our ranks fit to teach others also, and some who should become mothers in Israel. Most people are not only young in years, but very green in the things of God. Now, brother, if it is the state of affairs amongst your people, it is probably because the spiritual meat they have had has not been fit to feed their souls. I used to notice the wonderful appearance of the happy old Christian men and women who used to be members in Joseph Irons' and Harrington Evans' days. They looked as if they had been fed well, and great feeders they were, too, you could not satisfy them with a pretty little essay that had not a halfpenny worth of Gospel in it, and when you talked with them you found that they were judicious, kindly, holy, well-established, godly people. They were most assuredly saved, and they knew it. The devil knew it, too, and paid his attentions somewhere else.

If your ministry does not produce people like that, it is a sign that your preaching is not what it should be. There should be in every church, and will be if it is right, *great unity*. Now if your church members are not united, do not go and lay the blame upon the persons that make the quarrels, but upon yourself that you do not unite them together. I do not know how it is, but I always feel as if I could manage anybody. Many and many a strange thing has happened to me in the matter of quarrelling people. There was a brother who laid a very serious charge against a member in the church, and he never knew anything about it. I said to the one who felt aggrieved, 'You say it was so, and I am sure it was not, but I apologise to you for it.' It seemed strange that I should make an apology for what had never been done at all, and the man did not want to accept it, but I said to him, 'God has blessed me to your soul, so you must put down to my account whatever you think this brother has done wrong, for I humbly crave forgiveness on his behalf.' Of course, he forgave the other brother for my sake, and I commend to you the practice of smoothing over things like that, even taking the blame upon yourself. I do believe that there is an omnipotent way of knuckling under, and so dealing with a cross-grained person that he cannot resist you; you will either kill him or cure him. Somehow or other you must get the mastery, 'for every kind of beasts, and of birds, and of serpents, and of things in the sea, is tamed, and hath been tamed of mankind: but the tongue can no man tame,' so you had better leave that to him who is the great tongue-tamer. If people really love Christ, and get warm-hearted in love for souls, Mrs Smith will be seen earnestly working by the side of Mrs Jones, whom she could not endure before, and old Mr Grasp-all will be as ready to give as he was to grip before. Spiritual life is a wonderful cure for many evils. Let us judge ourselves—not the churches—by *our prayer-meetings*. You complain that so very few come out. Well brethren, it will be the safest way to act as if this were your fault, perhaps your members would say that there was not much in them to come for, you yourself prayed at such length, and did not pray very well either, and then you had not the moral courage to tell that poor old soul who prayed for five-and-twenty minutes that he had better pray at home. He persists in confessing his shortcomings, he ought to deplore his *long*comings. It always seems to me that if I have a good handful of corn ready for the Monday night prayer-meeting, there will be sure to be some chickens that will come and pick it up. When a man is in trade and says, 'I cannot get custom,' I should say to him, 'Let me see what you sell.' If he gave me for a pound of butter something very much like cart grease, and for tea something that I am sure never came from China or Ceylon, I should know why he does not get customers. I could show you an ugly little shop where a good man made a fortune. I said to him one day, 'How is it that you do such a good business, you seem to have next to nothing in your shop?' 'Why,' he replied, 'I really send my things away as soon as I fill in, for this reason, I never went to market without resolving to buy the best articles that money could purchase, so as I bought the best and sold the best I got all the trade of the district here in this little old shop.' If you keep the best, brethren, you will get the people.

Judge yourself also, dear brother, by *the mission spirit* of your people. We have not the full development of the mission spirit unless we have young men and women coming out and saying to us, 'Here are we, send us.' The question for each one of us to ask is, 'Have I been enough inspired myself with the missionary spirit?' Do not any of you be satisfied till you have a representative of your church at work for the Lord in the mission field.

And now, lastly, *do not let us have any sort of fear about us*. Let us go humbly and penitently before God, but let us be brave in the sight of men, to whom we give space by subjection, no, not for an hour. It is not for us to go about blowing our own trumpets, and exalting ourselves before our fellow-creatures, but we must remember that we are soldiers of Christ, and it does not become a soldier to put down his feet as if the earth was sinking under him. So let us march on with the tramp of men, confident of victory. If nobody else will believe God, we believe him, and say, 'Let God be true, and every man a liar.' A vain attempt was made to discover the philosopher's stone which should turn all things to gold, and other sages sought to find out a perpetual lamp. We have got it, the Gospel lamp which no damp can extinguish, but which must burn on for ever and ever.

Note

* A note in *The Sword and the Trowel*, May 1878, indicates that this was the address given on the morning of Tuesday 9 April 1878 at the Annual Conference of the Pastors' College.

What we aim at

Address at the commencement of the College session, September 1888

DEAR FRIENDS,—It is well known to you, as well as to the supporters of this College, that our great desire is to train men to maintain and spread the gospel of our Lord Jesus Christ. I have never professed, either at our public gatherings or on any other occasion, that this College was intended to teach modern views, or that our men were taught to preach liberal sentiments, or anythingarianism. I have never concealed the fact that the views we hold are pre-eminently evangelical, and of the form which is commonly called Calvinistic—not in any close or narrow sense, but in the sense of giving prominence to the grace of God. We have not attempted to tie men down to think exactly alike upon five points, or fifty points, of matters wherein there is fair room for difference without sacrificing foundation truths; but we have always held by the infallible inspiration of the Bible, and we have also held that the essence of the revelation made to us in Holy Scripture is salvation by grace through faith in the precious blood of Jesus. Exceedingly dear to us are the doctrines which we hold in common with all Protestant Christians, and also those which come more distinctly under the head of 'the doctrines of grace.' We are very pronounced upon the truth that 'salvation is of the Lord.' We hold the gospel as Paul preached it, and as the Puritans preached it. Brethren, if you find at any time that you do not agree with those truths, you are bound, as honest men, to acknowledge your change of opinion, and to go your way. All those who have not done so, but have gained their education gratis, and then have gone forth to assail the doctrines taught in this Institution, have—but I leave them to their own consciences. If it was announced that a dinner was to be given on this farm to Mr Allison's mowers, and a number of men came and partook of it, though they had never seen a scythe, and had an objection to its use, I should think that they were interlopers, and that they should at least pay the cost of the dinner of which they had partaken. Let that pass. It will apply to none of you.

We believe that our gospel is consistent with the highest style of scholarship. Our conviction is, that all the learning and culture that men can obtain, if it be true, will not hinder them from preaching the simple faith of Christ crucified. If we thought that learning would turn us aside from the simplicity of Christ, we would have none of it; and certainly would not carry on a college for imparting the dangerous gift to others. Brethren, light is never at variance with light, though the semblance of it may be. It is my earnest prayer that the Lord would raise up out of this College men of understanding, men of wide reading, men of deep acquaintance with the Word of God; but men who are too well instructed by the Holy Spirit to be wise above what is written. Oh, for brethren who have much grace, and many gifts; who will use great talents in the cause of God and truth! Give your hearts to your studies, my brethren. You cannot learn too much, if you salt your learning with grace. Kill yourselves with study, and then pray yourselves to life again.

Let me, at this opening festival, express our ambitions concerning you. First, *we long that you should become good preachers of the gospel*. Our chief object is, not that you may become classical scholars, but soul-winning ministers. You come here that you may be helped to know correctly, to think clearly, and to put the result of that thinking into good plain English, so that the people who hear you may understand what you say. We hope that you may become *attractive* preachers, so that your utterances may not weary your hearers, and disperse them. We are not anxious that the people should go to sleep under your ministry, or that they should be obliged to leave it because of its dulness. We would have you so proclaim the truth, that the people may throng to hear it, and may remain to listen to it with pleasure and profit, year after year. This will require the fulness of your manhood, and somewhat more. May you not be mere land-drainage preachers, who depend upon your laborious studies of other men's books for your supplies: but may you be springing-well preachers, from whom the fresh, living water will continually flow forth. May your preaching be lively because it is living. May it remain fresh and interesting year after year. Artificial eloquence is a miserable thing; but the natural eloquence which springs from a true heart is a most potent instrument in the work of God upon the minds and hearts of men. May you all be preachers, clear in style, instructive in matter, fervent in spirit, and, above all, filled with the Holy Ghost.

We would have you not only attractive, but *impressive*. You must not discharge fireworks, but red-hot shot. May you be abundantly *effective* in conversions! If you do not become winners of souls, we have laboured in vain. Dear brethren whatever else you are or are not, do become useful preachers—men who shall sow good seed, and in due season reap full sheaves. If you can *write* for the glory of God, I would exhort you to do so; and I wish all our brethren would endeavour to produce readable gospel tracts; but still, your chief business is not with the pen, but with the tongue. You are set to *speak* of free grace and dying love. Mind you do it well. My solemn conviction is that God will bless you as soul-winners in the proportion in which you and your preaching are fit to be blessed. Go in for a hundred-fold harvest.

Our longing is to see many of you good expositors. Preaching ought to be far more largely expository than it now is. The churches need more of the sacred text, and less of loose talk. Sermons frequently are essays upon a topic, rather than explanations of Scripture. At times we have dissertations upon things in general, with little or no relation to the text which is placed as a heading to the discourse. We must never introduce our text to the people, and then make a bow to it, and say, 'Good-bye,' as if we had paid it sufficient courtesy by reading it in the hearing of the congregation. We ought not to divorce our discourse from the text, but to feel that the two are happily wedded. We have a certain company of greatly earnest, but greatly rambling preachers. God blesses them, for they only ramble over holy ground; but I believe that the Lord would bless them more, if they honoured the inspired Word by sticking to their texts to a reasonable degree. Since men are denying the plenary inspiration of Scripture, it is all the more important that we should make our hearers feel that we have an unshaken confidence in the inspired Book. We should labour to discover that divine and deeper meaning of the Word which does not lie upon the surface, but only reveals itself to loving, God-enlightened eyes. Happy are those preachers who are so saturated with Scripture that their lips drop with its sweet-smelling myrrh! You cannot hear such preachers without seeing new beauties in passages which you had hardly noticed before. As they go along their beaten track, they point out vistas in the forests of truth, and green alleys of fresh teaching, all bedecked with flowers of promise. I have frequently learned more from what a discourse suggested to me than from what it actually discussed.

Brethren, be masters of your Bibles. Have the sacred writings at your fingers' ends. To this end, read your Bibles continually. To this end, expound the Scriptures which you choose as the lessons for the day. I should like you to explain them to the people; but, in any case, be sure that you understand them yourselves. You will get through a great deal of Scripture if you study all the passages you read in the congregation. Habituate yourselves to quote Scripture correctly. You ought to be as particular about the very words of Scripture as a classical scholar would be when he refers to a passage in Homer or Virgil. Let us have no false quantities, no omissions, no interpolations; but the *ipsissima verba*, the precise words which the Holy Ghost has given to us. Let this be your practical confession of faith in *verbal* inspiration.

Know your Bible so well as to be able to give its inward sense in a few short words, so that the people can understand what they read. Let the study of the Bible be the chief of your studies. We are not to treat the Bible as a Christmas pie, from which we pick out a plum here and there, in order to display our cleverness, according to the nursery rhyme; but we are to know the run of it, we are to enter into the meaning of each one of its books, and catch the spirit of the whole. How seldom this is done! but how important it is! When we come forth to the people we should be full of *Bibline,* and bring to them the essence of revealed truth. If you get a sponge full of water, wherever you lay it down, it leaves a wet mark; wherever you hold it, it drips. May you be so full of the Bible that, wherever you go, you leave traces of it behind you. You cannot take in too much of the precious truth which God has revealed in the Scriptures, nor can you give out too much of it: in proportion as you take it in you will give it out.

One admirable result of knowing your Bibles will be your confirmation in the truth. The essence of Bible makes moral and spiritual bone. I saw an advertisement the other day—'Thirty tons of bones wanted'—and I said to myself, 'Yes, *mostly backbones*.' *Bibline* is the nutriment which makes backbone, muscle, and, above all, heart; and no preacher can afford to be without these things. I could tell you of preachers who know so little of their Bibles that, when a question has been under discussion, and texts have been quoted, it has been needful to find the passages for them before they would believe that they were in the Bible. Gross ignorance of Scripture peeps out amid the pretentious learning of the evolution school! I fear that many ministers read less of the Scriptures than of modern literature, and this accounts for their vagaries of thought. Young brethren, go to the fountain-head, and drink from the well of truth, pure and undefiled! Drink from the Word itself! Know it yourself, and strive to make others know it. Have a deep reverence for our infallible chart, and fix your eye upon it till you carry it photographed on your soul.

The third thing that we much desire to see, as the result of the College training, is a host of good pastors. What is wanted, especially in the villages and country towns, is pastoral visitation. I hear constantly the outcry, 'He preaches very well on the Sunday, but we never see him during the week.' I have heard it said of some preachers that there were two things in which they imitated the Deity—for they were incomprehensible on Sunday, and invisible all the rest of the week. Let not such a remark be made concerning you. Remember the Scotch proverb, 'A house-going minister makes a kirk-going people.' Country people are glad for you to drop in, and have a cup of tea with them. Never let the pastoral visit degenerate into hearing and repeating gossip and scandal, but see to it that you converse upon spiritual things. Some of our brethren, who have not much gift in preaching, exert a great influence by their diligent pastoral labours. I had a visit, not long ago, from two deacons of a church that is without a pastor, and they said to me, 'Could you tell us of a minister like Mr So-and-so?' I asked them what there was about that gentleman which made them mention him as a model, and they answered, 'He works so hard for his church; he visits the people, and he throws all his energies into the cause!' I next asked them, 'Are there any ministers who do not do this?' They laughed; and that was the only answer I could get. I am sorry that I understood them only too well. If business men neglected their shops as certain professional ministers neglect their churches, they would soon be bankrupts; and deservedly so.

I fear that some brethren read one part of one of the parables too emphatically. It runs thus: 'As if a man should cast seed into the ground; and should sleep, and rise night and day, and the seed should spring and grow up, he knoweth not how.' Having sown their seed they sleep, and expect it to grow, they know not how. They neither drive away the fowls of the air by their watchfulness, nor water the seed with their tearful prayers. Alas! if *we* sleep the enemy does not; but he seizes the opportunity to sow tares. We must keep awake, and be on the watch against him; we must watch for souls as those that must give an account. In season and out of season we must labour for the good of our people. We are not like policemen, for we are never 'off duty'; but are more like those firemen who are required to be always within sound of the gong, and ready to rush to the fire. A shepherd's work is never done: his sheep may need him at any hour. A man who grudges labour had better quit the ministry. If he does not go into it with all his heart and soul, he had better be serving behind the counter, or sweeping chimneys, or doing some other honourable work. Our office is not an excuse for play, but a position for hard work. I pray that we may see many going forth from us who will be true pastors of the people, who will go in and out before them, and feed them with knowledge and discretion.

One thing more, and I have done. *We long to see born in this College a considerable number of good evangelists.* What a good evangelist should be I need not tell you, for you have examples before you in our brethren Fullerton, Smith, Burnham, Harmer, Harrison, and others. These earnest brethren have proved their qualifications for the office of evangelists by years of laborious and efficient work. The good that has been effected by our brethren Fullerton and Smith eternity alone will reveal; their visit to a place has been like a great cloud emptying itself in heavenly rain, refreshing the whole region. Our evangelists love their work, and I always feel quite safe in leaving them to do their work in their own way; the only fault I have to find with them is, that perhaps they exhaust themselves too much; but I do not think that the Lord will condemn them for that. We shall always need Christ-like itinerants who will range the country from end to end, and deny themselves the comforts of home-life, as these do.

In addition to this, we want all brethren who are good preachers, and expositors, and pastors, to be good evangelists also, to take their places under the trees on the village green, and in the streets of the city, or wherever they can get at the people. Do not imagine that your work is to be confined to your own little chapel, but invade the territories of Satan. Carry the war into the enemy's dominions. Be instant in season and out of season, and God bless you in all your efforts! I am sorry that I cannot often set you the example of going out to preach in the open air; but the Tabernacle is as large a place as any one mortal man can hope to fill with his voice for any considerable length of time; and so long as I have the thousands about me I do not care whether it is indoors or out of doors. The case is a very different matter with those whose meeting-houses are small, and their congregations still smaller. You *must* turn out. Get into the Town-hall for a series of special services; if a circus is to be had, hire it, or borrow it; go into the fair, and stand up among the shows and preach the gospel. By some means or other we must get at the people, and carry God's message to them. The Salvation Army has set an example of going right down into the midst of the people. They seem to be afraid of nothing, and ashamed of nothing, so long as they can reach the masses. We need not copy anybody's methods, but we may wisely learn from others how to do our work better. At any rate, let us never lag behind in our efforts for the good of our fellow-men. Wherever a man is wanted to bear the brunt of the battle, let a brother from the Pastors' College be forthcoming.

This year, as you know, I have passed through very severe trials; but I am yet alive, and alive to thank heartily the hundreds of my brethren outside the College, and the scores who are in it, for their loving faithfulness in the day of battle. I forget the few deserters in the joy of the hundreds who cling the closer to me because of the dreadful fight. Thank God, I have an army of friends as true as steel, who will support this College for my sake, and will sustain me for Christ's sake. God bless you all, my dear, loving brothers; and may he in great love bring back those few who have left their former leader. At any rate, may he make them faithful to his truth, whatever they may think of me. Amen.

A reminiscence and a warning

A College address on Jeremiah 45:5

D EAR BRETHREN,—I want to speak to you, this afternoon, upon a text which was once very useful to me. It may not convey to you quite the same lesson that it taught me; but it may be as much a word from the Lord to you as it was to me on a memorable occasion.

When I had been preaching for a little while at Waterbeach, in the year 1852, my father and other friends advised me to seek admission to Regent's Park College, or, as it was in those days, Stepney College. I believed that I might be useful without a college training; but I bowed to what I was willing to regard as their superior judgment upon the matter. I was living in Cambridge at the time, so it was arranged that I should meet Dr Angus at the house of Mr Macmillan, the publisher. I was there exactly at the appointed hour, and was shown into a room; the doctor also went to the house, but the servant put him into another room, and did not let anyone know that I was waiting for him. After a while, he had to leave, to catch the train for London; but I waited on for two hours, and as no one came to me, I rang the bell, and enquired the cause of the delay. When I discovered what had happened, I was very much disappointed; but I have often thanked the Lord since then that he directed me in a different path from that which my friends had planned for me.

Though the intended interview had not taken place, I had not given up the idea of trying to enter the college; but that evening, going to my service, I was crossing Midsummer Common, to the little wooden bridge over the river Cam, when I was startled by what seemed to be a loud voice speaking to me. I have not been one to take much notice of voices and visions; but I could not help hearing these words, as though they were actually spoken to me—

'SEEKEST THOU GREAT THINGS FOR THYSELF? SEEK THEM NOT.'

Thinking over this text, which had come to me in such a remarkable manner, I began to examine my position, and surroundings, and motives. I thought of the people at Waterbeach, many of whom had been brought to the Saviour under my ministry; and I determined not to leave them in order to enter college, and resolved that I would continue preaching to them as long as I could. It did seem to me, at the time, that poverty and obscurity would be the result of my decision; although time has proved that this was God's way of preparing me for the position that I was afterwards to fill.

It is too late for this passage to prevent any of you from entering college, for you have already entered. It may, however, contain as clear a message for you as it did for me on the occasion to which I have referred. These words are found in Jeremiah 45:5, 'Seekest thou great things for thyself? Seek them not.'

Let me remind you of the connection of the text. Baruch had been employed by Jeremiah to write out, on a parchment-roll, all that the Lord had told him to prophesy concerning Israel, Judah, and all the nations. When the roll was finished, he was to read what he had written 'in the ears of the people, in the Lord's house, upon the fasting day.' After Jehoiakim had burned the roll, Jeremiah dictated the prophecies again to Baruch, who wrote them on another roll, on which, the inspired record tells us, 'there were added besides unto them many like words.' Baruch occupied a very honourable office; and he appears to have faithfully discharged his duty. The Lord, however, saw that he was in danger through an ambitious or aspiring spirit; and he therefore sent Jeremiah to him with this message, 'Seekest thou great things for thyself? Seek them not.'

There is a warning here for any one of us who may be tempted to seek great things for himself.

The command is very peremptory and emphatic: 'Seek them not.' In any calling, seeking great things for oneself is wrong; but in the Christian ministry it is a doubly evil thing. Think of it for a moment. A follower of the meek and lowly Jesus, seeking great things for himself! One who ought to be an example to the flock, seeking great things for himself! You see at once, dear brethren, how incongruous it is; and yet we should not have to go back to the days of Jeremiah and Baruch to find those who have tried to join these incongruities together. They cannot do it; oil and water would sooner mix than a servant of Christ succeed as a self-seeker. He may succeed as a self-seeker; but not as a servant of Christ. Either the self-seeker will cease to serve Christ, or the servant of Christ will cease to seek great things for himself.

The man whose great aim is to reach the highest position in the ministry is, after all, a poor curmudgeon, and a wretched parody of a true minister of the New Covenant. Such a man is very likely to hear the words of the apostle Peter to Simon Magus applied to himself: 'Thou hast neither part nor lot in this matter: for thy heart is not right in the sight of God. Repent therefore of this thy wickedness, and pray God, if perhaps the thought of thine heart may be forgiven thee. For I perceive that thou art in the gall of bitterness, and in the bond of iniquity.' If a man thinks of trying to be 'the big man of the district', let him become town-crier or bill-poster! If he aspires to the great honour of being the wearer of a black coat, let him be a chimney-sweep! If he thinks he would look nice in a white tie, let him be a linen-draper, or an undertaker! But he will never win men for Christ by seeking personal prominence. Self-seeking in any shape is repulsive. Seek nothing for yourselves, brethren. It is easy to sing—

'My all is on the altar,'

but it is not so easy to lay all on the altar, not allowing even wife or children to come between our own soul and Christ, and our service for him; but letting Christ take the first place, the middle place, and the last place, and be all in all in our life and in our labour. If it be so with you, yours will be a successful life; but if not, there will be a worm at the root, which will destroy all your usefulness. Cardinal Wolsey charged Cromwell to 'fling away ambition; by that sin fell the angels!' I say to you, 'Students, fling away self-seeking; by that sin have fallen many angels of the churches!'

If we were to seek great things for ourselves, *we should be false and recreant to our profession.* We belong to Christ; we are not our own, we are bought with a price. Some of us sang, when we were baptized—

'Jesus, I my cross have taken,
    All to leave, and follow thee;
Destitute, despised, forsaken;
    Thou, from hence, my all shalt be.'

We professed then to be dead to our own interests, dead with Christ, and risen with him. We set our affection on things above, not on things on the earth. Jesus was all in all to us then; self was out of court. This was still more true of us when we were called to the ministry. Oh, what humble ideas as to ourselves filled our minds then! We could say then, with the apostle Paul, 'Unto me, who am less than the least of all saints, is this grace given, that I should preach among the Gentiles the unsearchable riches of Christ.' If, therefore, we live for ourselves, or seek great things for ourselves, we shall be telling one great lie, and taking a large part of our lifetime in telling it. Some have thought, 'What end can we gain by becoming ministers?' This is an awful view of our holy calling, and must be terribly like the unpardonable sin. I have seen some ministers who have lived to make money, and others who have striven to attain to worldly honour and political fame. They are nobodies now; mere wrecks of men, like Hymenæus, and Alexander, and others, who 'concerning faith have made shipwreck.'

To seek great things for ourselves is unwise. The highest wisdom lies in obedience to our Lord's words, 'If any man will come after me, let him deny himself, and take up his cross daily, and follow me. For whosoever will save his life shall lose it: but whosoever will lose his life for my sake, the same shall save it.' With us, the surest gain is to give up everything for Christ; it will be little enough when we have given up all. The man who sacrifices himself for God is the man whom God will not allow to sacrifice himself. The Lord never was in any man's debt, and he never will be. Peter seemed to think that he and his companions had made a great sacrifice, which demanded an adequate return from their Lord. He said to Jesus, 'Behold, we have forsaken all, and followed thee; what shall we have therefore?' Paul was a much better judge of the relative value of things, and he said, 'I count all things but loss for the excellency of the knowledge of Christ Jesus my Lord: for whom I have suffered the loss of all things, and do count them but dung, that I may win Christ, and be found in him.' The man who has right views of his Lord will think little of himself. The more we think of our Master, the less shall we think of ourselves; and the more we try to glorify him, the less shall we seek great things for ourselves.

No doubt there is a powerful attraction about great things. How we all wish to be great men! Every young French soldier hopes that he carries the baton of a field-marshal in his knapsack; and every young soldier of the cross hopes that he is destined to be the commander-in-chief of the armies of our Israel. If any one of you has such an idea, mind that you keep it in your knapsack, behind your back, and never look at it. Put it away out of sight, never think of it; be like the apostle Paul, 'Forgetting those things which are behind.' You remember John Bunyan's description of his model minister. The Interpreter showed Christian 'the picture of a very grave person hanging up against the wall, and this was the fashion of it. It had eyes lift up to heaven, the Best of Books in his hand, the Law of Truth was written upon his lips, *the world was behind his back;* it stood as if it pleaded with men, and a crown of gold did hang over his head.' Blessed is the man of whom this is a correct portrait! Many will speak of him as a good man, even if none call him a great man.

Perhaps great things would not be so attractive if men knew the burden they bring with them.

'Uneasy lies the head that wears a crown,'

is a saying that applies to many beside kings and queens. A great statesman said that he only remembered two really happy days in his life—the day that he entered upon his high office, and the day that he left it. The top of the tree is not the safest place, nor the most comfortable. You would do well to follow Agur's example, and ask your Lord to put you neither at the top, nor at the bottom; but to let you sing to his glory from one of the branches nearer the middle of the tree. The bird on the top of the tree is a target for every man with a gun, and every boy with a stone. You are often told, 'There's always room at the top;' that is quite true, but the top of the tree is a difficult place to reach, and it is a more difficult position to retain. Happy is the man who knows nothing of the trials and perils that beset 'a popular minister'! Many a man has become dizzy by the time he has climbed to the summit of his ambition, and then he has had a grievous fall,

A high position has its advantages; but it has its disadvantages, too. If the Lord calls you to eminence, he will fit you for the position; and then you shall 'dwell on high' in perfect security. But what is the use of seeking great things, if you are not qualified for them? A man with a small head is saving up his money to buy a big hat: what will be the good of it? It will be coming down over his nose. Some who seek great things are like the boys who put on their father's trousers or boots. If they are not big in themselves, at any rate they are wearing big trousers, big boots, and big hats. They think that, if people do not see anything big in them, they will surely see something big on them. How do you know, my young brother, that you will be able to fill a large sphere? If we set ourselves up on high places, for which we are not fitted, some impertinent person will be sure to ask the very pertinent question, 'Who put that beggar up there?' We shall then, with shame, be obliged to take a lower place, while a humbler brother will hear the welcome words, 'Friend, go up higher.' The man who pushes himself forward will be the one whom everybody will try to push backward; while the man who keeps himself in the rear will have many friends to help him to the front. 'Whosoever exalteth himself shall be abased; and he that humbleth himself shall be exalted.'

Those who seek great things lose greater things. A man seeking to be a great rhetorician loses the power of reaching the hearts of his hearers. You know some great word-spinners; but are they soul-winners? Some word-painters remind you of the angel who appeared to Manoah and his wife: 'The angel did wondrously; and Manoah and his wife looked on.' Oh, brethren, never try to preach grand sermons that will lead nobody to Christ! You may be thankful if you have not large churches to look after; for you will have all the more time to devote to the cultivation of your own mind and heart. Yield yourselves wholly to God, and your life cannot be a failure. Even though you are never heard of beyond the little country village where you labour for the Lord, you will have true success. The greatest success does not depend on the greatness of your position. A circle is never praised for its size, but for its roundness; and it is not the surface you have covered, but the completeness of the work you have done for God in the sphere where he has placed you, that will entitle you to his 'Well done, good and faithful servant.' 'Seekest thou great things for thyself? Seek them not.'

Besides all this, *self-seeking will be ruinous to any minister's career.* The people soon find out the difference between the man who lives for the Lord, and the one who lives for himself. I do not know how they get to know it; but they do. If, in our preaching, we are evidently intent upon preaching ourselves, they scent it out; and the greatest sinners discover it as well as the greatest saints. Two women were conversing about their pastors, when one of them said, 'Our minister always impresses us with the idea that he is a great man; but your minister always sends you away simply thinking over what he has said about his Master.' Let us be like number two.

Two ministers were talking together, and one of them said to the other, 'Who is going to preach for you at your anniversary?' His friend answered, 'I am going to preach myself.' The brother did not mean quite what he said; but that is what a great many ministers might say. There are some who could never say with Paul, 'We preach not ourselves, but Christ Jesus the Lord.' They do preach themselves; and a fine subject they have for their discourses! Brethren, let us not belong to that company: whoever else preaches himself, let it always be true of us, 'We preach Christ crucified.' This is a theme worthy of your loftiest powers. You will never reach the height of that great argument, not even when unto the principalities and powers in heavenly places you make known the manifold wisdom of God. Exalt Christ crucified: nothing will so crucify self as the uplifting of the crucified Christ. Remember how Paul wrote to the Galatians, 'If a man think himself to be something, when he is nothing, he deceiveth himself. ... But God forbid that I should glory, save in the cross of our Lord Jesus Christ, by whom the world is crucified unto me, and I unto the world.' If you find any self-seeking in the Lord Jesus, you may be a self-seeker, too. His disciples were often seeking great things for themselves; but you know how their Master rebuked them. The Lord of all became the servant of all; he washed their feet, setting them an example. Again and again he laid down the rule of his kingdom: 'If any man desire to be first, the same shall be last of all, and servant of all.' May our Lord make us all willing to take the lowest place in his blessed service, and keep us faithful even unto death! Amen.

Beaten oil for the light

An address to the students of the Pastors' College

'Thou shalt command the children of Israel, that they bring thee pure oil olive beaten for the light, to cause the lamp to burn always.'—Exodus 27:20.

JEHOVAH is the God of light, and he would not have his service performed in darkness. As there were no windows in the Tabernacle in the wilderness, the holy place was lighted by the seven-branched candlestick or lamp. This lamp was to be fed with oil, and the oil was to be supplied by the Israelites. In the Church of God there must always be light; light within herself for the delight and instruction of those who dwell in the courts of the Lord, and light which, unlike that of the old Tabernacle, shall shine forth in the midst of the dark world. The Israelites were a nation of priests, and so were typical of the children of God; and as it was their business to supply the oil for the sanctuary lamp, so is it the privilege and province of the children of God to keep the lamp of knowledge perpetually burning by bringing forth the precious oil of divine truth. Upon the ministers of God this work is especially binding, but every believer, according to his ability, is called upon to take his share therein, for it is not written of ministers only, 'Ye are the light of the world,' but of all the disciples of our Lord Jesus Christ; even as Paul said to the Philippians, 'Do all things without murmurings and disputings: that ye may be blameless and harmless, the sons of God, without rebuke, in the midst of a crooked and perverse nation, among whom ye shine as lights in the world; holding forth the word of life.' From the rubric before us, in reference to the character of the oil to be supplied for the sanctuary, we may gather not a little of the duty of preachers and teachers with regard to the instruction by which they endeavour to feed the lamp of knowledge.

It is clear that it was intended, by this precept, that *the oil furnished for the sanctuary should be the very best*. That oil which comes from the olive under heavy pressure, or after being subjected to heat, is of a secondary quality, thick and cloudy; whereas the virgin oil, which flows forth under a more gentle pressure, is clear, and of the highest value. God is to be served at all times with our best; the clearest thought, the deepest study, the truest conception, and the most excellent utterance, should all be displayed in preparing to 'speak on God's behalf.' We must burn nothing but the best oil. For a preacher to rush into his pulpit, to fill up the time with talk of the sort which first comes to hand, is to present to the Lord the very dregs of the oil-press. God forbid that we should serve him with so little reverence! For a teacher to go to his class, to weary the children with dry, uninteresting talk in which there is no real instruction, and no gospel unction, is to treat the Lord as if we had no awe of him, but felt that anything was good enough for his service. Such negligence may be covered over with the notion of trusting in the Spirit of God, but the veil is too thin to conceal the sloth. We should endeavour to bring our minds into the best possible condition by prayer; we should labour to draw from them their noblest ideas, and most spiritual conceptions; we should also search the Word of God, and the choicest of books, selecting with care everything that is most apposite and suitable; and thus we should come forth to edify others with valuable knowledge worth communicating. The Lord would not have his lamp supplied with any common kind of oil which stood handiest in the house, or with that which could be produced most quickly, or with that which had stood so long as to become stale and rancid; but the very best oil in the country was to be consecrated to the golden lamp which burned before him continually. Is not this right? Should such a God as he is be served with anything but the choicest? He bestows upon us the richest imaginable gifts; should we not in return offer to him that which is most costly, and the noblest of its kind? We would impress this upon all who undertake to feed even the least of the lamps, and we would especially urge it upon those whose public position causes them to supply oil to hundreds, and perhaps to thousands. How shall the Church of Christ shine with a clear radiance if the oil supplied by her ministers be coarse and impure?

The ceremonial law fixed everything, and allowed no latitude. The filling of the lamps was commanded, and the exact manner of doing it was prescribed. *The oil to be used was not left to choice or chance; it must be olive oil, and nothing else.* The precept is specific, and cannot be misunderstood. As Dr Gill very properly remarks, 'the oil to be brought and used there was not any sort of oil; as what is got out of fishes, as train oil, or out of nuts, as oil of almonds; but what comes from the olive-tree.' Even so, we are not left in ignorance as to what we shall preach; the doctrines of the gospel are revealed plainly and definitely, and it is not our business to make discoveries, or to frame inventions, but to proclaim the very truth of God. There were, no doubt, excellent reasons for the choice of olive oil, and the refusal of every other oil; and there is the best of reasons for our bringing forth Scriptural truth, and nothing else; for it is the entrance of God's Word which giveth light, and not the entrance of human opinions. 'The law of the Lord is perfect, converting the soul;' nothing else but the living Word of God will convince, convert, renew, and sanctify. He has promised that this shall not return unto him void; but he has made no such promise to the wisdom of man, or the excellency of human speech. The Spirit of God works with the Word of God; and if we get away from that Word, we depart from the track of the Holy Ghost. All his paths drop fatness; but man's paths are barrenness.

Much stress is to be laid upon the word 'pure' in the statute now under consideration; for it was not enough to bring olive oil; but it must be in a refined and undiluted condition. There must be no dregs in the oil; it must run clear, and appear transparent. This was the reason why the olives were to be bruised and beaten, and not ground in a mill; because in the mill the stones are broken and ground, and so the oil is not so pure. Everything in the process was chosen to promote purity; so must it be with all our teaching, truth and nothing else but truth must be brought forth for the enlightenment of God's people. Our own opinions and imaginings must not be substituted for the infallible mind of God. We must not declare the dogmas of councils, or the creeds of churches, or the dicta of learned men, as if they had an authority co-ordinate with Holy Scripture. We must keep to 'Thus and thus saith the Lord,' for it is the Word which giveth light; and of all teaching which is not according to that Word, it may safely be affirmed, that there is no light in it. It will not be a service done unto God; but rather an insult to his majesty, if we smuggle into his sanctuary the sayings and traditions of men. The words which the Holy Ghost teacheth must alone be the oil which feeds the lamps of God; and it is at our peril that we substitute the inferences of reason, the hypotheses of philosophers, or the drivellings of superstition.

Nor will it suffice for the Lord's priests to replenish the lamp with oil of which the major part is pure. The oil must have no admixture of any sort; as far as possible, we must endeavour to remove from it the scum and dregs of our poor fallible interpretation, and we must entreat the Holy Spirit to enable us to deliver, not our rendering of the Scriptures, but God's Word itself. Jealously must we fight against the temptation to tone it down, to soften it, and dilute it, where the truth seems to be harsh or unpleasant. It is no business of ours to please men; our sole object must be to please God. We ought to speak the truth, and the truth just as we find it; we may not even attempt to increase its force by purposely exaggerating its expressions, or placing those truths in the forefront which the Holy Spirit has put in the rear. The exaggeration of a doctrine may lead to an error as gross as that which comes out of lessening its importance. To add to the Book of the Lord, is denounced in the same text as that which forbids taking from it. As the Israelite was commanded to bring the best olive oil without dilution, without mixture, and without dregs, even so must we bring forth in our teaching 'the truth, the whole truth, and nothing but the truth.' To return to the figure before us, it must be pure olive oil, and nothing else.

The oil was to be prepared by heating the olive. The Israelites were not to bring the olives whole; but they must be crushed, and the oil must be extracted by manual labour. The Holy Scriptures must be searched with diligence by those who would find instruction in them worthy to be imparted to others. The apostle saith, 'Meditate upon these things; give thyself wholly to them; that thy profiting may appear to all.' Superficial talkers upon holy things do not bring to the lamps beaten oil. A little of the precious fluid of instruction exudes from the berries, and they are content to present this to the Lord; but they are not acting according to his commandment. Idleness invents excuses, but God does not accept them. The oil was to be prepared, and so must our teaching be; there must be force of mind, effort, energy, hard study, laborious thought, or otherwise our testimony will not be such as the children of God require to make their light clear and steady, and acceptable with God. The oil was not to be such as flows from the berries when they are ground beneath the rough machinery of a mill. The major part of olive oil is produced by crushing between stones, and such oil is good enough for ordinary purposes; but for the lamps of the sanctuary the oil must be prepared in a mortar with a pestle, by the personal labour of the individual, judiciously applied, and not with the rude roughness of mere force. He who prepared the oil must bruise the olives and press them with discretion; no heavy grinding-stones were to run their accustomed round, but the living force of a willing hand was to extract the choicest juice. We have heard of ministers preaching other men's sermons, and we have even been informed of the existence of mills in which the olives of doctrine are bruised wholesale, and the extract is sent forth bottled up for immediate use. We refer to lithographed discourses, whose manufacture is an important branch of trade. Those who purchase and habitually use such substitutes for personal study hardly deserve the name of ministers of Christ; and if they do not meet with the divine acceptance in the course of their ministrations, they need not marvel. If the Israelite had presented the very best oil which had been produced at the mill, he would have been acting in violation of the divine ordinance which required of him oil beaten with the hand; and we are persuaded that sermons which are borrowed, which cost their reader no thought, no emotion, no prayerful agony, are not at all the offerings which the Lord requires at the hands of his true ministers. Before we venture upon the high and honourable service of instructing the Lord's people, let us go to the Lord himself for a supply of his grace, and when he has directed our minds to the chosen subject, let us further ask his aid that we may, in devout meditation, extract from the Word its fatness and unction; and then let us spare no effort, but cast our whole strength into the endeavour to prepare that which we hope to present to the people of God. It must be beaten oil. McCheyne was wont to say to young preachers, 'Mind, it must be beaten oil, beaten oil, for the lamps of the sanctuary!' Such a work must not be entered upon with half-heartedness: casual thoughts, and superficial observations, platitudes, and everyday expressions, are not worthy of the people whom we would instruct, much less of the God whom we would honour by our service.

It may be instructive here to observe that, *although a measure of force was needed to bruise the berries, yet this had to be used with discretion,* lest even by the gentler mode, as well as by the mill, an impure oil should be produced. What was wanted was such a bruising as would express from the olives their first and readiest juice. What was called 'the mother-drop' flowed forth of itself as soon as the berries were a little bruised, and this was much purer than that which was obtained after the olives were put under the press. You can soon squeeze a text too much. It is even possible to extort from it what it never contained. The plain meaning of the Scriptures is the best and purest. Ingenuity is often presumption. When we go about to force a sense upon God's Word which is not natural to it, we are rolling the olives under the grinding of huge stones, and are not beating them according to the commandment. Let all readers, and writers, and preachers, remember this: there must be the pressure of study; but not the force of violence. Beat the oil for the light; but use not the mill-stones.

Another thought strikes us. Much of the teaching which is given forth by the servants of God, flows from their experimental acquaintance with the Word of God, and this they can hardly obtain without affliction. No doubt, God's best ministers are sorely bruised and passed through many a crushing trial in order that they thus may present unto the Church of God beaten oil, the truth which they have procured by suffering, which has become their own by the breaking of their hearts and the bruising of their spirits.

'Spices crushed, their pungence yield,
 Trodden scents their sweets respire;
Would you have its strength revealed,
 Cast the incense in the fire:
Thus the crushed and broken frame
 Oft doth sweetest graces yield;
And, through suffering, toil, and shame,
From affliction's keenest flame
 Heavenly incense is distilled!'

Adam of St Victor (d. 1146) translated from Latin

Certainly, no testimony for the Lord is so much valued by his saints as that which comes from men who have tried and proved the loving-kindness of the Lord in dark hours of adversity. These, like ships which have been tossed upon the mighty main, bring treasures from afar, and, like victors in a great war, return with mountains of prey. Gladly, therefore, do we glory in infirmity if thereby the power of Christ doth rest upon us, and we the more fully bring forth for the lamps of the sanctuary 'pure oil olive beaten for the light.'

Doubtless the reason why the purest kind of olive oil was used in the sanctuary lamp was that there might be less of smoke and smell than would be caused by any other kind of oil. If we endeavour to feed the lamps of God with mere human thought, and the production of talent and ability, there will always be the smell of human fallibility and error, perhaps of pride and self-sufficiency; and with this ill savour will go forth the blackening smoke of man-worship and creature-confidence, which will be exceedingly displeasing to the great God who takes up his abode in his Church. It would have been a sorry thing for the vessels of the sanctuary to have been smoked and blackened by the lamp that gave light to the holy place; and it is beyond all measure deplorable when those who should give light in the house of the Lord dim the lustre of the glorious doctrines which it is their duty to reveal. Purity of heart and life and teaching are beyond measure essential: that which defileth can never be tolerated in the courts of the Lord's house. Our doctrine must be according to holiness, our speech must minister edification, our lives must be sanctified, and our whole spirit must be gracious. We are to wear 'HOLINESS UNTO THE LORD' upon our brows, and all our teaching must be godly and pure.

We have been viewing the text from the human side of it, and interpreting it as representing what the priestly nation was to bring into the Lord's service for the maintenance of light in his house; but there is another side to the type. Oil usually represents the Holy Spirit. The golden lamp typifies Christ and his Church, and the light which streams therefrom is produced by that Divine Enlightener, the Holy Ghost. All his influences are pure and holy; he is never the author of any doctrine which leads to sin; all his teachings tend to the production of holiness in the heart and in the life. Any fancied spiritual light which does not come from him is mere darkness; and any professed 'light of the world' which burns with blackness and smother of smoke, is not of his kindling, and is not sustained by his influence; for that is pure in itself, and produces a pure light. Let it be ours to magnify his name by sensibly feeling and openly confessing our dependence upon him, without whom we shall be like the foolish virgins, who took their lamps, but took no oil with them. Our lamps, instead of being fit to do honour to the heavenly Bridegroom, will bring despair to our own souls, if they be without the holy oil.

Gifts neglected and gifts stirred up

An address to the students of the Pastors' College

THERE are two texts upon which I should like to speak to you this afternoon. I will put them together. 1 Timothy 4:14, is a text for all students, and all ministers of the gospel, 'Neglect not the gift that is in thee.' 2 Timothy 1:6 is another text equally applicable to us all, 'Stir up the gift of God, which is in thee.' The first text we are to consider at this time is this,—

'NEGLECT NOT THE GIFT THAT IS IN THEE.'

Our heart, our whole nature is like a garden; and it can only be kept in cultivation so as to bear fruit by diligence and by pains. In order that a garden should produce weeds, and be worthless to its owner, all he has to do is to neglect it. It is a sad thing when a man neglects himself. You must have known, in your time, some young men, if not some older men, who have neglected themselves, sadly neglected themselves; they allowed themselves to grow up learning no more than was beaten into them at school. Afterwards, they spent their evenings in frivolity instead of giving themselves to study, and now they are good for nothing, they cannot be placed in business because their minds have been so sadly neglected.

Can a ministerial student neglect himself? I think he can. He may get up his lessons for the class in a slovenly way, until it is reported to me by his tutor, 'I do not think young Mr So-and-so makes much out of his studies; I do not know how it is, but somehow or other he does not learn, he does not grow, he knows no more now than he did when he entered the College.' Some old divines are called 'painful preachers of the Word', the old sense of the word 'painful' being laborious, taking pains. If a man is a painful student in this sense, he will become a pleasurable student to himself, and a pleasurable preacher to others. That is what you all ought to be. Do not let a single gift that is in you rust for want of using; you will either be better fitted for the work of the ministry every day that you are here, or else you will be daily getting worse than you were when you came to us. There will be a gain or a loss constantly going on in the commerce of this house; therefore I say to each of you what Paul wrote to Timothy, 'Neglect not the gift that is in thee.' Look up every faculty of your being, and give it a cleaning; examine every portion of your mind, and dust it now and then; water every plant that God has put into the garden of your nature; prune every tree that is found there, dig about it and dung it, and do all for it that you ought to do, and that you can do, to make it bring forth fruit unto God.

There are some who neglect the gift that is in them because *they are exceedingly earnest to possess the gifts of somebody else*. They so greatly admire the style and manner of some eminent divine whom they have heard, or whose works they have read, that they are scarcely thankful for the gift that is in themselves. Never you mind about the renowned Dr This or Mr That: 'Neglect not the gift that is in *thee*.' What if you cannot illustrate a text with all the beauty and exuberance of a Guthrie? Perhaps you can apply to it a clear, calm analysis like that of Candlish. You have not a tremendous, voice, you say, you are not like Boanerges, you cannot make many thousands hear; then try to train that thinner voice of yours to be more clear and bell-like, so as to make up in sweetness for the lack of strength; but anyhow, 'Neglect not the gift that is in thee.' You are very sorry that you have not a mathematical brain; yours is a more classical type of mind; very well, then, study the classics diligently. 'Neglect not the gift that is in thee.' It may be that you cannot address the learned and the educated; perhaps you are a soldier-student or a sailor-student; well, use that rough talent that you have. Never mind about the gift that is not in thee; but 'Neglect not the gift that *is* in thee.' You have not every gift, no man has, it were a pity that any man should have all gifts; it has frequently happened that one who has seemed to be an 'Admirable Crichton' has turned out to be a dreadful apostate in the pulpit. I do not know how it is; but often an excess of cleverness is often accompanied by an excess in other directions, and so a man's brains get turned; he carries much sail, but little ballast, and his vessel becomes top-heavy, and in an unexpected storm gets capsized.

If, on the other hand, you have only one talent, remember that you are the man who is in the greatest danger of neglecting his gifts. The man with the five talents did not bury them, nor did the man with the two talents; but the man with the one talent was the one who buried his. He said he never should be the foremost man, so he gave up trying to be anything, took a napkin, wrapped his talent in it, and buried it in the earth. If he had put out his talent to interest, he might have made two of it, and turning it over again, it would have been four, and then it would have been eight, and soon he would have beaten the man who had five talents, for his eight would have become sixteen. If you have only a few talents, seek to turn them over a great many times, and so increase them. A man who starts in business with a large capital, and who only turns it over once in the year, will not do so well as the man who, with a smaller capital, manages to turn it over every week, and so has rapid returns. The Jew over in Houndsditch says, 'I lent Israel eighteenpence, and set him up in business.' Israel takes his eighteenpence, and it is soon three shillings; and that before long becomes six shillings, and soon he is able to take a shop, and perhaps makes his fortune; while the man who has eighteen hundred pounds to begin with takes many years to make his fortune. Well, you Israelites with the eighteenpence, do not neglect the gifts you have; do not say, 'I cannot get on in the ministry, because I have so few talents; I cannot get on because I have only eighteen pence.' No, but imitate the young Jew who goes and sells his oranges somehow or other; like him, 'Cry aloud, and spare not.' You must take care, then, brethren, not to neglect your gifts if you have only a few talents.

If you have great gifts, do not neglect any part of them; if you have five talents, remember that you will be held responsible for using five well. Suppose that you who have five talents do only as much as a brother with one talent, that will not do, for you have to account for the five talents which God has given you. If you have the swiftness of the hare, it is not enough for you to be a little ahead of the tortoise; you can go much more rapidly, and God expects you to do so. Then do not neglect any part of the gift that is in you, use it all, even to the last ounce.

Next, remember that *you may neglect your gift so much as not to know that you have a gift;* there are some who even do that. Here and there we stumble upon a man whose opinion of himself is not so high as it ought to be, because he has never fully appreciated himself; it is not a common fault, but it is a fault that does exist. The brother I refer to is a man of a very retiring spirit; he has probably been frightened through mixing up with some rough fellows at College, and his spirit has been so broken that, although he is worthy to take a front rank, he is now generally found in the rear. He never puts his best foot foremost; when he speaks, he generally makes a blunder of things because of his diffidence. Now, brethren, I do not want you to have self-conceit, there is too much of that already in the world, but do you know what true humility is? Humility is not to think too little of yourself, but to appraise yourself at your real value. That is the best definition of humility that I can think of; for it is not humility for a man to think, 'I have only one talent,' when he has five, or at least two. What will his Master say to him, when he says, 'My Lord, I never thought I had more than one talent'? Will that let him off? I trow not. If he had the five, or the two, it will not do for him to think he has only one. Here he is, six feet high, or very nearly so, a fine, good-looking fellow, with a beard and moustache, and yet he talks like a little baby. I admire the spirit of the Suffolk labourer who, when the lawyer asked him, 'Can you read Greek?' replied, 'I do not know.' 'Now, Hodge,' said the lawyer, 'you do know whether you can or not.' 'No, I do not, for I never tried.' I think you had better have Hodge's spirit, and resolve that you are not going to say you cannot do a thing until you have tried; but rather believe that you can do it, because there is a text which should encourage you greatly in this matter: 'I can do all things through Christ which strengtheneth me.' I do not say that I can read Greek without having tried, or learned the language; but anything that God meant me to do, and that ought to be done by me, I can do in his strength. There is a period in which every man who can speak wakes up to the belief that he can do so. I recollect distinctly that, when I was speaking to myself one day as a lad, I said to myself, 'Well, now, that was put so that I can understand it; and I think that, if there had been any persons here who could have heard me, they would have understood it, too;' and I felt, from that moment, that I ought to begin speaking to others.

I do not know what your special talent may be; but whatever it is, use the talent that is given to you. 'Neglect not the gift that is in thee.' Some of you have a talent for poetry; use it in the same prudent way that men do when they send some of their compositions just to give us pleasure, but not wishing to have them published. Write an epic as long as *Paradise Lost,* but do not have it printed. It will make good pipe-lights if you have friends who smoke, or it will be useful for pasting in boxes; but do not print it; we have far too much poetry in the world already. Write poetry if you can, you may cut out Milton and Shakespeare if you only try long enough, though it is a pity to dislodge them after they have held their positions so long; still, do your best. Do not let me, by anything that I may say, nip a flowering Watts or Cowper in the bud. Even if you are not a poet, perhaps you have a talent hidden away that you know nothing about. Rummage out your old stores, clear out your boxes, turn out all your £5 notes. It is a great pity when a man, who has a little business, is in financial difficulty when, all the while, between the bottom of the drawer and the drawer where he put it in, there was actually a £100 note. Some of you have a wonderfully grand faculty lying hidden away somewhere; fetch it out, scratch your head as hard as ever you can, and see whether there is not something or other comes out of it. Never believe, brethren, but that there is something in you that can be used for God's glory. It is said that, whenever a great sculptor looks upon a block of marble, though another man sees nothing in it, the true artist says, 'I can see a statue in it; all I have to do is to take a chisel and hammer, and knock away the superfluous marble; my work is not to create the statue, it is inside there already, and only wants bringing out.' There is a wonderful power of usefulness inside every one of you, brethren, if you can only get the marble knocked off. Christ sees it in you, God sees it in you, and he will help you to get it brought out, if you ask him to do so.

Another way of neglecting the gift that is in you is by *allowing it to run away with you.* How some fellows do talk! When they get up in a pulpit, there is no knowing what they will say, and they do not themselves know what they will say. They will never break down; oh, that sovereign mercy would give them grace enough to do so! They seem to say by their action, like Tennyson's 'Brook',—

'Men may come, and men may go,
    But I go on for ever.'

There is nothing in what they say; but they can talk on, and on, and on, and on. It is a fearful disease, that extreme facility to talk. It is like a whole train of mules going along the road with nothing inside their packs; or like a number of engines, with screaming whistles, rattling along, but with no passengers in the carriages, and no goods in the trucks, all tearing ahead, but carrying nothing at all. Pope well says:—

'Words are like leaves, and where they most abound
Much fruit of sense beneath is rarely found.'

We have known men carried away by the faculty of imagination. Talk of the Pantomime at Christmas, it is nothing to them, not a tithe of what they can do; see the phantasmagoria that flits across their brain. How they soar on the eagle's wings that they have borrowed, how they take us down into the deeps, and do the diving-bell business, how they come out again on all fours! Oh, I have heard them; with such imagination that I could not imagine what they meant, there was nothing in it; a horse gaily caparisoned, a winged Pegasus with nothing on his back, only a piece of imagination! And there are some ministers who are carried away with the gift that is in them. As you listen to them, you feel something like Manoah and his wife when they looked upon the angel. How wondrously they do! They are like the six cream-coloured horses of the Queen's state coach; only there is no Queen, and no coach either. And they use such long and ugly words, too; it sounds almost like swearing. I have heard some such preachers; and I have felt inclined to say, as the men of Lystra did about Paul and Barnabas, 'The gods have come down to us in the likeness of men.' It has been Dr Johnson-Redivivus, the whole of his dictionary crammed into a sermon. Oh, these brethren! Oh, these brethren! It is a great shame when a preacher does this, because the gift of language is a glorious gift when it is properly bitted and bridled. It is a gem rich and rare; but it must be cut and polished, and put in a golden setting. The power of speech is a grand thing when it is rightly trained and kept in order; but if it is unchecked, it will be the ruin of a man. It is bad when a vine is allowed to make too much wood, and to trail along the ground, so that its purple clusters are eaten up by the worm and the mildew. Take care that it is not so with your speech; do not let it be the master of you, but be the master of it.

Another way to neglect your gift is *by using crutches*. It is a very shameful neglect of a man's legs if he does not use them, but goes about on crutches; and it is an equal neglect of a man's eyes if, long before his sight fails him, he wears one small eye-glass, which he puts up and down every few seconds. There is great wisdom in wearing spectacles when you need them. I like to see some of our brethren wearing spectacles, it is a sign that men are growing in grace as they grow in years, and their infirmities make them need spectacles. I do not deprecate the use of them under such circumstances; but I do not like to see men making spectacles of themselves while they are still young, by using glasses which they do not really require. There is a way of neglecting your eyes by over-much care of them; and I think there is many a man who has neglected his gifts in the same way. Dear old Mr Rogers used to say that a memory was a faithful friend if you trusted it, and there is a great deal of truth in the remark. The power of free speech is never known by the preacher who learns his sermons off by heart. Have you not heard what a servant said to some one who wanted to see her master, 'You cannot see him, for he is commutting'? Those who cannot speak must 'commut' their sermons; but do not 'commut' yours, or read them either, if you can help it. Do not neglect your gift by using crutches.

You may neglect your gift by not trying it, by needing everything to be made up for you unnaturally, and apart from yourselves. I suppose you never heard of the gentleman who said to the waiter at night, 'Here, I want you to take one of my eyes out, please.' The man was astonished at the request; but he wondered still more when the gentleman said, 'Take my arm off first, and then unscrew my leg.' The waiter was afraid that he would have to be all taken to pieces. Do not be ministers of that kind, like those who could not preach if they lost their manuscript, or if their notes were gone, or unless they were in their own library, where they could …, where they could think original thoughts! I am sure, brethren, it is possible for us to sit still until we shall feel that we have no legs, and we may neglect our gifts until we believe that we have no gifts at all.

I have mentioned these somewhat special gifts, but the text applies to all our gifts, and the command to each one of us is, 'Neglect not the gift that is in thee.'

Well, now, for our second text,—2 Timothy 1:6.

'STIR UP THE GIFT OF GOD, WHICH IS IN THEE.'

First, neglect not the gift that is in thee; then, stir it up. There is an allusion to a fire in the words, 'Stir up the gift of God, which is in thee.'

First, you must get your gift set on fire; for it is no use stirring a fire-place, or stirring the coals before they are set on fire. What a difference in appearance there is between the grate filled with wood and coal, and the same grate when they have caught alight! There is all the difference to those who look on, as they will soon find if they will put their fingers between the bars. It is just so with a young man with plenty of ability, but who is indifferent to his work; he is nothing but a cold grate. If he will put his whole heart into the work, and if the Spirit of God shall come upon him, and set his talents on fire, if every gift be all ablaze with zealous consecration to God, then will he be of some service.

But the best fire sometimes wants a little stir, and so do your gifts. Get a poker, brethren; I manage generally to be the stoker, on Friday afternoons, when I come to stir you up to fresh zeal and devotion, and poke your fires with my little black poker. Do you not feel, even as students, that you want to be stirred up every now and then? When you are settled in the ministry, and you get thinking about your straitened circumstances, and the trials of life, your wife will be a little bit of a poker to you. She will say, 'Now, John, you must be more zealous, you must preach better, or else the people will complain, and there will be no blessing upon your work.' It will be no small privilege if you have such a wife as that. If you do not poke yourself up, God will send the devil to do it. He employs him, you know, in the kitchen to clean his pots; Satan is nothing better than God's scullion, and he takes some of us when we are getting rusty, and brightens us up a bit. Rutherford used to say, and so did Ralph Erskine, that 'a roaring devil is better than a sleeping devil'; but the less we have to do with either kind of devil, the better for us. I hope you will each one say to yourselves, 'I do not want to be poked about by him, therefore I will poke myself up. I must get all the cinders and the dead stuff out of the grate, for this state of things will not do; I cannot go on smouldering in this miserable fashion any longer. I will have a special day all to myself, and I will get into my study, or into the country, and lie down in a ditch or on the grass, and see to this matter; but I will poke my fire up; I will get a good blaze somehow or other.' Sometimes it may be well to gather a few earnest Christians together, that you may provoke one another to love and good works. When you are settled, and are in danger of settling down too quietly, you will perhaps say to yourself, 'I will go and make a trip up to the Tabernacle, and spend a little time there, and see if I do not get stirred up again by some of the earnest friends I shall meet there.' Everyone's fire will seem to go to sleep at times; therefore we must manage, somehow or other, to break the monotony of the life we are all too apt to lead, that we may be aroused to deeds of nobler daring.

The way to stir up the gift that is in you is, in general, to *try to improve it every day*. That man will be wise who every day grows a little wiser, who every hour learns a little more wisdom. The man who does not preach better every time probably preaches worse every time; and if he does not do more good than he used to do, he will probably do less good by-and-by. 'Stir up the gift of God, which is in thee.' Fan the flame to something brighter than it has ever been. When you get to be as enthusiastic as Whitefield was, try to rise to something higher even than that seraphic spirit reached. Stir up the fire, blow upon it, get a tremendous blast upon the furnace, that you may to the utmost of your capacity be consumed in the service of God.

One way to stir up your gift is to *remember the responsibilities that lie upon you*. I wish that all of us would think more about this matter. I now and then have to say to a brother, who has thought so much over his responsibilities that he has been depressed by the weight of them, 'Do not make too much of your responsibility, because that will be as great an evil as thinking too little of it.' You may think that you are responsible for saving your hearers, but you certainly are not; you are not responsible in God's sight for what you cannot possibly do, and you cannot save them. You are responsible as a watchman unto the house of Israel. 'If the watchman see the sword come, and blow not the trumpet, and the people be not warned; if the sword come, and take any person from among them, he is taken away in his iniquity; but his blood will I require at the watchman's hand.' It is not his perishing that brings any responsibility upon you; but you are responsible for giving him due warning of his danger. The Lord speaks to you as he did to Ezekiel: 'When I say unto the wicked, O wicked man, thou shalt surely die; if thou dost not speak to warn the wicked from his way, that wicked man shall die in his iniquity; but his blood will I require at thine hand. Nevertheless, if thou warn the wicked of his way to turn from it; if he do not turn from his way, he shall die in his iniquity; but thou hast delivered thy soul.' If you do not live a holy life, so as to commend the gospel, you put a slur upon it, and by your inconsistency you put a stumbling-block in the way of those who are coming to Christ. You cannot save men, but you can help to ruin them. It is for you to tell them how they may be saved, to reason with them of righteousness, temperance, and of the judgment to come, to tell them all you have learned from the Scriptures about heaven, and hell, and the precious purchase of souls by Christ, and of what must be their eternal state if they live and die without him. Think much of such topics as these, and you will be likely to remember your responsibilities. But I feel certain that, after you have lived for a few years in a country village, with nothing to stir you but the scandal and gossip of the place, when they talk about that young Mr So-and-so, who walked with a married woman because she happened to be going the same way home that he was going, if you are not careful, you will get your mind degraded to the level of the people among whom you live. There will be no excited and earnest gatherings, perhaps not even a political meeting, to cause any break in the universal dullness. It will be with you as dull and dead as it was with Coleridge's 'Ancient Mariner.' Then will you need indeed to pray, 'Awake, O heavenly wind, and blow, and make the ship that lies becalmed to fly before the gale!'

You must, sometimes, brethren, get away for a while from the same people; get away from the Hodgsons, and the Browns, and the Jones, and the Smiths, and all the little tailors in the village, and try to get among some fellows who have a little life in them; but above all, you must get away to the Lord himself, and ask him to stir up the gift of God, which is in you.

Keep the pot boiling, brethren, to come back to the old simile. Your deacons will come in to you, some wintry Sabbath morning, when there are not many people at the chapel; and when you ask what they have brought, they will say, 'Snowballs, sir; to help to keep the fire up!' That is their way of stirring up your gifts; and lots of your people will keep the fire up in the same way. You must not let their iciness freeze you; you must be so much alive, and so full of zeal, that you will make them alive and zealous too.

I once saw a picture, painted by that quaint artist Weiss, in which he had represented the resurrection, and people gradually getting alive. One man had his head alive, while the rest of his body was dead; another had his bones covered with flesh only as far as the ribs; another had no toes, but here and there were bits of flesh just coming to clothe various parts of his body. Well, there are fellows that I know who do not seem more than half alive; they have their heads alive, and they eat vigorously enough; and they have their pockets alive, for though they have but a very small salary, they look after it pretty sharply; but their hearts are not alive. We have had one or two brethren who have gone out into the ministry, and we have been obliged to hold a coroner's inquest on them to try to find out if they were alive. They could speak capitally, they could say a sharp thing as nastily as anybody could, and they delighted in it, too; but they never seemed to have any care about other men's feelings. We have had them carefully examined, but we never could detect a heart anywhere in them. Such men never do any good, because they are not thoroughly alive unto God. Here is a big fellow, with sixteen ounces to the pound of talent, fully up to the mark in his knowledge of the Bible, and well-up also in classical and scientific knowledge; but he is only partly alive, going about his work with a dignified and yet lackadaisical manner that makes everybody who sees him disgusted with him. They said of a man I know, that he would have made a capital preacher if he had ever been converted; and that another would make a master-preacher if he could only preach; and of another man's sermon, 'What a wonderful sermon it might have been! How it would have run if it had only had any legs!' but it was a lame sort of a sermon, and down it dropped. Its great fault was that it had no life in it. Let none of your sermons be like that, brethren.

I recollect that, at one of our closing meetings at the College, many years ago, I said that I was a poor man, or I would give every student a present, and I told them what I would have given them if I had been rich. I remember one brother to whom I said that I would give him a corkscrew, because he had a good deal in him, but he could not get it out. 'As to you, my brother,' I said to another student, 'I should give you a sausage-stuffer, to put something into you.' There was one friend to whom I was to present a canister of Chapman and Hall's gunpowder. He was to have two pounds of it, and someone was to set it alight exactly at the second head.

Now, I beg to suggest that some of you should try that last article. Better men than you have done it, you know. You are not acquainted with history, or you would not laugh. You read 'Foxe's Book of Martyrs', and you will see that Mr Rowland Taylor and Bishop Hooper both had a friend, who came with a bladder of gunpowder, to put under their arms when they were going to be burned. I do not want to do it that you may be made to die, but that you may be made thoroughly alive. Just a little of the stuff that the Czar of Russia is so fond of, would be a fine thing for sleepy ministers. Oh, for about half a pound of dynamite just underneath some pulpits! I think I will talk to my wife when I go home tonight about supplying dynamite as well as books to poor ministers. Well, something of the sort must be done. Oh, do put some dynamite into the sermons! Stir the people up! But, first of all, put the dynamite into yourselves, and stir yourselves up. May God stir you up, and make you a blessing! Amen.

The first Baptist minister

A College address

DEAR BRETHREN, in trying to stir up your hearts to preach the gospel of Christ, I thought I could not do better than to give you a sort of sermonic-lecture upon some of the great preachers of the New Testament, beginning with John the Baptist. Our text for this afternoon will be found in John's Gospel, fifth chapter, thirty-fifth verse:—'HE WAS A BURNING AND A SHINING LIGHT: AND YE WERE WILLING FOR A SEASON TO REJOICE IN HIS LIGHT.'

It may serve as a preface to this discourse if we notice that we have a brief yet instructive account of John the Baptist in the sixth verse of the first chapter of this Gospel. I trust that these words would be a true description of each one of you: '*There was a man sent from God.*' Can this be said of each of us? 'There was a man sent from God.' What right have we to profess to be the ministers of Christ if we have never been sent? Our Lord Jesus Christ himself was 'the Messiah'—'the sent One'; and if we are not sent of God, if we have never said to the Lord, 'Here am I, send me,' and have never received the consecrating touch of the live coal from off the altar, the sooner we are out of the ministry the better. We must all be missionaries, or persons sent; and if we are not so sent, we are not going upon God's errand, but only upon our own.

In order to be men sent from God, as John the Baptist was, it is quite certain that we must have been, first of all, *brought to God*. No man can be sent forth from God unless first he has been *with God*. We are not so while in our unrenewed nature, for we are far from God by wicked works; we must therefore be sure of our own conversion, that we have been brought out of darkness into God's marvellous light, that we, who were as sheep going astray, have returned unto the Shepherd and Bishop of our souls. It is clear that we can never be sent from God unless we have been brought to God, and it is equally involved that we must have dwelt with God. Our Lord Jesus Christ himself could not have said that he came forth from the Father if he had not been with the Father; and if we want to prove that we are men sent from God, we must really come from communion with God, from sitting at the feet of Jesus to learn his message, and from drinking in of the Spirit of Christ wherewith we may preach that message with power. I want you, brethren, to desire no higher title than this—'a man sent from God.' By-and-by, you will be spoken of as 'a man sent down from Spurgeon's College'; well, I hope that will be no disgrace to you; but, unless you are 'a man sent from God,' you will be no credit to us.

A man who is sent from God will prove it by having *God with him.* You remember how our Lord Jesus Christ said, 'He that sent me is with me: the Father hath not left me alone;' and it will be the same with you if you are 'a man sent from God.' You shall hear the sound of your Master's feet behind you if your Master has sent you. Just as Christ sent his seventy disciples before his face into every city and place whither he himself would come, so, if he really sends us, he will shortly follow us; nay more, he will go with us if we are sent of God. This, therefore, should be our prayer, 'If thy presence go not with us, carry us not up hence.'

Here, then, is a true description of John the Baptist,—'a man sent of God,'—conscious of that mission, girt with the power of that mission, resolved to fulfil that mission even to the last jot and tittle. You see in him a noble specimen of the man upon whom the hand of God is still resting, and in whose heart burns a devout enthusiasm to fulfil the commission which he has received from on high.

In our text we have our Saviour's further description of this man sent from God; and, in considering it, we shall note concerning John, firstly, *his character:* 'he was a burning and a shining light;' secondly, it will be well to notice *his treatment,* as some of you will receive the same: 'and ye were willing for a season to rejoice in his light;' and thirdly, *the praise he received from his Master:* 'he was a burning and a shining light.'

I. HIS CHARACTER. John's character was indicated by his Master's words: 'he was a burning and a shining light.' Notice, first, that *he was a light.* Read it thus, please, 'he was a lamp;' for that is Calvin's rendering, and that of De Wette, and many other learned scholars. Christ was *the Light*; John 'was not that Light, but was sent to bear witness of that Light.' He was not a light as we speak of light in its essence; but in the same sense as we call a candle or the gas, light, so was he a light. John was not the Light of the world, but he was a light-bearer, a lamp, a torch.

'He was a burning and a shining lamp,' from which it is evidently implied that *he had been lighted,* and that he still had light. He was not, so to speak, like the sun, which gives light to all things, though even there the figure is not exactly correct, for the sun itself was kindled from the Supreme Light which existed long before; but, speaking after the manner of men, Christ was the great and glorious Sun, but John was like a mere candle, and gave no light till the Celestial Spirit had illuminated him. It is, dear brethren, a most solemnly important thing that, if we profess to be men sent from God, we must have received a divine light. If we have not received that, all the light we have obtained from books, or from our instructors, or from our own imagination, will be of no service; the only light that can avail for God's work is the light divine. It is an awful thing for a man to say that he is moved by the Holy Spirit to take upon him the office and work of the ministry, and to declare that, neither directly nor indirectly, has he given a halfpenny for a living, when all the while he knows that it was bought at a public sale. May we never fall into such terrible sin as that! May we truly feel that the Spirit of God has illuminated us, or we should not dare to undertake this sacred work! It was so with John the Baptist; he had been lighted from above, his was divinely-derived light.

We shall not all have the same measure of light, or the same amount of ability and diffusive power. 'There is one glory of the sun, and another glory of the moon, and another glory of the stars.' In the great Reformation, they were not all Luthers; in the Methodistic day, they were not all Wesleys or Whitefields; and we ought not to expect today that all candles shall have the same number of wicks, or that all lights should be exactly alike. There is one glory of the gas, another glory of the rock-oil, and another glory of the electric light. There are all sorts of lights; and you and I must not resolve that we will not shine because we are not great magnesium lights, but only little candles. Only, brethren, you must give more light than your predecessors gave. A minister must always have more light than his hearers. The lesser lights were sufficient for the night of the nation's ignorance; but now that School Boards are educating the children, we must have the greater lights to rule the day, and unless you really become sun-burners, you will be certain to be despised by the people. I reckon that ministers ought to be ahead of their people in all respects, as far as it is possible; but especially in respect to that great Light which we are to diffuse, we ought to have the greatest powers of illumination, because we have received so much of the light divine.

John witnessed against the darkness, even as his Lord did. In a measure, it might be said of him as of Jesus, 'the light shineth in darkness; and the darkness comprehended it not.' A light is a protest against darkness. Darkness was upon the face of the deep, yet the Lord never scolded the darkness; he said, 'Let there be light,' and there was light. There is great darkness in the spiritual world, and we shall probably find that our best plan is not directly and impatiently to rebuke the darkness; yet is the darkness to be rebuked at fitting seasons. How bravely John did it! 'Repent ye; for the kingdom of heaven is at hand.' 'And now also the axe is laid unto the root of the trees.' How sternly he denounced the Pharisees and Sadducees! 'O generation of vipers, who hath warned you to flee from the wrath to come?' John had a strong witnessing faculty as a light against the gross darkness of the times in which he lived.

Light, however, is mainly intended to reveal the body which we wish to see; and that John did. 'He was not that Light, but was sent to bear witness of that Light.' His constant preaching was that he was not the Christ, but that he was sent to bear witness to him; therefore, he pointed to him, and cried, 'Behold the Lamb of God.' In this way we also ought to be lights; and, like John, plainly point men to the Lamb of God, the Sin-bearer, the Sin-remover, who taketh away the sin of the world. All our life long, may we be able to say, as we can, I trust, say even now,—

'E'er since by faith I saw the stream
    Thy flowing wounds supply,
Redeeming love has been my theme,
    And shall be till I die.'

I have little enough of light, therefore would I focus it upon the Lamb of God. Little enough shall I be able to reveal to men, for my knowledge is limited; but I can say, with Paul, 'I determined not to know any thing among you, save Jesus Christ, and him crucified.' John was a light, then, and he did reveal that which he was sent to reveal, which was that men were to be saved by the sacrifice of the Lamb of God.

But the text also tells us that *he was a burning light,* by which is meant that he was a real light, not a sham one. John was not a painted light, a mere reflector, like that which we put in a dark room; which gives no light; in fact, it repudiates it for itself, and throws it upon other objects. You are not to be like those reflectors which reject the light, you must absorb it into your own substance, and then you must make it to shine out of yourself to others. John was a real torch, flaming and burning. It is an awful thing if a man's ministry is not a reality, when you can truly say, 'That fellow took up the business of preaching simply and only because he thought it would pay better than any other; he rather liked to wear an all-round collar, and to be admired by the young ladies, and to see himself in a pulpit; but he would quite as gladly have been an auctioneer, and he may go into that line yet.' No, no, brethren, let us be real in our ministry. A man sent from God, not who merely says he is, but who really is so, and who comes because he cannot help himself, the divine impulse is so strong upon him, he is a real minister, and all he does is very real.

I suppose, however, the chief allusion is to John's energy: 'he was a burning light.' John was like Elijah, whom the Rabbis called 'the candle of God.' Elijah burned like a torch, brightly blazing, but soon quenched, his ministry was short. So was that of John; he was not long before the public, his was not the lengthened ministry to which some aspire; but his was an earnest, blazing, burning ministry, which all might well desire, for he soon accomplished the work which God gave him to do when he sent him into the world. I wish we had more ministers like John the Baptist. Weight is important, but pace somehow is more important. If you could have a very large cannon ball, and hurl it through this room at the rate of ten miles an hour, some of us would be where the late Czar of Russia has not gone; but if we happen not to be great cannon balls, if we are only like little bullets about the size of a boy's marbles, yet if one of those bullets passed through this room at the pace it would go when fired out of a Minie rifle, it would be very awkward for any man whom it struck. If you are but small shot, take care to go at such a pace that you make up in speed what you lack in size, make up by the momentum for the force that you might otherwise lack. After all, I do think that man usually succeeds best who throws most energy into what he has to do. I have seen people ready to go to sleep, and I have been very sleepy myself when listening to some sermons, but as soon as ever the preacher woke himself up, his hearers also became wide awake.

There was no sleepiness about John the Baptist. When he stood preaching in the wilderness, there was nothing dull or heavy, cold or lethargic about either the man or his message; he was just a burning firebrand in the midst of the people. Like him, we must have these three letters, N R G; it is not exactly the pronunciation of the word here, though it would be quite correct if we crossed the Tweed, or the Irish Sea. Energy is what is wanted in the ministry, plenty of it, the more the better, energy! *energy!* ENERGY!

In John the Baptist's ministry there was real zeal; he was a *burning* as well as a shining light. Some men's ministries shine, but so does the moon, and they are just as cold as moonlight. You can see everything by their light, and the shadows are quite dense through their brightness, you are often astonished at the clearness of their views; yes, they *shine,* but God's true servants *burn.* Our God is a consuming fire; and his ministers should burn with holy zeal against sin. John was not one of those who wear soft raiment, who dwell in kings' palaces, and speak of the royal mistress as 'Her Highness'; he had other titles than that for Herodias, he burned with indignation against sin, and rebuked the tyrant Herod to his face. He also burned just as fiercely against error, even that which some do not care to touch. 'Think not,' said he, 'to say within yourselves, We have Abraham to our father: for I say unto you, that God is able of these stones to raise up children unto Abraham.' There is nothing wrong in sin or in error but what John smites it. They say to us, 'Why cannot you leave other people alone, and mind your own business?' It is our business to interfere with everybody and everything that is opposed to Christ. We came into the world on purpose to do so. If we do not, what is the ministry for? You may say to the shepherd, 'Leave the wolves alone,' but he would answer, 'If I do leave them alone, I cease to be the shepherd;' and if we do not meddle with the sins of the times, and the errors of the times, we cease to be the ministers of God, and we are unfaithful to our vocation. John was not afraid to rebuke even the greatest sinners; he burned with indignation against them, and, of course, they did not like it, and they will not like it if we do as he did.

He was full of zeal also in that sweeter way by which he could show his love for his Master. How happily he cries again and again, 'Behold the Lamb of God, which taketh away the sin of the world,' speaking with his finger as well as with his voice! How graciously he speaks of his Lord when he says, 'He must increase, but I must decrease,' and bids those who have followed him as his disciples look to Jesus, and follow him! How he delights to be able to say, 'I am but the Bridegroom's best man, and I rejoice greatly because of the Bridegroom's joy'! He had a great zeal for his Master, of whom he humbly said, but none too humbly, 'There cometh One mightier than I after me, the latchet of whose shoes I am not worthy to stoop down and unloose.'

Great, too, was John's zeal for the souls of men. You can see him in the wilderness, and in prison, ever thoughtful of others, and labouring for their good; it is for them that he bears all that he is called to endure. It must be a horrible state of mind for any minister to get into, when he does not care for the people committed to his charge. Even Xerxes, who was one of those men of war whose bowels seem to be made of stone, and who drove myriads into the battle-field without a regret, yet even he, when he saw his armies pass before him, wept when he thought that, out of all those thousands, so few would be alive in a short time.

Our outlook goes much further than that of Xerxes, for we look into eternity, and when we reflect how many may lose their souls as well as their lives, and find immortality in death, we may well weep and sigh as they pass before us. We shall never be burning lights for God unless our heart itself burns with an inward anguish for the woes of men, and our inmost spirit is wrung with a pain unspeakable on account of those who are hurrying on towards the wrath to come. With Dr Doddridge, let each one cry,—

'My God, I feel the mournful scene;
My bowels yearn o'er dying men;
And fain my pity would reclaim,
And snatch the firebrands from the flame.'

I think I have said almost enough to you about John being a burning light; but I must just add that burning seems to imply self-consumption, as a candle burns itself away as it gives light. John's was a life of self-sacrifice, and his martyr-death worthily crowned his noble life. His raiment was not soft, it was made of camel's hair, and he had a leathern girdle about his loins; his diet was not rich and rare, he never quarrelled with his food, for 'his meat was locusts and wild honey.' I remember how Dr James Hamilton, using the words of a grumbler, says, 'Only that cold mutton!

Only this cold water! Two covers on the table; under one of them only manna, under the other only water from the rock!' That is the style of many men, alas! even of some ministers, forsooth, for even they must have the very best food and raiment. I read of a priest who, when he was cooking a chicken for his dinner, burnt his fingers, and then said, 'Ah! how much we ministers do have to suffer in the cause of God!' No such calamity as that ever occurred to John the Baptist. 'His meat was locusts and wild honey,' and his death fittingly crowned his life. He was imprisoned because of his faithfulness in rebuking Herod, his spirit had been revived by the return of the messengers whom he had sent to the Master, and he was perhaps meditating upon all the glory of the kingdom which he had been permitted to usher in,—the brightness of that Sun before whom he as the morning star rightly faded away,—when the executioner entered his cell in a hurry. No notice was given to the prisoner, he had short shrift. As soon as the daughter of Herodias asked for the head of John the Baptist, we read, 'Immediately the king sent an executioner, and commanded his head to be brought: and he went and beheaded him in the prison, and brought his head in a charger, and gave it to the damsel: and the damsel gave it to her mother.' Thus the 'man sent from God, whose name was John,' went back to God, and proved the fulness of 'the favour, or gift, or grace of God,' for such was the meaning of his name, and such had he been all his life long.

But John was *a shining light* as well as a burning light. I have known some men who have been very full of zeal, but there has been no shining in their ministry. I have heard that it was a lucifer match that kindled their light; it was so in the case of the man who had a fierce temper, for that is the lucifer match which has made some into burning lights. Such fire as that is as hateful to God as the strange fire that Nadab and Abihu offered. The zeal that is wanted for the Lord's service is that which is accompanied with knowledge, and consecrated by love. 'He was a burning and a shining light.' John shone so brightly because of the fulness of his testimony. He kept back nothing that he knew concerning Christ. He had not much to say; but, little as it was, he said it all. One thing I warn you against, brethren, that is, trying to save up some of your light. It is no good attempting to do so, for light is an article that will not keep, it must burn on and burn out. I have sometimes told you that I compare myself, not to one of our vast vats, the reservoirs of learning that you will find in some

Colleges,—not marked XX, but D.D.,—enormous vats they are; I should like to speak of them with all the reverence they deserve, but it seems to me that the tap was fixed up at the top of the vat, and very little runs out. Now I am a very small kilderkin [half a barrel or two firkins], but I take care to empty myself right out every time I preach; if there are only eighteen gallons in the cask, the people get it all; but some of these thousand-gallon vats only pour out about half a pint, and keep the rest themselves. I think that you and I had better tell the people all that we know; we must not keep our knowledge to ourselves, else it will be like the manna which was kept beyond the appointed day, it will stink, and breed worms. Get more manna fresh continually, and use it all up, let none of it be kept until the morning.

John was not a light shut up in a dark lantern; he was a *shining* light, and one reason for his shining was that his speech was so plain. Everybody who heard him could understand him. He was a sort of John Bright or William Cobbett among preachers. There was not about him even the mystery which you sometimes notice in his namesake, the beloved apostle John; it is all downright hard hitting and straight firing with John the Baptist. The words that came from his lips were very plain and simple. Brethren, do be shining lights in this sense. Cut out all those long words that you have put into your sermons; do not carry a silver pencil-case, to note every word of fifteen syllables that you meet with, in order that you may roll it out to the people next Sunday. Give them as many words of one syllable as ever you can; make your preaching as plain as a pike-staff, and let nobody have to say of you, 'What a fine preacher he is!' for 'a fine preacher' will go to hell if he does not mind. It is one of the greatest of all sins to be 'a fine preacher.' Look at the Church as John saw her in the Revelation. She was clothed with the sun, the moon was under her feet, and upon her head was a crown of twelve stars. The Church of Rome makes the woman very fine, but she cannot compare in glory with the woman in heaven, so they put on her all kinds of nick-nacks and ornaments, and thus produce the harlot of Babylon, 'arrayed in purple and scarlet colour, and decked with gold and precious stones and pearls, having a golden cup in her hand full of abominations and filthiness of her fornication.' Do not so with a sermon, I beseech you; but clothe it with the sun, and put the stars about its head, deck it with celestial ornaments; and as for the moon, put that beneath its feet. Never expect to be a burning and a shining light by hanging the gaudy trinkets of oratory about your sermons, for John the Baptist shone by the brilliance of his plain speech, and of him his Lord said, 'Among them that are born of women there hath not risen a greater than John the Baptist.'

Still more, John was 'a shining light' in his holy life. All men knew that John was a prophet, not only because he was such a powerful preacher, but because of his consecrated life. There was something even about his asceticism, his total abstinence, his evident self-denial, that made him all the better preacher. May God make us holy men! Men cannot make head or tail of some of us; but if ever this question is asked, 'the ministry of Thomas So-and-so, was it from heaven or of men?' oh, that the devil and all his emissaries may be forced to be silent because they dare not say it is not from heaven, even if they will not admit that it is! The baptism of John vindicated itself; so may the life of each one of us be the justification of all our preaching! There is a story told of Origen that, in great stress of trial, he denied the faith. Afterwards, going to Jerusalem, he was asked to preach. He was very much averse to doing so, but was at last persuaded to attempt it. He took the Bible that was in the pulpit, and you may imagine what was his dread when he opened it, and his eye caught these words, 'Unto the wicked God saith, What hast thou to do to declare my statutes, or that thou shouldest take my covenant into thy mouth?' He sat down before the crowded audience that had gathered to hear the celebrated preacher, read the text, and said his tears must be his only discourse; and unless you and I live godly lives, we shall have to be silent in God's house. Until repentance has been shown, and God's infinite love sets us on our feet again, we must be quiet. The better thing, however, will be not to sin, nor turn aside from God, so that we may be able to say with Paul, when writing to the Thessalonians, 'Ye are witnesses, and God also, how holily and justly and unblameably we behaved ourselves among you that believe.'

Further, John was 'a shining light' from the fact that he had a striking style and manner. There was a diffusiveness about him, he scattered what light he had. All men heard of John; even Herod heard of John the Baptist, and for a very good reason. I do not believe he ever put an advertisement in the weekly or daily papers stating that 'the Rev. John Baptist had become the Pastor of the Church in the Wilderness, that on a certain day there would be "a locust and honey meeting", and he would preach a special sermon, and at the close of the service, the ordinance of believers' baptism would be observed.' No, no, John's preaching was his only advertisement; he stepped forth into the wilderness, and began to preach; there was a voice crying, and men could not help hearing it.

Brethren, we must do something striking, but the most striking thing nowadays is to preach the gospel. It will not do for us to preach the gospel inside a missionary box, for unless all the people were to gather round the little slit in the top, they would never know anything about it. Well, brethren, you smile, but you know what I mean; there are some ministers who are quite content if about a dozen people come to hear them; let it not be so with any of you. If you are sent of God to a town, or a village, make a stir somehow or other. Let it not be done with any idea of self-glorification; but say to yourself, 'People who do not hear the gospel are not likely to believe the gospel. If I preach to empty pews, I shall save nothing, not even myself. I shall be the loser by it, and not the Saviour; but if I get the pews full, "faith cometh by hearing, and hearing by the Word of God," and by that means I may hope to help to get heaven full.' One Catholic priest said to another that 'virginity peopled heaven.' 'Ah!' replied the other, 'but it would not people earth.' If the earth was never peopled, I do not see how heaven would be. We may say that modest, genteel, lady-like preaching gathers together the *élite* and the eclectic; but I do not know where they are going to pick out these *élite* and eclectic people about whom we hear so much unless they have some ordinary sinners from whom they may select them. So, brethren, preach in a simple, earnest, striking manner, as John did, and like him you will be a burning and a shining light.

Put together all that I have said, and I think you will have a true description of the character of John the Baptist, of whom his Master said, 'he was a burning and a shining light.'

II. Secondly and briefly, let us consider HIS TREATMENT: 'ye were willing for a season to rejoice in his light.' I call your special attention to this point, because this will be the kind of treatment that some of you will receive.

There were some who had *a temporary delight* in John the Baptist's ministry. Calvin translates the whole verse, 'He was a burning and shining lamp, and for a time you were willing to amuse yourselves in his light,' and then he goes on to explain his translation, 'as if,' saith he, 'the head of a family were to light a lamp for his servants by night, that they might perform the duties which he had enjoined on them, but they, instead of doing so, employed it for debauchery and every kind of licentiousness.' Well, now, there are many churches that do just this with their minister; they have a very beautiful, bright lamp, and they amuse themselves in his light. Oh, how they praise the preacher! The ladies especially cry, 'What a dear young man he is!' 'Well,' says one, 'I cannot help admiring his charming looks;' and another praises the musical tones of his voice, and the sweet key in which it is pitched. They are full of admiration of the new lamp. Brethren, if this is happening to you, do not be so very proud, because all of us have in our measure passed through the same process; many men, as good as you, and better, and *worse*, have received just the same sort of treatment as you are experiencing from your hearers. They are willing for a season to amuse themselves in your light. But remember that we were never sent to amuse people, we were sent to enlighten them, and to be the means of burning sin out of them; but they are willing for a season to amuse themselves in our light! There is many and many a ministry of which it can be said, 'it is gold in the morning, silver in the afternoon, and lead at night.' There is a grand welcome meeting, an enthusiastic recognition service, the newspapers announce that 'the Rev. So-and-so commences his work under the most happy auspices,' everybody rejoices, and the whole town rings with the praises of the brilliant young minister. Whether it is that the promising young man has not many sermons, and so is soon spun out, or whether he came into the world to be 'sent of God' to speak with power only two or three times, or whether it is that he gets very lazy, and does not work, or whether it is the fault of the people, I am sure it is still true that 'they are willing for a season to amuse themselves in his light.' The Greek is ἀγαλλιαθάναι, that is, they danced gaily, up and down, backwards and forwards, across the room, with hands joined, all praising this splendid young man. Well, brethren, that is the way that they often go on, as they did with John the Baptist: 'they were willing for a season to dance,' and frolic, and play at games, like boys at a bonfire, 'in his light.'

The quieter people do not make so much fuss, in fact, they do not approve of it; they are the sort who never gush, and never go into ecstasies, but still they are willing for a season to rejoice in his light, such as it is. They do not think it is as good as they might have had from another College; but still, the minister is a useful young man, and may be made into something in course of time, especially if they are all of them properly unkind and cruel to him! It is *an intellectual pleasure* which these people feel. 'Ye were willing for a season to rejoice in his light,' not in his burning, mark you; and they did not rejoice in *the* Light; no, they did not care much about that, they rejoiced in John's light, his little penny candle, his small illumination, they rejoiced in that which appertained to the man, not in the message which the man brought. Oh, how many of our hearers think more of us than they do of our Master! They go out saying to one another, 'Was not that a splendid climax?'—a peroration, I think they call it. If it had been because of the Light that John's hearers, or ours, rejoiced, it would have been a different matter.

There is an old story about Hercules trying to drag Cerberus, the three-headed dog, out of the pit. He seized him by his huge dog-collar, and for a time the cur came out with him; but when they reached the gates, the dog pulled so hard, and the ground was so slippery, that Hercules had to let go, or the dog would very soon have dragged him down with him. Men of the world are very like that dog. If it is God's light that you want them to see, you may pull them till you get them nearly up, but if the light once begins to shine on them, they will roar at you, they will bite and bark, and you will need all the strength you have to keep from being dragged down to them. Still, if you will proclaim the truth very cleverly, if you will preach the gospel very nattily and prettily, it may be even good strong Calvinistic theology, you will find that, as it was with John, so it will be with you, the people will be willing for a season to rejoice in your light so far as to have an intellectual pleasure in it.

But afterwards, what then? Why, then, they are willing, after that season is over, to put the light out. There will be *the ultimate rejection* of the light, as there was in John's case. Herod was the extinguisher, and most effectually was John the Baptist's light quenched. The king said that, with an oath, he had promised the daughter of Herodias that he would give her whatsoever she should ask of him, even unto the half of his kingdom, and he was obliged to kill John for his oath's sake. There is one of the old Fathers who says, 'Herod was a liar even in making that excuse, for he had promised to give her anything to the half of his kingdom, and John's head was worth more than the whole of his kingdom;' so he might have replied to her shameful request, 'I said that to the half of my kingdom I would give you what you asked, but I cannot give you the head of John the Baptist, for that is worth more than the whole of my kingdom.' As was said of Chrysostom at Constantinople, 'much better that the sun should cease to shine, than that Chrysostom should cease to preach,' so much better would it have been that the kingdom of Herod should all have been destroyed, than that the head of John the Baptist should have been cut off.

Expect, brethren, that in all probability people will treat you as they treated John. They may take away your character, they may take away your reputation, and it may be necessary for you to remove to some other place, and let your light shine there. If so, do not be so 'stoppish' as not to move, and do not go running home to tell the President, as if such a thing had never happened to anybody else. If they rejoice in your light during a long season, be glad; but if it is a short season, do not be too much cast down, but pray God to trim your light so that others may be able to rejoice in it for a season elsewhere.

III. But now, lastly, what was John's reward? John's reward, dear brethren, was, so far as my text is concerned, HIS MASTER'S PRAISE, for it is the Lord Jesus who says of him, 'he was a burning and a shining light.'

If we can have our Master say of us what he was able to say of John the Baptist, it will be all that we can want. Oh, for that approving word from our dear Lord's lips, 'Well done, good and faithful servant!' I earnestly beseech you, brethren, to expect no other reward, because, although there may seem to be other rewards, there are none of them that are satisfactory or satisfying to a man of God. You may think it is a great thing to gather around you a large church, and to be a person of influence; but I can assure you, from my own experience, that there is nothing really satisfying in it all, for as in 'making many books there is no end; and much study is a weariness to the flesh,' so, it is just in proportion as you succeed that you will be weary, that you will be worried, that you will be worn, and that you will scarcely know what repose of mind means. If your own comfort were to be sought, you might be content to abide in some humble sphere of service, for as far as success is concerned, there is nothing in it worth toiling for. But it is worth while aiming at pleasing Christ. If you do not live for that, if you are seeking to make your preaching pleasing to your people, you will get broken-hearted one of these days. I like to feel, 'I do not preach to please my people, I do not preach to please myself; but I do preach to please the Lord Jesus Christ.' A toad under a harrow is better off than a minister who preaches to please men, one spike or another is always running into him. He feels that he has as many masters as there are people, and he gets to dread even the silly remark of a servant girl. He has five hundred masters if he has that number of hearers in his congregation, and every Tom, Jack, and Harry can kick him as much as he likes. Let not one of you be such a cur as that; but live for something nobler and better, and seek to please Christ, even as John the Baptist did.

Now, in summing up, I want you to notice that there are four testimonials to John's ministry, which I hope we may all have when our work comes to an end. The first is in John 5:33: '*He bare witness unto the truth.*' That would make a capital epitaph for any one of us. If that be the truth, it will be a fine memorial of any man's ministry. Take care that you know the truth, and the whole truth, bear witness to the truth, and nothing but the truth, so shall you have won an encomium from your Lord like that which he gave to John: 'He bare witness unto the truth.'

Another passage concerning John the Baptist is in John 10:41: '*John did no miracle; but all things that John spake of this man were true.*' I should like each of you to have that for your epitaph; it is perhaps preferable even to the other. The first part is true of us all, 'John did no miracle.' John did not crowd the place, John did not build a new chapel, John did not have half-a-dozen plated teaspoons and an inkstand presented to him, 'John did no miracle: but all things that John spake of this man were true.' He spake about Christ, and what he said was the truth; he was no great wonder-worker; he was a faithful preacher, and souls were saved and fed by his preaching. People might have said, if he had lived nowadays, 'he will never set the Thames on fire.' 'John did no miracle: but—' oh, what a blessed 'but'!—'all things that John spake of this man were true.' May that be truly said of each one of us!

Another high encomium, and one of a different character, because it comes from the other side of the house, is recorded in Mark 6:20: '*Herod feared John*'. John did not fear Herod, but 'Herod feared John.' John had nothing to lose, but 'Herod feared John,' for John came to him, and said, 'it is not lawful for thee to have thy present wife.' There were some preachers who came to Herod, and he paid them well for their very excellent discourses; but 'Herod feared John.' Herod told other preachers to mind what they said, and especially never to say anything against the Herodian government, or else he would let them know who was master; but he never said anything like that to John, for 'Herod feared John.' It is a grand thing when it can be said of a minister that men fear him, and that they do not dare to act in his presence as they do when he is not near them, for they are afraid of his righteous rebukes. The devil himself is afraid of some ministers; I know he is by the nasty tricks he plays upon them; he is a devil of a devil, there is none like him in devilry, he will go any length in evil; but I hope it will be true that even Satan will tremble when he sees us on our knees, or when we enter the pulpit.

There is one more testimony concerning John the Baptist; it is in Acts 13:25: '*John fulfilled his course.*' There we read Paul's testimony concerning him, 'John fulfilled his course.' His father, Zacharias, you know, was a priest, and was fulfilling his course when the promise of John's birth was conveyed to him. John was a priest, too, and he fulfilled his course. That would be a noble epitaph for any one of us. He was not the greatest man who ever lived, the least in the kingdom of heaven is greater than he; but 'John fulfilled his course.' Some men's lives are broken columns, snapped off before their work was half done; others are like Penelope with her web, undoing in the dark night of forgetfulness and sin what they had woven in the light of day; but 'John fulfilled his course,' what he began to build, that he finished.

I think any of these four, or all four together, might serve for mottoes for a man of God, that he might be able to set before him as his ideals of what his ministry ought to be. May you all be such men, for Christ's sake! Amen.

Young preachers not to be despised

A College lecture, delivered in 1887

D EAR BRETHREN,—I want to address you, this afternoon, not quite in the form of a sermon, but yet somewhat in that fashion, taking for my text Paul's first Epistle to Timothy, fourth chapter, from the twelfth to the sixteenth verses:—

'Let no man despise thy youth; but be thou an example of the believers, in word, in conversation, in charity, in spirit, in faith, in purity. Till I come, give attendance to reading, to exhortation, to doctrine. Neglect not the gift that is in thee, which was given thee by prophecy, with the laying on of the hands of the presbytery. Meditate upon these things; give thyself wholly to them; that thy profiting may appear to all. Take heed unto thyself, and unto the doctrine; continue in them: for in doing this thou shalt both save thyself, and them that hear thee.'

I. My first observation is, that THERE IS A GREAT TENDENCY TO DESPISE YOUTH, especially among those who wish they were themselves youths, whose age is their only authority for despising those who are younger than they are, and whose years are the only proof of their wisdom. Such men are very likely to sneer at those whose knowledge is far greater than their own, and to look down upon them simply because they happen to excel them in one thing that they cannot help. I do not believe that wise old men despise youths in the least degree; of course, they do not look up to them, it would be a reversal of nature if they did. Yet they do not despise them; they are more likely to be encouraged by them, they often feel quickened by them; as they look at their younger and more vigorous brethren, they have bright reminiscences of their own early days, and they themselves seem to grow young again. I know some old men of this kind; they have grey hairs on the top of their heads, but they are not grey within, they are rejoicing in the perpetual verdure of their youth even at seventy or eighty years of age. Still, it is the tendency on the part of many old men to despise the younger members of society.

Yet, *if it were necessary, youth could be vindicated.* Why, there is no road to age except by way of youth! A young man cannot help the fewness of his years; and, as they increase, he is getting rid of that which some seem to regard as a drawback; and all the while he is swiftly riding on the wings of time, and speeding towards the period of discretion *and infirmity.* He cannot help being young; but even during his youth there is no reason why he should be despised. Young men have done a great deal in this world; if they have not accomplished more than old men have, they have at least done as much for the people among whom they have lived.

We could mention, you know, such names as that of Samuel, called of God while yet a child; and who was more noble than he among all the judges of the chosen race? There may have been some of them more valiant in fight; but none were of braver spirit, none were more full of wisdom, none were more worthy to be leaders of God's ancient people. No man could wish to have a grander testimony to his integrity and uprightness than that which was accorded to Samuel when Saul had been chosen king of Israel. Hear how this truly grand old man addressed the whole assembly:—'And now, behold, the king walketh before you: and I am old and grayheaded; and, behold, my sons are with you: and I have walked before you from my childhood unto this day. Behold, here I am: witness against me before the Lord, and before his anointed: whose ox have I taken? or whose ass have I taken? or whom have I defrauded? whom have I oppressed? or of whose hand have I received any bribe to blind mine eyes therewith? and I will restore it to you. And they said, Thou hast not defrauded us, nor oppressed us, neither hast thou taken ought of any man's hand. And he said unto them, The Lord is witness against you, and his anointed is witness this day, that ye have not found ought in my hand. And they answered, he is witness.' Samuel, even while yet young, was a man after God's own heart.

Then there was that other man after God's own heart, young David, who was never perhaps so fully a man of God as when he was hardly a man; his later days were far more obscure, and dim, and misty, than those bright morning times when the Lord was his Shepherd, and he was made to lie down in green pastures, and was led beside the still waters. It was a grand part of David's life when he was hunted like a partridge on the mountains, yet all the while was soaring like an eagle above the hills. So may I say, in a measure, of his famous son, Solomon. It was not in his old age that he was noted for his wisdom; even in middle life, strange women had turned away his heart; but it was while his heart was young and tender that he made the wise choice that the Lord approved. Solomon as a young man certainly shines far more brightly than Solomon the aged; it was while he was comparatively young that all nations heard of his wisdom, and the wisest of sages came to learn what the young man had to say.

I scarcely need mention Daniel, the wonderful total-abstaining young man. There is hardly one of the ancient saints who seems to have been so perfect as he was; I do not know of any fault that is recorded of him. He is the John of the Old Testament, the man who saw more visions than any other prophet, the man greatly-beloved, even as John is called the beloved disciple. Under divine inspiration, Daniel wrote a Book of Revelation long before John came into the world; indeed, there are many interesting points of resemblance between Daniel and John. I should say that John, too, was a young man, probably the youngest of all the apostles, and certainly the best of them.

If we were to descend from Scripture times, there would be no difficulty in finding a long list of young men, who never lived to reach any other age, who yet did a splendid life-work, and whose service deserves throughout all ages to deliver young men from being despised. I am sure that, if anyone were to read the stories that have been written or that might be written about the exploits of young men, he would never afterwards think lightly of them.

Yet, brethren, we must admit that *youth certainly has some disadvantages*. We cannot speak with the authority of experience concerning things which we have never gone through. We are obliged to borrow from others, to act by faith upon the observation of others, because we have not yet made these observations ourselves. Some of you have no notion what it is to be over fifty years old, and I have no idea what it must be to be seventy; but we shall have one day, if we live long enough; and so, by experience, we shall understand what are the peculiar trials and troubles of middle life and declining years. We have our own drawbacks; but we have not yet tasted and tried many things that our 'grave and reverend seigneurs' have done. We speak of such subjects as a young man understands, whereas the old men talk of themes that are more appropriate to the whiter wigs that they wear. To some people, there is a great deal in the manly appearance of a minister; and there are some who will only receive instruction from one who looks like a man of wisdom.

I hope you will consider that, in this year of grace, 1887, I can be no longer reckoned among young men, yet I trust that you will not put me down as having at present any affinity to the old men. I have left the period of youth, and reached middle life, wherein all wisdom is, or ought to be concentrated; but I have not yet arrived at anything like old age, I must leave that honour to Mr Gladstone and 'Father Rogers.' I believe I have just arrived at the best time of life. I may whisper to you, brethren, that I used to think the same when I was nineteen, and I had an exactly similar opinion at thirty-five. At *our* age, brethren, we have many advantages. What if we are not so weighty as the old men? We can make up for that by moving faster. We cannot speak with the authority of so many years; but it may be that our speech is more fluent than that of our elders, so that we can say more in the time, and thus make up in quantity what, perhaps, we lack in quality. We are not so solid as our seniors; but then, at the same time, we are not so heavy. We have force and elasticity, our blood does not creep in our veins, our breath does not freeze in our lungs, we have energy, we have faith, we have confidence, we can wake men up as the old men cannot, we have vigour and daring and dash, and we often lift up a church from the very dogs where some dear old fogie has dragged it down.

But what is it about youth that people despise? How dare they despise youth? They know that they would like once more to be young themselves; would they not? They would give their grey beards to have none at all; they would give their eyes, and their spectacles, too, if they could only see as we see; they would give their legs, and their walking-sticks, too, if they could only run as we run. Why, if they try to run up a hill, they puff like a pair of bellows; they are getting old and feeble; yet they dare to look down with scorn upon us! What can there be in us to despise?

I fancy, brethren,—and I speak as the mediator between the old men on the one hand and the young men on the other,—I fancy that what they despise in you of this playful, fickle, juvenile age is *that which they see when youth is too juvenile.* That is to say, there is a measure of playfulness which even my old friend over here likes;—I am not now referring to any individual,—I am, metaphorically, putting the old man on the right side and the youth on the left. Well, my old friend likes some fun; but he does not care to have row, and noise, and larking, and joking always going on. There is a tendency that way in some young men, who seem to think that play is the main business of life. It ought to be the sauce and curry of life, not the chief dish upon the table. Old men will despise you if you are all playfulness; and I should think that you will despise yourselves, when you are in your sober minds,—if that ever occurs,—therefore it is no wonder that the old gentlemen despise you when you are nothing but frolicsome, and frothy, and foolish.

Then, too, *young men are often too hasty*. They jump at conclusions, they must do the thing they are about, offhand, there and then. I believe that many a noble enterprise has been the result of that dashing, unhesitating spirit, and that a glorious hastiness has often driven the devil like chaff before the wind. Yet there is an unseemly hurry-skurry for which there can be no excuse whatever; and it is that sort of thing which often causes young men to be despised. Still, it is a grand thing, while so many are sound asleep or carelessly indifferent, to see an earnest young fellow riding along, on a bare-backed steam-engine, red-hot, and never so much at home as when he is trying his hardest to beat the lightning or outride the whirlwind.

We notice, sometimes, in a young man, *a positive silliness*. You would think he was a great boy, and you ask yourself how much it would cost to put him in knickerbockers. He is five feet ten inches in height; but, bless the dear child! he would be in his proper place if you put him in a kindergarten class. Give him some toys, especially a rattle, pretty little darling! Oh, what a poor, weak speech it was that he delivered at the tea-meeting, the other evening! Do you never meet with young men of that sort? Of course, they never come within these walls! The older men tell me that they see a great many of these very silly young men, and that when these young idiots preach, they say to their hearers, 'Pat us on the back, dear friends, say that we have preached very nicely.' They do not put it quite in so many words, but that is what they mean. Such a simpleton said, 'Mrs Grundy was *so* pleased with my sermon,' and other ladies paid him such pretty compliments, and told him what a dear young man he was! All that such a creature as this is fit for is to take cauliflowers round the town; he would do admirably for that kind of work, as he is such a donkey! There are some young men who will not be bigger fools than they are now even when they get old, for that would be quite impossible; they are already as asinine as they are ever likely to be. May the Lord speedily change their nature by his grace!

The old men sometimes say that *the young men are very proud*. Dear brethren, do not let anybody ever have cause to despise your youth through any display of pride on your part. You can easily get yourself up in the proudest possible manner; pride can be shown in your dress, it can be shown in your speech, it can be shown in all your habits. As soon as ever it is discovered, I do not say, 'Go and hang yourselves,' but I do say, 'Hang your pride at once.'

I must admit that there are some young men who act so foolishly that you may very well despise them; and one or two of you, brethren, may easily bring a bad name upon the whole College by foolish, silly ways. Young men now are despised because of what some of these old men whom I have mentioned did when they were young, and they are only too ready to believe that we must be as bad as they once were. My hope is that we shall not be as our fathers, who were a stiff-necked generation.

II. The apostle Paul has given us, in our text, admirable advice as to HOW THE YOUNG ARE TO AVOID BEING DESPISED. He says, '*Let no man despise thy youth; but be thou an example of the believers.*' Nobody can despise a person, be he young or old, who is an example of believers. If our lives are such that they set the pattern for our fellow-Christians, and especially if they are fashioned according to the pattern given us by the Lord Jesus Christ, nobody can despise us because we are young. Even a holy child is honourable in the sight of God and men, and the youngest saint who lives like Christ is worthy of universal reverence. A holy old man is venerable, but a godly young man is also to be venerated and highly esteemed.

Paul exhorted Timothy to be an example of the believers '*in word.*' That, I suppose, means, 'in preaching.' We are to be exemplary preachers, such preachers that, if anybody wants to know how to preach, he may come and hear any one of us, and so learn how to do it. If we are such preachers as this, when the old men hear us, they will not despise us, but will honour us notwithstanding our youth.

'*In conversation,*'—or, in behaviour, in general conduct, in everything we do. When we are about to do anything, let us reflect and consider how it will appear in the eyes of other people, and especially, let us consider whether it will be approved by the Lord Jesus Christ; and if we are not quite certain on both these points, let us not do it.

Paul says, next, 'Be thou an example of the believers … *in charity,*' that is, in love, ever manifesting a loving spirit. We ought to be an example to all the rest of the church in love to the brotherhood, and love to sinners, and love to the truth, and love to God. May we all be examples of the believers in all these respects! There are some men, and some ministers, too, whose love is very cold, and whose charity is almost *nil;* let them see that, if we cannot testify from a long experience, we can at least love with a warm affection.

'*In spirit,*' that is, in the general tone of our life; our spirit being unselfish, prayerful, happy, holy. If there is a deeply spiritual tone about us, people will not despise our youth, I am sure. If any of them are so foolish as to despise us for being under twenty-one, we need not mind what such persons say, or what they think.

'*In faith.*' Now, years ought to add strength to our faith, because we have had a longer time in which to prove the promises to be true; yet, brethren, that is the truest faith that has had no experience. We ought to have a glorious, fearless faith, like the first-ripe clusters of the vine, or like the virgin drops from the honeycomb. Faith should be sweetest and strongest of all when the dew of our youth is upon us. I am sure that old men, when they are doubting and trembling, rejoice to see us believing in God, marching on with a dash and a swing, confident of victory.

One other point Paul mentions, and that is a most important one: 'Be thou an example of the believers … *in purity.*' Oh, my brethren, do give good heed to this apostolic injunction, especially in your connection with the female sex! Ministers are sometimes called into intercourse with men and women under peculiar circumstances, and we are necessarily with them occasionally in private. Be not only pure in your connection with them all, but be careful not to do or say anything that can be fairly construed into evil, for the tongue of slander has often spit its venom even upon a pure character, and the stain has not been wholly wiped out during a long lifetime. I should advise you to keep out of the way of certain people when you have cause for suspicion as to what they may do or say. I remember being at Mr Stott's chapel one night; I had preached, and the people had responded very heartily to the appeals I had made to the unconverted, and many of them seemed to be impressed. I was praying with one man, and Mr

Stott was talking to another, when someone came to our friend, and told him that a young woman wanted to see him. When he heard her name, he said to his friend, 'You go and see her.' 'But she says she will not see anyone but you.' 'Well,' replied Mr Stott, 'I will not see her alone; I would not be in the vestry with only that woman on any account.' Afterwards, he said to me, 'That is a woman whose tongue would slander any man, or even an angel if she had the chance; her tongue is very lightly hung, and she speaks without thought, and says this and that when there is nothing in it, and I do not mean to let her say it about me.' I know that you young men are sure to be hunted up by silly women; some of them take to the red-coats, but others look after the black-coats. Don't you let them catch you; but when the right time comes, you catch one of them; meanwhile, when there is not one to be caught, don't you go courting them. Avoid everything that might by any possibility lead to evil. I believe, many a time, the act of sin begins in a very small matter; perhaps an impure word was uttered, or it may have been only a look, or a thought; and ere the man has been aware of the consequences, it has come to something that is altogether wrong, and has made him a wreck for life. I believe that you single men are generally safest the further you are off from the females; but, anyhow, a good rule for you will be, never to do anything that may not be done by any member of the church, and always to aim at being the purest of the whole. The minister, like Cæsar's wife, must be above suspicion; mind that it is always so with you, my dear brethren.

This is the kind of thing that makes old men despise youths; I could tell you of a man who, to my certain knowledge, had no less than four young ladies to whom he was supposed to be engaged at one time; and I used to wonder which one would really have him at last. By the infinite mercy and goodness of God, he escaped a trial for breach of promise, and he is all right now; but he had more than one narrow shave, and if he had been severely punished, it would only have served him right. I should not advise you, brethren, to have any strings to your bow just yet; and when you do begin this archery practice, mind that you do not have more than one string at a time, otherwise you will deserve to be despised.

The apostle Paul thus continues his advice to his son Timothy:—'*Till I come, give attendance to reading, to exhortation, to doctrine;*' and you, brethren, will do well to obey his injunction. There are three things, you see, to which you are to give attention,—reading, exhortation, doctrine. There is, first, your own 'reading.' Give diligent attention to your private study of Scripture; read it frequently, read it carefully, read it prayerfully, read it with an earnest, anxious desire that the Holy Spirit, who inspired it, may teach you its hidden meaning. Next, you are to give attention to 'exhortation', speaking to the unconverted, exhorting them to repent of sin, and trust in Jesus, and stirring up the saints to more complete consecration to the Lord's service. You are also to give attention to 'doctrine.' You cannot put the doctrine into the sermon if it has not been first put into yourself; those foolish fellows who think they have a fertile soil within their own brains, wherein everything that is good will grow of its own accord, must be themselves very verdant. Their foes and their friends, too, will discover that fact first, and they will find it out themselves afterwards. If any of you are unwise enough to think that you are going to bring out of your brains what has never been put in, a very few weeks ought to be sufficient to convince you of your mistake.

'*Neglect not the gift that is in thee, which was given thee by prophecy, with the laying on of the hands of the presbytery.*' Timothy seems to have received the *charisma,* which in those times was imparted by the laying on of the hands of the elders. We do not practise the laying on of hands in the Baptist ministry now because we have nothing that we can communicate by such a process. As soon as we have anything to impart in that way to our brethren, we will put our hands on them; but we do not see the good of laying empty hands on empty heads. If any of you have special gifts which have been received from others, whether you have birth-gifts, or gifts obtained by education or practice, do not neglect them; for they will grow smaller if they do not grow greater. They will be like a fire that is left alone, it must go out unless you stir it up; therefore, put the poker in, and make it burn. Use your gifts, or they will soon be of no use to you or anyone else. Nobody who is sensible will despise a man's youth when he takes care of his gifts, when the people can say, at the end of the first six months of his ministry, 'He preaches better every time we hear him,' and when he has been with them three years, they say, 'He was only nineteen when we first had him, and you would hardly think he is the same man, he is so much improved. Visiting among the poor has taught him many useful lessons; then, too, he has had trials of his own, he has been married, he has had a suffering wife, and he has been ill himself, but he has grown wonderfully; he is a much more gifted man than when he first came to us, in fact, we are always afraid that we shall lose him, and that he will be called away from us to a much wider sphere.' On the other hand, if he neglects his gifts, this is what they will say, 'Oh, those first two or three sermons that he preached! They ought to have been published, for they were really wonderful productions. He did pretty well for about six weeks, and then his preaching became very dull; he went up to the Conference, and when he came back he seemed to waken up for a Sunday or two; but he soon went off to sleep again. We go to chapel, and home again; but we generally feel that our minister has given us nothing at all for our souls to feed upon. The fellow appears never to get out anywhere except when he crawls into his garden in his dressing-gown and slippers, and smokes his pipe, or goes out to tea with some old gossip or scandal-monger. He never seems to read or study, he never tries to improve himself, and there are some of our young members who would beat him hollow at preaching.' When this is the state of affairs, the deacons write or come to me, and say, 'Could you not move our minister to another place?' Move him! I wish I could; but men of his stamp are steadfast, unmoveable, *never* abounding in the work of the Lord! Oh, brethren, do not any of you get into that dreadful state!

What next does Paul say to his son Timothy? '*Meditate upon these things.*' Turn them over in your mind; often be thinking of the doctrines of grace, and of these precepts of the apostle. Think of the things that he had mentioned—your word, *i.e.,* your preaching, your conversation, your charity, your spirit, your faith, your purity, your reading, your exhortation, your doctrine. 'Meditate upon these things.' That meditation is a thing to which some brethren never seem to attend; they borrow out of other people's books, but they never meditate on their own account. A book that suggests thought is one of the best works you can have in your library, but you must never rely so much on what others have written as to neglect your own personal meditation. Do your own thinking, do not put it out as you put out your washing, have a thinking-machine at home, and do your own thinking. Do not send your coffee out to be ground, grind it yourself. Keep a mill, and grind your own corn. Set apart a certain portion of every day in which you resolve to be all alone for quiet meditation upon the Word; and if people want you at that time, let them want you. Bore your way into the truth as the little maggots bore their way into the nuts, and eat a road right through. 'Meditate upon these things.' Meditation is the chewing of the cud. After you have had a good feed of truth, just imitate the cows when they have been browsing, ruminate, turn it over and over in your mind till the blessed morsels become part and parcel of yourselves. I do not believe any meditative young man is despised; meditation gives a kind of age to a man, and if it does not set grey hairs upon his head, it sets them upon his heart, not to indicate decay, but ripeness.

'*Give thyself wholly to them,*' or, 'Be thyself wholly in them.' Get inside the gospel. I believe naughty boys in the street, when they see a man on a horse that he cannot ride properly, tell him to 'get inside.' The same advice might often be very rightly given to a preacher of the gospel. I have seen many a minister who seemed to me as though he wanted a piece of rope tied round him to keep him on his creed, for he could not ride it. Why did he not get inside it? The inside of the gospel is where the ladies and gentlemen ride; it is only poor silly fools who ride on the outside. 'Be thyself wholly in these things,' that is, put your whole self into your preaching; there is not much of it at the best of times, therefore, put yourself into it, and so make the most of it. Go right at the people; as I once before said to you, take yourself, and ram yourself right into the gospel gun, and then fire yourself point-blank at your hearers. The apostle says to the Thessalonians, 'We were willing to have imparted unto you, not the gospel of God only, but also our own souls, because ye were dear unto us.' When you do that, your people will say, 'Why, here is our minister himself come home to us! If we reject Christ, we must reject our minister as well, and we love him, and would not willingly grieve him for all the world;' and very likely they will accept both you and your Master also.

I do not say that we may not have a little recreation at times; but I do say that a minister must not have a divided aim. I do not know any reason why a Christian minister should not play a game of cricket; but I never knew one get much credit for the superior style of his bowling or batting. There was one preacher whom I used to know, and when he was wanted the answer generally was, 'He is at such and such a cricket ground. He and another minister, and three or four other sporting characters spend four days a week up there during the season.' The Lord have mercy upon the people who have to listen to such preachers! The man who always has his bat in his hand, I would bowl him out, and send him home to his books and his work. There is a difference between anything that is taken up for relaxation and that which is pursued as a regular occupation. For instance, there is one of our brethren whose people tell me that nearly all his time is employed in seeking to raise prize chickens. Now, a man who keeps a few fowls for an amusement, or to supply the needs of his family, would be quite right in doing so; but it is another matter when his whole time and strength are devoted to such pursuits. When one of our brethren kept a few pigeons, he was only imitating Noah when he was in the ark; but if a minister is noted as a pigeon-rearer and pigeon-flyer, he will not be likely to see the people come flying as doves to their windows.

You ought to have one great aim in life, and to be able to say with the apostle, 'This one thing I do.' I would be willing to be a fool at everything else if I only knew everything about the gospel; at the same time, I would try to know a little about everything that was worth knowing, so that I should not be a fool at anything. Still, the main thing for you and me, brethren, is to know all about Christ and his salvation. There are many ministers who are very great tale-writers. Well, a man may very properly write much, as it will assist him to speak correctly and easily; but when his whole mind goes into the tales that he is writing, I am persuaded that his preaching cannot be up to the mark. If anything diverts your mind from your main work, you will not do it well. I hope, however, though you are young, that the people will say of you, 'Well, he does his best, he is not very experienced, and he often makes us smile, but his whole heart and soul are in his work. He has the spirit of a man of God, he is just the right kind for the Lord to bless, and he will grow into the very man we need as a pastor and teacher.' They will not despise your youth if they are able to say that of you.

'*That thy profiting may appear to all.*' That is, that they may all see that you are a growing young man. Congregations and churches do not like a minister who cannot grow any bigger. I always fear for any man who thinks he knows all he ought to know, or imagines that he is all he ought to be. You do, sometimes, meet with a man who prides himself on being absolutely perfect; he never makes a mistake, and even if we all differ from him, we are all mistaken, he is not. Here is a young man who has finished his education. Very likely! He never went to College, and he looks with sovereign contempt upon all who have. He is not one of your 'man-made ministers'; God has made him, and a beauty he is! In his own time and place, he might let you give an address to his people; how condescending he is! He means to see how far you fall short of what he is. Though you are as old as he is, he will correct you. There is one of our students who left the Baptists some years ago. Occasionally he favours me with a criticism, for which I am exceedingly obliged to the ninny. These donkeys cannot err, they cannot make mistakes, so they think; they are all that they should be, and, consequently, they cannot grow, there is no room for them to develop. Their house is so big that it covers eternity, and fills infinity; it would be impossible to add a new wing to it. Men of this size are despised by everybody; and young men may easily get as big as this in their own estimation. The people will soon observe that you are not everybody, even though you say you are; they will soon perceive that you do not know everything, even though you pretend that you do. On the contrary, let them constantly have to say that you do know more than you did, that you are growing and advancing men. If you do this, nobody will despise you; or, at least, nobody can rightly despise you.

Now, to finish, notice the sixteenth verse: '*Take heed unto thyself.*' Many other things beside charity must begin at home. Keep yourselves right. Take heed to your whole bodies, minds, spirits. A Christian man ought, as far as possible, to try and keep his body in a healthy condition; he should regard it as a temple of the Holy Ghost, that is to be kept with the utmost purity. I have always admired the saying of that good man, who said, 'I shall die today; therefore, I must be washed. I would not like to leave even this body with a speck of dirt upon it, for the body should be clean that is redeemed by Christ, and consecrated to the service of God.' Dirty ministers ought never to be Baptists; it ought to be true of us in a double sense, 'but ye are washed.' Never look untidy in your appearance, brethren; if any of your garments do get worn and seedy at any time, brush them up, and make the best of them. We have known some young men who have not been as careful as they ought to have been in these little things, but sometimes these lesser matters are of great importance. We must in all things take heed to ourselves, even to that which concerns the body; much more to that which relates to the mind, and most of all to that which affects the soul.

'*And unto the doctrine.*' Take heed unto the doctrine that you preach, brethren. Do not go forth, in the name of God, and say what is not according to his will; otherwise, the people will have cause to despise your youth. Give them the Word of the Lord in all its fulness, and they will not despise you if they are what they ought to be. Do not go and make blunders about doctrine; do not mix up different doctrines, and make a mingle-mangle of them, as some do. Read Hodge, read Dr Gill, read Calvin, John Owen, and others who are worth reading; get all the theology that you can into your mind and heart, for you will need it if you are to be 'throughly furnished unto all good works.' Still, take heed to yourself first, because, however sound your doctrine may be, it will not be of much service to your hearers if you are not yourself right with God.

'*Continue in them.*' Be one of those who, when they have found the right track, keep in it; cleave to what you know to be the truth. There is a minister to whom I say whenever I meet him, 'Well, what are you now?' He has changed his views so many times, that I never expect to find him what he was the last time I saw him. Once, when I put the usual question to him, he said, 'Well now, Spurgeon, I think I really shall take this question as an affront.' 'All right!' I replied, 'but what are you now?' 'Well, you see, I left that place where I was when I last saw you, I could not get on at all there;' which was exactly what he had told me about every other spot where he had been. I knew him first as an Arminian, violently preaching against me. He read my sermons, and became a Calvinist; not content with that, he became a hyper, and denounced me. He continued to read my sermons, and he joined the Baptists. The last time I saw him, I felt that the course of nature could no further go, for he had reached the Plymouth Brethren! He is now, I suppose, somewhere or other in space, like a comet. Do not be like that, brethren. 'Continue in them, continue in them, continue in them, continue in them.' I would like to say that sentence over and over ever so many times; say it to yourselves—'Continue in them, continue in them, continue in them.' No wise gardener would think of transplanting a tree just as it is bearing fruit, but he would leave it to grow where it is. So let it be with you, brethren, take fast hold of the ground where you are planted, and bring forth much fruit to God. Lay hold of the truth; be like a young man who is learning a business in which he hopes to succeed, and secure a competency; only let it be the business of your life to master all the truths of the gospel. 'Continue in them. Continue in them.'

'*For in doing this thou shalt both save thyself, and them that hear thee.*' Some people would have a suspicion that Paul could not have been sound when he used language like this. It is enough to make the hair of our hyper brethren stand on end; they would consider the apostle to be a rank Arminian. One of them actually said, 'As if a man could save himself! How can we save them that hear us? We were not called to save them; it is the work of the Spirit of God, we cannot do it.' I have heard the most solemn objurgations as to man's inability. 'Save themselves! They can't do it. Why, there ain't not none of 'em that can't do not nothing at all!' There brethren, you cannot get over that sentence. I remember hearing a man of this school before I was nineteen,—I do not suppose I was scarcely seventeen. He said to me, one day, as we stood outside the chapel, 'Do you believe that a man has any power of himself?' 'Well,' I replied, 'you have power to stand where you are, have you not? You have power to go up the chapel walk if you like.' 'No,' said the old gentleman, 'a man has not the power to go into the house of God at all until the Spirit gives it to him; he can walk to the public-house, but he cannot walk to the house of God.' 'Well, but,' I said, 'when the gospel is preached, surely the man can go in and hear it if he is so inclined;' to which the only answer that I received was, 'May the Lord teach you something that you have not learned yet! You do not know the very vital truths of the gospel. How can a man hear when he is deaf? His ears must be first of all unstopped, and they cannot be unstopped until the Holy Spirit begins to work in him.' I once preached a sermon from the text, 'The forts and towers shall be for dens for ever, a joy of wild asses, a pasture of flocks; until the Spirit be poured upon us from on high, and the wilderness be a fruitful field, and the fruitful field be counted for a forest.' My dear father and grandfather honoured me by listening to me, but some of the congregation had gone out, believing in that horrid idea of man being a log of wood, and doing nothing at all. I remember so well noticing their departure, and saying, 'I hope there is a sign and token for good already, for the wild asses have begun to move.' I am sorry to say that that particular work ceased from that moment.

We believe thoroughly in the grace of God, and yet we perfectly understand what the apostle meant. If you obey this command to Timothy, you will save yourself from the rebuke, 'Thou wicked and slothful servant.' You will save yourself from being idle; you will save yourself from being despised; you will save yourself from the corruptions that are in the world through lust; and you will save your hearers from getting dissatisfied with you, you will save them from neglecting the means of grace, you will save them from getting into a dead, cold, lukewarm state, and instrumentally your preaching will be the means of saving their souls eternally.

Finally, brethren, let each one of us say, 'I cannot preach as I would like to do, and as I hope to do by-and-by, but I am going in for winning souls; and, by the grace of God, I will win them.' Do not complain as some young ministers do, 'What right has that old deacon to tell me that I do not preach as well as the minister who was there before me? Why does he speak to me in such a dictatorial manner? He ought to defer to me, and not expect me to defer to him. Am I not Sir Oracle? When I speak, let no dog bark. If people despise me, I will despise them. Why, I was at a meeting, the other night, and they did not ask me to speak; yet I am a minister as much as that old gentleman who prosed away for nearly an hour, and I do not see why I should not have as much honour as he has.' Yes, you talk like that, and then everybody will despise you, and it will serve you right; but if you will carry out Paul's injunctions to Timothy, and bide your time, you will have no wish to despise anyone else, and no one else will have any good reason for despising you. May you all be such ministers as Paul desired his son Timothy to be! God grant it! Amen.

Points never to be forgotten

An address to the students of the Pastors' College, delivered on a Friday afternoon, twenty years ago [1879]*

I HOPE no brother, who comes into this College, will ever forget that he is A CONSECRATED MAN. I presume that is what each man here really is; if not, he certainly has no right to be in our ranks. He could not have been accepted as a student merely because he was a man of ability, or a fluent speaker. This College was never founded merely to impart knowledge;— that work can be better done at the Universities, and it was and still is well done in many a Collegiate establishment. My object, in founding this Institution, was that consecrated men might here receive suitable training for the Christian ministry. It was my purpose that they might here have their natural powers developed and increased, that they might discover their latent capacities and abilities, and use them to the greatest advantage, and that they might here become better acquainted with the methods and implements of our holy warfare, and so go forth well equipped for the service to which we trust they have been called of God.

Hence, brethren, there are none of you who can ever live for the sake of making money, or for the purpose of winning honour or fame among your fellow-men, without breaking your vow of consecration to the Lord. It is impossible for any one of you to live for himself, unless he becomes a traitor to his King and Lord, and to all the professions he has made as one of the disciples of the Master who have heard the Divine command, 'Follow me, and I will make you fishers of men.' It remains impossible for any man here henceforth to live for any aim but the highest; he cannot have other than the loftiest desires perpetually actuating him. You have come now to give your whole souls up to the one end of glorifying God by the winning of your fellow-men unto Christ. First and foremost, as the centre of the target you are aiming at, must be the glorifying of God. The heavens and the earth are proofs of the Creator's power; but a higher honour has been conferred upon you than upon them. You have been ordained, from before the foundation of the world, that, in your body, soul, and spirit you should glorify God. He separated you from your mother's womb, and called you by his grace for this express purpose. There was something about your very birth which proved that you were the Lord's, set apart unto him for ever. Possibly, there are prophecies, that were long ago uttered concerning some of you; and, certainly, with regard to those of you who came from Christian homes, multitudes of prayers surrounded your cradles. What the Jesuit says he is, that you really are if you are what you ought to be. His motto, 'For the greater glory of God,' is truly yours. His name is yours, far more than it is his; you are the true 'Society of Jesus,' pledged to live, henceforth, for Christ and his gospel, and for no other object.

Remember, brethren, that you are to be consecrated men always. It is not merely at certain times and seasons that you are to be consecrated men, but always;—in your work, but equally so in your recreation; for, if there are recreations that are not in harmony with your consecration to Christ, they are not such as should be engaged in by you. Take care that your recreation is always what the word implies, a re-creation; not a desecration. You are to be sanctified men in your domestic relationships;—sanctified when alone, and sanctified in public, dedicated for ever to the one sole and only purpose for which you were made, that you might 'glorify God, and enjoy him for ever.' You are called, beyond the rest of mankind, to make this your one aspiration; and to carry it out into practical effect by seeking to win souls, and to feed the flock of God. Do not imagine that you will ever fulfil the Divine purpose if you do not aim at the winning of souls. I do not believe that God is glorified by the reading of pretty little essays, or the delivery of grand oratorical addresses. If ever the harps of Heaven ring with new melodies, it will not be because of the matchless oratory of a marvellous speaker; but it will be when sinners' tears are made to fall through the rod of the gospel striking their rocky hearts, and causing the penetential floods to flow forth. Then is there wrought a miracle of mercy, and sinners are converted, while saints are encouraged, and instructed, and made to adore the Lord.

David said, 'Awake up, my glory;'—'my tongue, the glory of my frame,'—I suppose he meant. A human being is exalted infinitely above a mere brute beast because he can speak; and a minister of the gospel is vastly superior to an ordinary man because he can speak with lips which have been touched with the live coal from God's altar. Our tongue is the two-edged sword with which we smite the enemies of the Lord; yet there must ever be much tenderness manifested in the use of that sharp weapon. Our lips should be lips of persuasion, that convince with love. They should be like hives full of honey stored by the bees; they should drop with sweetness for the refreshing of the sons and daughters of men; yet all we say must be for the glory of God alone. That a man should seek to be a minister, in order that he may get a large following, and be called great and successful, seems to me to be sad indeed; but brethren, you and I will never do so, will we? We are God's men, we belong to him, and to him alone. Do you not remember what Jonah said to the shipmen even in that time of unfaithfulness when he tried to run away to Tarshish, instead of going to Nineveh as the Lord had bidden him? He was in a wicked temper, and no mistake;—cross-grained, and disobedient to the Word of the Lord; yet, even under such unfavourable circumstances, when the mariners asked him, 'What is thine occupation? and whence comest thou? what is thy country? and of what people art thou?' he gave them a noble answer, 'I am an Hebrew; and I fear the Lord, the God of Heaven, which hath made the sea and the dry land.' That was a strange description of his occupation, or his country, or his people; but it must be true of you and of me, too. If we ever do get into an ugly temper, and try to run off Tarshish way, we must still remember that we 'fear the Lord.'

That is one thing never to be forgotten by you, brethren,—that you are consecrated men, set apart, dedicated unto God and his holy service. The sacred chrism is as much upon you as ever it was upon the heads of kings, or priests, and even more so, for 'ye have an unction from the Holy One.' I can say, with the prophet Samuel, only more truly than he could say it, 'Surely the Lord's anointed is before me.' Well, then, brethren, do not desecrate that sacred head, do not pollute those consecrated lips, do not prostitute to minor objects that noble spirit in which God the Holy Ghost himself deigns to dwell.

Next, I want to say to you that, *as you are consecrated men, you must lay yourselves out to serve the Lord*. I hope we all feel that we really want to serve God; and the way in which we can best serve him is by doing our duty, and the duty of today is today's duty. That sounds very much like a platitude, but it is not one. You have not merely to be preparing for the labour of tomorrow, and speculating about what you will be and do in ten years' time. Do not be always talking about what you mean to do when you are settled, or what you will be when you get to your work. If you do not do your duty now, you will not be likely to do it then; if you neglect the duty of today, you are not likely to attend to it by-and-by. I do not want to hear you say what you expect to do on the first of April, 1889; but if I wished to know what you will probably be ten years' hence, I should form an opinion from what you are in this year of grace, 1879. Well, then, as I am a consecrated man, and I am, therefore, to glorify God, I will endeavour to do it by serving him faithfully today. You cannot do today's work tomorrow; all that you can do tomorrow, you are bound to do when tomorrow comes. If this day passes without God being honoured by you, there is one day of your lives that will be a blank for ever. If a particular obligation that comes upon you today,—whether it is to sit in the class, to take part in your College prayer-meeting, or to talk to some little child at home,—if that duty, whatever it is, is left undone, this day will have a flaw in it which cannot be removed. Perhaps, the most important obligation upon you, at this time, is the acquisition of knowledge that will be of service to you in the future. Then, attend to it with all diligence.

Another point that must never be forgotten is, that *today's opportunities of usefulness will never come again.* This I do know, that the opportunities of usefulness this current Friday, Saturday, and Sunday, never can return to you. There may, possibly, be opportunities very like them on the next Friday, Saturday, and Sunday, but the special and peculiar opportunities of this particular time never will come back to you. You may tell me that, if a certain wave breaks upon the shore, and rolls back towards its native element, it will be met by other waves, and perhaps be carried once more to the same spot; but that is not possible. Other waves will come, but *that* wave will never again return, it is gone for ever. So, as students, you have opportunities, at the present time, which you will not have again; and if you do not utilize each of these years, and months, and weeks, and days, and hours, and even minutes, as they come and go, you will never be able to use them at all.

Then remember, also, that you are to get all the good you can as well as to do all the good you can; and it must never be forgotten that *the advantages of today will not return to you.* I have frequently heard a very sorrowful confession made by those who are now in the ministry. Again and again, a brother has said to me, 'Oh, Mr Spurgeon! I am sorry I did not make better use of my College course; I am persuaded that I should more highly value certain studies now than I did when I had the opportunity of pursuing them.' Ah! they regret what they lost by neglect, but the regret cannot make up the loss to them; and it will be the same with you, brethren, if you do as they did. You cannot have that class over again if you do not make use of it ere the time for it goes by. Other harvests may come to the world after the present one; but the farmer who does not reap his corn this year, will lose this year's harvest, and he will lose it irretrievably; no other season's bounty will be a compensation for his loss of the crop that God gave him for the present time. It ill becomes a consecrated man to lose anything that he can use for his Lord; so take care, brethren, that you wisely utilize all your advantages, occupy your opportunities, and fulfil your duties, while you can.

Here is another very great platitude, yet it is one that must never be forgotten by you;—*Nothing will ever come out of you that is not in you.* I pray that you may not have either empty heads or empty hearts; I have heard of both those evils having existed in remote ages, if not in later times. You have probably known or read of people who have been afflicted with that troublesome complaint, *cacoëthes scribendi,* a propensity for scribbling; and there have been men who have suffered from a still worse disease, which I have sometimes called 'diarrhoea of the lips.' It has seemed as if oceans of verbiage have flowed from their mouths, yet there has been nothing whatever that has been worth hearing. Through want of sense, they talk nonsense; for lack of consolations for the righteous, they have plenty of abuse of everyone who does not agree with them; and not being themselves established in the truth, they teach all sorts of errors. You must yourself be filled with good matter, or else you cannot pour out that which will be of service to others. Set your poor earthen pitcher right under the place where the springhead sends forth its streams; let it stand there till the water flows in, and flows out, and flows over, let it keep on flowing in sweet and clear, and when the time comes for it to be carried away, that the thirsty may drink from it, it will not disappoint their longing desires. You cannot expect to be of service to your Lord, and to your fellow-creatures, without studying, acquiring, and retaining all that you possibly can of the truth of God. It must be allowed to run in, but it must not be permitted to run out again until the time comes for you to pass on to others what you have received. Some brethren have a fine way of giving the truth free course; they let it go in at one ear, and out at the other! In their case, it would be well if we could stop up one of their ears, so that, when the truth once went in, it would remain in.

If you are really to be full, in the right sense of that word, it is not merely reading and study that are required, but your own experience of the things of God will be a grand preparation for preaching. The best preachers are those who can say, with the Lord Jesus himself, 'We speak that we do know, and testify that we have seen.' To retail second-hand wares, may be left to those who buy their sermons at nine shillings a dozen, or get them supplied for nine-and-sixpence a quarter; but you and I, brethren, have no money to spare for buying sermons of that sort; and we would not buy them, however much money we might have. If we are really called of God to preach the gospel, we shall be enabled by the Holy Spirit to make our own sermons, even as the spiders spin their webs out of their own bowels. A Christian minister has to go through many experiences, not only on his own account, but for the sake of others. So, my brother, when you are depressed, glory in it, for you are now learning the way to cheer the depressed; rejoice, for you are now being qualified to become a comforter of others. If it should be your lot to suffer affliction, to endure penury, to be the subject of scorn, slander, and misrepresentation,—whatever the trial is, accept it joyfully, and sing, amid it all,—

'Since all that I meet shall work for my good,
The bitter is sweet, the medicine is food;
Though painful at present 'twill cease before long,
And then, oh how pleasant the conqueror's song!'

Let all your experience assist to complete your fulness. Do not be empty, brethren; especially, be not like those who are full of their own conceit, and therefore are more empty than if they had not even that in them. Do not be what we generally call 'sticks.' There are great bundles of them to be seen, and we do not wish to increase the number.

Another thing that must never be forgotten is, that *every day your character is being formed*. I think that, especially during his time in College, a man is forming himself, or being formed, for life. What you are here, is very much what you will be throughout your whole career. You are now like the clay on the potter's wheel, you are being turned, and shaped, and fashioned for the future. I have no doubt that some of you will, throughout your entire ministry, bear the mark of the tender touch of your tutors; and I should not wonder if you carry away impressions of the graving tools of your learned fellow-students, who so kindly try to improve you by their gentle and kind criticisms. In any case, your character is being formed; so be careful to cultivate everything which will be helpful, and seek to root up anything that would be harmful to yourself or to others. We are, all of us, a little better or a little worse, and perhaps a great deal better or worse, every day we live; we are, constantly, either hindering the work of the Spirit, or else we are feeling, more and more, the force and power of his gracious working. Therefore, yield yourselves absolutely up to him, to be moulded and fashioned according to his blessed will; yea, as Paul pleaded with those in Rome, who were 'called to be saints,' so do I say to you, with all my heart, 'I beseech you therefore, brethren, by the mercies of God, that ye present your bodies a living sacrifice, holy, acceptable unto God, which is your reasonable service. And be not conformed to this world: but be ye transformed by the renewing of your mind, that ye may prove what is that good, and acceptable, and perfect, will of God.'

Note

* Published in *The Sword and the Trowel*, September 1899

The preparation of sermons

A Friday afternoon address to the students of the Pastors' College

DEAR BRETHREN,—I thought I would talk to you a little while, this afternoon, about the preparation of sermons. It is a good practice, sometimes, when you have listened to a discourse, to try to analyze it; to see what are the materials of which it is composed, and to seek to find out how they were put together. It may be a useful exercise to treat your own sermons in a similar fashion after you have delivered them. Your best messages to men will be the outcome of the grace of God working in your own heart; for, to a large extent, as the preacher is, so will his preaching be. Some ministers, as soon as they get into the pulpit, become mere machines, grinding out chaff on which their hearers will never be able to feed. Many men, the moment they close the pulpit doors behind them, seem to shut out all their humanity, whatever becomes of their divinity. Perhaps that is one of the reasons in favour of the abolition of the preaching-boxes of which our forefathers were so fond. Yet it is possible to be quite as stilted and unnatural when speaking from a platform as wide as the one on which I am at this moment standing.

In the preparation of a sermon, there are several steps or stages. There are various modes of making sermons just as there are different ways of preaching them. Probably, each one of you differs from all your fellow-students in your methods of sermon-building, so far as certain details of your work are concerned; yet there are some general principles to which we must all conform if we would be workmen needing not to be ashamed, 'rightly dividing the word of truth.'

The choice of the subject and text of your discourse is a very important matter. You may not have the difficulty which often perplexes me; for, frequently, when I have fixed upon what I hope will be a suitable subject, I find that I have already several printed discourses upon the same text. No doubt, my new sermon would be quite distinct from the previous ones; but I have to think of my readers as well as my hearers, so I start out again in search of an appropriate theme. In choosing a text, I always like to have one that lays hold of my own heart and soul, and will not let me go. Then I make terms of peace with it, and promise to give it a good character, on the following Sunday, if it will only let me do so. We can never preach with power from any passage of Scripture against which we have the slightest antagonism; we must be reconciled to it before we can go and commend it to our people. The Bible is, to me, like a long row of iron safes full of precious treasures; I try my key in a great many of them, and presently one opens at my touch, and there is my sermon. At another time, I am like a gold miner who finds the quartz in which the precious metal is imbedded, and my great concern is to get out all the gold, that it may be minted and used for my Master's service.

Many preachers lose a great deal of time in searching for subjects. I have found it very helpful to have a pocket-book handy, so that I might jot down texts, and thoughts upon them, in the course of my reading or conversation with others; and I would advise you, brethren, to do the same. Our old proverb says, 'Make hay while the sun shines;' and it is wise to do so. The day will come when you will gratefully see, in such a book of reference as I have suggested, the very topic for some emergency that has arisen. I should not care to imitate those ministers who announce the titles of their discourses for weeks or even months ahead. I should indeed feel fettered if I were tied down in such a fashion as that. I always like to be free to follow the leadings of the Spirit both in the preparation and in the delivery of my message. More than once, as some of you know, I have been led to change, even in the pulpit, the theme upon which I was about to speak; and I believe it was God who guided in making the alteration, and who gave me, in that selfsame hour, the words that he would have me speak in his name. When the truth comes to us with power, it will also go from us with power.

It is a good thing to keep a record of our ministry, so as to notice that all truth is presented to our hearers in due proportion. Some ministers always remind me of barrel-organs, from which the one set of tunes is ground out over and over again *ad nauseam*. It must not be so with us, brethren; we must be like the 'householder' of whom our Lord speaks, 'who bringeth forth out of his treasure things new and old.' There are certain doctrines that must have great prominence in the whole of our preaching; the atonement, the office and work of the Holy Spirit, the three R's,—Ruin, Redemption, Regeneration,—are not set before all congregations as frequently as they should be. But while we make them prominent, we must not neglect any revealed truth, for 'all Scripture is given by inspiration of God, and is profitable for doctrine, for reproof, for correction, for instruction in righteousness.'

We need more expository preaching; and for that, we need more diligent and intelligent study of the Scriptures. I hope you will all endeavour to read the Word of God in the original languages in which it was written, and to ascertain its meaning from the Holy Spirit who inspired it. When you do take a text, do not say 'Good-bye' to it as soon as you have announced it; but make it the real theme of your discourse, and seek to bring out of it the special teaching which it is intended to convey. Let your aim and object be, to bring God's mind *out of the text* rather than to put your own mind *into it*. You must have a clear idea of the truth yourself if you are to set it plainly before your hearers. A preacher in a fog will produce a sermon of a similar character. So mind that you get the true teaching of your text, and then expound it to your congregation. The true art of preaching consists in the easy and natural development of the main and central thought of the passage under consideration, and that one idea so persistently impressed upon the minds of the listeners that they carry away with them a distinct perception of the truth that the preacher wished them to receive.

In preparing for the pulpit, I sometimes make many outlines before finally settling upon the one that I follow in preaching.* I note the various lines of thought as they occur to me, not at first trying to reduce them to exact order and symmetry. If the mind will not freely work, I find it helpful to take a walk in the garden, or even to go round my study table a few times if the weather is not favourable for outdoor exercise. Then it helps me, sometimes, if I turn to what others have said upon my subject; although, often, I have to wade through a mass of verbiage with very little result. Of course, I am taking it for granted that much prayer has preceded, accompanied, and followed all the processes of preparation of which I have been speaking. Without that, all would be useless; for we are absolutely dependent upon the Holy Spirit both in the study and in the pulpit.

If you write out your sermon in full,—a very useful practice, for many reasons,—I would earnestly urge you not to commit it to memory, or to read it to your people. I might almost repeat the advice that is given concerning cucumber;—Peel it, cut it into thin slices, put salt, and pepper, and vinegar to it, let it lie awhile, and then fling it on the dunghill! So, rather than read or recite your written discourse, burn it, or cast it to the four winds of heaven. Reading from manuscript, or repeating what you have learned, can never take the place of that glorious gift of speaking straight to your hearers out of the fulness of your heart.

When your material is all ready for arrangement, you must take care that it follows the natural or logical order. Some young beginners, when trying to put their 'skeletons' together, make strange blunders with regard to the anatomy of their discourses; they place the back-bone in the foot, the fingers where the eyes ought to be, and so produce an utter monstrosity. They might learn a lesson from an architect who is drawing the plan of a house. He knows what the dimensions are to be, and what style of architecture he is to follow; but he is careful to see that the doors and windows are in their proper places, and in proportion to the rest of the building. Sermons, too, must have windows in them; that is, openings to let in the light. Illustrations are useful for this purpose.

It greatly helps the hearers, as well as the preacher, if the divisions of the discourse are plainly indicated. All great political orations, and leading articles in the newspapers, must be divided and sub-divided if people are to understand and remember what is spoken or written; and it must be the same with our sermons. We need not imitate the Puritans, with their main divisions, and sub-divisions, and sub-sub-sub-divisions almost *ad infinitum;* but what grand teaching they gave to their congregations! I should have liked to have heard some of those two or three hours' discourses. Sometimes, when I have been preaching in the North of Scotland, I have had pointed out to me a sturdy old Highlander who has walked twenty or thirty miles in order to be present at the service. When a man has done that, he expects to get some good substantial spiritual food before he starts back on his long tramp home. But, nowadays, the minister often has nothing to say that is worth hearing, or the sermon comes in at the tag-end of a musical entertainment which disgusts the most godly people in the congregation, and very likely drives them off to the Plymouth

Brethren. This should not be; and I hope it will not be the case with any of us, brethren. We shall never grow men unless we give them men's meat. Big, brawny fellows, six feet high, need plenty to eat; and they must have something better than lollipops. Mind that you always give it to them; yet take care also to have a good supply of milk for the babes amongst your hearers.

After all, the proof of the preparation is seen in the results that the sermon produces. If it is such a discourse as God can bless, it will be owned in the conversion of sinners and the edification of saints. Perhaps I need not warn you against putting too much into any one sermon, though there have been preachers who have done that. It is to be a loaf of bread rather than a field of wheat. Your hearers' heads are not large enough to take in all the world of thought at one time. Many of them have to work hard all the week, so they ought to be allowed to rest on the Sabbath day; mind that you do not give them undue labour in trying to understand your message. Whatever material you have gathered, make sure that it is all aflame with love to God and love to the people, for fire is certain to spread. The Lord make each one of you to be 'a flaming fire' in his service, for Christ's sake! Amen.

Note

* A full-page *facsimile* of the rough notes made by Mr Spurgeon, on one of these occasions, is given in Vol. IV. of his *Autobiography* (Passmore and Alabaster), which also contains other interesting information concerning his preparation for the pulpit.

The Church at work

An address to the students of the Pastors' College

IN order that his people may be kept in a thoroughly healthy spiritual state, the pastor will be wise to KEEP THE WHOLE CHURCH AT WORK TO ITS UTMOST POSSIBLE STRETCH.

A Christian church is not like a steam boiler, which is apt to blow up if you work it at too high a pressure; but the more pounds to the square inch that you can put upon the church, the more sure may you be that it will not blow up. Make the fire burn as fiercely as possible in the furnace, and then sit on the safety valve, if you like; it will be all right, and you need not have any fear as to the consequences. But if you work the church slowly and let the fire get low, then something will burst.

Every Christian minister should seek to utilize the entire church and congregation under his charge. You will probably find a few members of your church whom God has intended to be preachers,—men who could, would, and should preach, but perhaps they have not had any opportunities of doing so. Try to find village stations for them. In connection with the church in every market-town, there ought to be five or six village stations, like satellites around a central luminary. The church, with which I was connected at Cambridge, had, and still has, I think, about a dozen stations, which are, on the whole, very well worked. The men who can preach are the most dangerous men in the church unless you keep them at work; for, otherwise, they are sure to criticize you, and, possibly, to put thoughts into the minds of others of your hearers, which would never have entered their heads if it had not been for these unoccupied amateur parsons. Send them out, brother, send them out to preach, and keep them always at it. If they can preach, it will do them good to be so employed, they will be the means of blessing to their hearers, and to you also.

In the next place, look out all the young men who should preach, but who are too modest to begin. Modesty is an almost universal fault among young men. Some of you smile so loudly at that remark that I suppose you do not think the fault is universal. Well, I do not know how many exceptions to the rule can be found in the present company; but, gentlemen, if you do not find the fault to be so common as I have suggested, you may find, among your flock, some of these modest young men, and also discover that the better sort of Christian workers are often not so forward as some who have less ability, and less grace. Get some of those young men, who say they cannot preach, to walk out with those who can, when they go to the village services. Perhaps you might give a hint to the elder brother to get his young friend to begin to speak, by some means or other. Then you might arrange for meetings where the young brethren would have opportunities for speaking,—discussion classes, preparation classes, and anything that will help to train their minds, and to develop their oratorical powers. You do not know whom you may have in your church; you may have some Whitefield, or Wesley, or other powerful preacher of the Gospel, among those horny-handed, shock-headed boys, that now follow the plough. If you can gather them together, and give them some mental and spiritual training, and frequent opportunities of speaking, who can tell what good you may be doing? You may be helping to prepare those who will occupy Metropolitan pulpits in days to come.

Look after all the young men, whether they can preach or not; and do try, as far as ever you can, to get them well instructed in the things of God; and it will be well if you can help them also to be better educated in secular matters. There are many things, that you ought to be able to teach them, which would make them better equipped for fighting the battle of life. Perhaps you fear that, if you did so, you would lose them just when they might be most helpful to you in your work. Certainly, in the country, you would do so; but, still, it would be a great gain to the general cause of God if those who come up to London, and our large towns, were not only well educated, but also thoroughly trained for various forms of Christian service. So, brethren, have plenty of societies for the young men. Let them have their Evangelists' Association, and Bible-classes, and prayer-meetings, and let them feel that they have an important part in spreading the knowledge of the Saviour's name. If it is their lot to remain with you, these young people, whom you have thus trained, will be your best helpers in after years; but if you let them rust while they are young, they will not get into habits of spiritual industry when they grow older.

Do not neglect the female part of the community. They have their own work to do; and if you do not give them plenty of it, they will find, or Satan will find for them, some work to do that will be far less useful. The sisters will be well employed in their Dorcas Societies, Mothers' Meetings, and Maternal Societies, and such work as comes under their special departments. You can pay them an occasional visit at their meetings; read a chapter to them, pray with them, and give them a word of encouragement. They will be glad to see you, and will work all the better because they have the countenance of their minister.

Keep the younger women at work, too, for they, also, can do plenty of mischief if they are idle. I think there should be Young Women's Classes, and prayer-meetings, in which they could meet by themselves, and pray together. I strongly recommend prayer-meetings specially for females, but I hardly think they ought to pray in the general public assembly, though there is not praying like theirs. I do not know whether you agree with me, but I do not think that men know at all how to pray as women do. There is a wonderful tenderness, and a peculiar power about a woman's prayer, so that, when I have heard it, it has done me vastly more good than twenty of the usual prayers I have heard from our brethren, and it brings down unnumbered blessings from God.

For the sake of all your young people, mind that you keep the Sabbath-school in a high state of efficiency. The Sabbath-school is a perfect nuisance to some ministers. I have heard of some places, where difficulties have arisen because the superintendent has taken too much upon himself, or the school is quite a separate institution from the church. It is well, as a general rule, for the superintendent to be a deacon or an elder of the church; and the school should always be a branch of the church, and not an organization by itself. The minister should visit the school, on suitable occasions, and give an address, and so should the other officers of the church, who are qualified to do it. I do not think the teaching of the young ought to be given up, so much as it is, to those who are themselves little more than boys and girls. It seems to me that this service is so important that the very best ability we have should be devoted to it. Then you will often find a number of boys and girls, who do not like to be thought so any longer because they are getting to be their own masters and mistresses. Try to arrange classes for them just a little above the Sunday-school range, so as to retain your hold upon them rather longer than is usually the case. One of the drawbacks of the Sunday-school system seems to be that it loses the children just at the time when they are most likely to be able to understand the truth. So, have classes for the hobbledehoys,—those who are neither men nor boys, and for the girls who fancy they are young women. I think our church system ought to be such that we could take a child as soon as he is old enough to leave his home, and, God the Holy Spirit being our Helper, educate him right up till we could lead him to the pulpit to preach the Gospel, or land him safely in Heaven. I think there ought to be means of grace adapted to every stage of growth, both among the godly and the ungodly,—food convenient for the whole household of faith, and for all outsiders as well. He who shall succeed in doing this will have proved himself a master-builder in God's Israel.

You ought certainly to have a good Loan Tract Society, and to push its operations vigorously. You can take the Gospel by that means where you could not take it by any other. Be careful to get good tracts; and I should recommend you always to read them yourselves before you circulate them. If you do, there are some of them which you will never send out. Some tracts you will never be able to read; they are too soporific. They really ought to be placed in the pharmacopœia to be used instead of chloroform and opium and other things of that sort. There are many striking narrative tracts, which tell out the Gospel plainly; and if they have good illustrations to attract attention to the letterpress, so much the better.

Then there must be plenty of open-air preaching; and not only tell others to do it, but do it yourselves. Many of your people will find employment for themselves by going out with you. When I was at Waterbeach, I used to do a great deal of open-air preaching in the villages around. Sometimes, we went down the river in a barge, and several of my own people went with me, so we always had a congregation on board, beside those who were attracted by our singing. A few sturdy, strong men pulled the barge along, and we had grand times. Much good was done by that means, and some of the rough men, who helped to drag the barge, were amongst the converts. If I were in your place in the country, I would turn out into the fields, on summer evenings, as often as possible, and stand against a five-barred gate, or on the village green, or at the cross-roads, and fire away at all I could reach. Preach with all your hearts, and make the squire of the parish hear the Gospel if you can. If he will not come out to hear it, send the message through those big open windows, and make him listen to it.

In the winter, you will do well to hold plenty of cottage meetings, for you will find these exceedingly useful. Poor people often like to lend their rooms for such a purpose. They will sprinkle a little fresh sand down on the cottage floor because the minister or a deacon is coming to hold a prayer-meeting or a service. The most heathenish parts of England are not our great towns and cities, where people can hear the Gospel preached if they are willing to listen to it; but they are the hamlets, where there are but half-a-dozen houses quite away by themselves, where there are not sufficient people even to support a 'Ranters' chapel' or a Baptist mission-room. In such places, you must hold cottage meetings, and your gleanings there may yield to God's granary some of the very finest of the wheat.

In a word, keep the whole church earnestly at work. Keep every member of it doing something, just as God keeps every part of our bodies to its own special service. I do not suppose that there is any one limb, or organ, or faculty, that lies dormant when we are in a healthy state; but all are moving just like clock-work, all working unanimously, harmoniously, steadily, almost involuntarily, under the power and pressure of the inner life, and so life and vitality are sustained in our whole being. So let every member of the Church be zealously at work, every one attending to his or her own special department, and all striving together for the glory of God and the good of the whole community.

The minister's three Gs

An address to the students of the Pastors' College at a meeting held at 'Westwood'

DEAR BRETHREN,—I thought I would say a few words to you, this afternoon, on a topic suggested by this short paragraph, which I recently read in a newspaper:—'Grace, Gumption, and Greek are the Three Gs with which a speaker, at the Congregational Union meetings at Edinburgh, wished ministers might be endowed.' I was very glad to see those three words, all beginning with G, put in such a connection; and, in talking to you about them, I will begin with the last, go back to the first, and finish with the one in the middle.

First, as to GREEK, brethren,—I do not know how much of that fine old classic language you have acquired. I have rather more than a suspicion that some of our brethren have not made much progress in it, and that they never will, while they are with us, notwithstanding all their tutors' efforts. I hope you will all learn as much of the Greek tongue as you possibly can; I am very gratified to find that so many of you are anxious to know more of it. I believe that some of you, as the poet says,—

'Speak Greek
As naturally as pigs do squeak;'—

and, to finish the quotation, it may be said of such brethren, that—

'To them the Latin is no more difficile
Than for a blackbird 'tis to whistle.'

Samuel Butler, Hudibras, Part I

I trust that you will go on learning more of both languages, and especially the Latin, for Latin lies at the very root of our own language, and we cannot thoroughly understand English unless we know at least a good deal of Latin. I do not think that there can be a better language than the English, for it contains the means of expressing every form of thought; and if there is any thought which you cannot express in English, you had better suppress it; I find that all my thoughts, except my 'unthunk' thoughts, can always be uttered in English.

But the Greek is specially useful to us as Christian men, and as Christian ministers, because, by means of it, we can understand the New Testament; and he who can understand the New Testament is in possession of greater mental and spiritual wealth than if he had all the discoveries that have been made by modern thought. I believe that, to know the exact meaning of each Greek word, so as to comprehend the correct and precise sense of it, is of the utmost advantage to us. I shall never pose as a classical critic, but I know enough of Greek to be able to use other people's criticisms; and, by setting one critic against another, I am able to become a critic myself by criticising the critics, and finding out between them what is the exact meaning of the various words under consideration. I never dare pronounce upon the meaning of a text, upon my own authority; nor may you do so. You would need to be very proficient in Greek before you dared to do that. Still, to be able to read and understand the Greek tongue, is a great acquirement, which must not be neglected by any of us. I suppose the word Greek, in the connection in which we have it here, means all kinds of science, languages, and everything else that helps to make up a thoroughly educated man. Well then, brethren, get plenty of Greek into you, for it is certain to be useful to you in your future ministry.

Now, going back to the beginning, and putting the beginning in the middle,—which is very irregular, but we are irregular here today;—we have next to consider that which is all-important to a minister,—GRACE. That is the foundation, not only of our ministry, but of our whole spiritual life. Grace is the most needful thing for the upbuilding and perfecting of a minister of Jesus Christ; yet, alas! how many ministers there are who do not appear to have any of it! There are some men whom I know, and very able men, too, who would have made admirable ministers of the Gospel if they had only been converted. There are some, who are eminent as lecturers; but, if they only knew the grace of God in truth, what a power for good they might be! It is a horrible thing for a minister of the Gospel to be without the grace of God in his heart, yet we must have met with many in that sad condition. When Mr Haldane went to Geneva, to speak to the students there, young Merle D'Aubigné was selected to be the spokesman to reply to him. The good man spoke about the doctrine of the depravity of human nature, and the young man admitted that he saw that truth in the Bible. 'Yes,' said Mr Haldane, 'that is all very well; but do you know it to be true in your own soul?' And that pointed question was used by the Holy Spirit to open the door of the young man's heart; it was the means of his conversion, and so prepared him for the great work for the Lord which he afterwards accomplished. That is the way you must know the grace of God, brethren. I believe that we really know nothing thoroughly until we know it in our inmost soul,—until it is burned into us as with a hot iron,—until it becomes part and parcel of our very being. I believe that the best possible education for a minister is for him to become impregnated and saturated with the Word of God. When that is the case with you, then you can go, and speak of the truth as a thing that you have tasted, and handled, and felt; and going forth to preach thus you will be sure to be blessed. Get plenty of grace, brethren; you know where it is to be had. If you want Greek, you must go to Mr Gracey for it; but if you want grace, you must go to the source of all grace, that is, to God himself. It is to be had, freely, to the full extent of our need; and we can get it by crying to God for it; and by continuing to trust the Holy Spirit to fill us with it.

Then, the third thing needed is GUMPTION. I do not know exactly what that word means, nor from what root it is derived. I do not think it is a Suffolk word, because Suffolk is called 'Silly Suffolk.' Where does gumption come from? It is generally found in certain districts; there are immense crystalized masses of it among the Scotch. They are usually supposed to be the canniest of all people, but that is not exactly what gumption means. Gumption is, well, what *is* gumption?

Well, brethren, when you cannot define a thing, it is a help to remember what its opposite is. So, gumption is not making a bigger fool of yourself than you are by nature. It is needless for some men to make fools of themselves, for they are ready-made fools; but there are others, who seem resolved to make themselves bigger fools than they are by nature. When I think of some brethren, I am really astonished at the amazing profundity of their stupidity. I know a brother, who seems to take a delight in going out of his way to get into a mess; he appears to be always trying to find out how it is possible for him to spoil everything that he touches, and to spoil himself, too. Everything is getting on well in the church; and then, all of a sudden, he upsets the whole coach. One brother, whom I know, fell foul of his deacons for no earthly reason that I could find out. They appeared to have been quite satisfied and even pleased with him; but he got the notion that they were a bad lot, and therefore nothing would do but that they must be stamped out. Of course, the result was that *he* had to stamp off. When I heard the story, I thought the brother was a little wrong in his upper storey. There is another man, who was as happy as possible with his people, and they with him; yet he went, and deliberately, as if with malice aforethought, married a young woman, who was the very person from whom I would have taken care to keep away,—a woman without any education, and utterly unfit to be a minister's wife. She soon picked a quarrel with somebody in the church; and, as a consequence, her husband had to resign his pastorate, and now he cannot get another. He preaches very well, and the people would have him, but his wife is such a dreadful woman that they cannot. Why did he do such a foolish thing as to marry her? There are so many difficulties in the ministry that, for a man to go and select an opportunity for creating some more, does seem sheer madness. I have seen a brother pick out something in himself, that is evil, put it under a glass, knock up a forcing-house, and do his very best, or worst, to increase it to an enormous extent. There is really no need for any of you, brethren, to do anything like that; on the contrary, do try to get all the gumption that you can before you go forth to the work. Of course, in the College, there is such a stock of wisdom and common sense, that one student borrows from others; but when you get out into the world, you will need all your wits, and all the grace you can get from God, if you are to make full proof of your ministry. Therefore, brethren, be men of God to the full; seek a full endowment of grace, gumption, and Greek, and then you will do well anywhere, at home or abroad, wherever the Lord may please to send you.

Preaching the doctrines of grace

An address to the students of the Pastors' College

I AM going to give you, brethren, the reasons why I most earnestly urge you to preach the doctrines of grace, and to keep on preaching them right to the end of your ministry. I am going to tell you my own reasons for preaching the Gospel in what is called the Calvinistic manner in preference to preaching it after the Arminian fashion.

And, first of all, I preach the doctrines of grace *because I believe that the Calvinistic system,* as we call it for shortness, *is the most Scriptural.* I do not say that all Scripture truth could be arranged under the head of Calvinism, and I am quite certain that it could not be arranged under the head of Arminianism; but I do think that a much larger part of the truth, revealed to us in the Word of God, is included in the Calvinistic system than in the Arminian system. That system, which makes God to be the Author and Giver of all grace, and makes man to be the unworthy receiver of it; that system which shows God working in us to will and to do of his own good pleasure, and man working out what God has worked in; that system which finds in God all grace, and mercy, and power, and gives him all the glory, and that makes the creature to be condemned, and ruined, and undone, in God's sight; that system which represents God as giving his grace and favour where he pleases;—that system I believe to be Scriptural. I do not understand how a man can read the Bible without seeing these truths. An Arminian brother said to me, the other day, 'When I read the eighth and ninth chapters of the Epistle to the Romans, I do not feel easy in my mind.' 'I do,' I replied, 'I feel perfectly at ease when I read them, and that glorious Epistle to the Ephesians; in fact, I do not know any portion of Scripture that troubles me in my doctrinal belief.' Sometimes, I meet with a passage of which I have to say, 'I do not exactly understand how this truth squares with other passages of Scripture; however, I believe it, and I must go on reading, and learning, and praying until I do understand it. It is not by giving up any portion of the truth, nor by twisting it, that I shall get set right, but by remembering that there are more things in Heaven and earth than I have dreamed of in my philosophy.' Of course, a man, who is a thoroughly sound Calvinist, will find other difficulties; but, in the other system, he will find ten times as much to puzzle him, and he will not find anything like so much that is clear and plain, I am sure of that. After searching the Scriptures for thirty or forty years, I still stand to it that, in preaching the doctrines of grace, we have Scripture to support what we preach. Even Arminianism has Scripture to support that part of it that is true; but, as a system, we cannot receive it, because it has not Scripture to warrant it.

Another thing that always makes me love this system is that *it is so coherent with itself.* If any man believes in one of the doctrines of grace, it follows, as a matter of course, that he must believe all the rest. If you believe in the total depravity of the human race, you must believe in effectual calling; that is to say, that it is by the power of God's grace that men are called out of spiritual death into spiritual life. If you believe in effectual calling, you must believe the doctrine of election; because, if some are called out of death, and they owe their life entirely to the grace of God, there is an election, seeing that all are not called; and you must ascribe the calling of some, and not of others, to the sovereign grace of God. I do not see how you are to get off it if you receive the other doctrines I have mentioned. Neither do I see how you can deny that there is a speciality and peculiarity in the redemption by Christ Jesus; for, surely, it cannot be that he died just the same for Judas as he did for Peter; it cannot be that he did the same for Cain, who was already in hell, that he did for John, who leaned upon his bosom. It is quite true that the Scripture says that 'He is the propitiation for our sins: and not for ours only, but also for the sins of the whole world;' but it is equally explicit when it states that he laid down his life for the sheep, and that he has redeemed us from among men. 'Having loved his own which were in the world, he loved them unto the end.' The special, discriminating, distinguishing characteristics of the grace of God are clearly taught in his Word; and if you once believe any part of this system, you must believe the rest, for one doctrine follows inevitably upon another by stern logic, and by blessed relationship. There is such a thing as the analogy of faith, and in Calvinism we have a practical illustration of it.

Moreover, I am able now to say what a younger man cannot say,—that I have received great confirmation of my faith in the Calvinistic form of truth *from experience*. I find that, the longer I live, the things that I meet with in my own heart, or in my daily circumstances, all tend to confirm me in the doctrines which I have received. If I did not believe in the alienation of the human heart, I should have been driven to believe in; it, for I know that my own heart was 'deceitful above all things, and desperately wicked;' and I find that the flesh still 'lusteth against the Spirit,' and 'is not subject to the law of God, neither indeed can be.' Looking back over my past experience, I feel certain that, before the Lord called me by his grace, I was so estranged from him that I should never have come to him of myself. I cannot help believing the truth of our Saviour's words, 'No man can come to me, except the Father which hath sent me draw him.' That is a truth which I have proved by experience; and now I also perceive, by experience, that, if there be any good thing in me, it must be by Divine grace that it is within me; for I do not find that, even now, as a quickened man, I am what I ought to be; and if I, being now alive, do not the things that God desires, how much less could I have done them when I was dead in trespasses and sins; and if, now that I am reconciled to God by the death of his Son, I still grieve him, how could I please him when I was his enemy, and my heart was estranged from him? Experience also leads me to believe that God casts not away his people; for, otherwise, he would certainly have cast me away. If God wanted to find any reasons for casting away his people, he would have found plenty of reasons for casting me away. If ever the sheep of God could be left to themselves, as Hart sings,—

'My fickle, feeble soul, alas!
Would fall a thousand times a day.'

That is just what I think about myself. I know that we are to be watchful and prayerful; but if our salvation depended upon our own watchfulness and prayerfulness, we should be in a sorry case indeed. Who can keep himself watchful and prayerful? If we are watchful and prayerful, that is the evidence of the working of God's grace within us, for these are the gifts of God's Spirit, as every man must know. When a man has neither God, nor Christ, nor hope of Heaven, he may well be an Arminian; he cannot claim anything as his own, for even if he has anything good now, he is not sure whether God will not take it from him by-and-by; but when a man comes to have faith in an unchanging God, who does not predestinate a man to be saved, and then permit him to be lost after all; or who does not love him today, and hate him tomorrow, then he gets to deal with God after a different fashion from that of the man who holds Arminian doctrines.

I used, sometimes, to go to see a man, whose name I will not mention; he was a well-known Wesleyan minister, and he used often to come to hear me preach. One day, he said to me, 'I am an Arminian, but I believe in election, and I believe in the final perseverance of the saints, and I am quite certain that, at my age, I could not live in peace if it were not for those grand truths.' I could not quite see how he could be an Arminian; and, only a little while ago, a very eminent Wesleyan minister said to me, 'I do not think that you and I differ on a single point of doctrine.' I replied, 'Why, how is that? I am a Calvinist, and you are an Arminian.' 'No,' he answered, 'I am not, and there are very few of us who are.' I know, for a fact, that if you want to hear a good Calvinistic sermon, nowadays, you must often go to a Wesleyan chapel to hear it. Not to all Wesleyan chapels, for I remember another minister of that Connexion, who was a thorough Arminian, and for whom I once preached. Some time afterwards, he met me, and he said to me, 'I do not wish to say anything unkind, but I do not think I will ever ask you to preach for me again, for there are lots of my people, who sucked in the doctrine you preached, and I cannot get it out of them; and what is more, if I had received it myself, I would never give it up, for it is a deal more comforting than ours is.' Experience does teach us this; and I do not see why young men should not learn the same lesson that others of God's children have been taught. It is well for preachers always to begin as they mean to go on, and I hope all of you will be found preaching such things from the beginning as you will wish to preach right to the last.

Another thing that makes me preach the doctrines of grace is *my observation*. Take that expression on the largest possible scale, for I do not mean simply what I have seen with my own eyes; but, from wider observation, from reading history, I notice that those periods, in which the Church of God has most flourished, have been the periods when Calvinism has been to the front; and so far from it being true that the preaching of the doctrines of grace does not tend towards holiness, it only needs the historian, whose pen will write the truth, to inform us that there never was such holiness in this world as when Calvinistic doctrine was predominant. Have we not proved it to be so in England? Think of the state of morals during the Puritan period; even when there was the Cavalier faction to do all the mischief possible, those were the days when devotion, prayerfulness, and godliness were seen beyond anything that you and I have seen, and I was going to say beyond anything that we are likely to see again in this land. But the moment that Laud came in, with his Arminianism, down went godliness in England directly; and, very soon, not only godliness, for, in the degeneracy that followed the Puritan period, there was little enough even of morality, and still less of true religion. Whatever power there is in Arminianism,—and there is some,—it cannot hold a nation right, as Calvinism does. You just watch where that wave rolls up, and you will see that the wave of godliness also rolls up; and when that wave goes down, godliness goes down, too.

I have observed also that *there is a great holdfast* in these truths that are called Calvinistic. I remember a remark of old Dr Thomas Jackson, who was once President of Richmond College, and also President of the Wesleyan Conference. He said to me, at the house of my friend, Dr Campbell, 'I have been very grateful to God that you are a Calvinist.' I replied, 'My dear friend, I am astonished to hear you say that, knowing that you are not a Calvinist yourself.' He answered, 'There are no Arminians in the world, except the Wesleyan Methodists, who hold Evangelical truth.' That is quite true, for all other Arminians, sooner or later, let it go; but, somehow, within the bounds of Wesleyan Methodism, it is always preached thoroughly; but if you take other Arminian preachers, you will find that, as a rule, they leave out, not only the doctrines of grace, but the grace of the doctrines; and, by-and-by, they get preaching 'modern thought', and then they glide away, further and further, into Unitarianism, and Rationalism; and that is about as straight a road down to the devil as I know; and, alas! many there be that take it. But you never heard of anybody becoming an infidel because he had received and taught too much of the Calvinistic form of truth. That is not an inclined plane down towards Deism, or Atheism. A man may be so extreme in his Calvinism that he becomes a fatalist, and so falls into errors of another sort; but, certainly, never will he give up Evangelical truth because he preaches the doctrines of grace. He will never fail to preach that the Son of man is come to seek and to save that which was lost, and he will bear a clear testimony to the Deity of Christ, and to the personality of the Holy Spirit. Calvinism is a great sheet anchor; and the young man, who has got that down in the deeps, may feel perfectly safe whatever storm may arise. You cannot depart from the faith while you have this holdfast; but if you go off to a mingle-mangle, which is neither Law nor Gospel, you will gradually turn aside until you will not know where you are.

One great reason why I delight to preach the doctrines of grace is *that they seem to me to be the very essence of all theology*. Other doctrines appear to me to be like laying the plates, and knives, and forks; but this is meat, of which our soul may eat till it is satisfied. In these doctrines of God's eternal, unchangeable love, Christ's matchless atonement, and the effectual working of the Holy Spirit of God, you have something which you need never be ashamed to speak. These doctrines reveal the truth as to man's condition as utterly lost, and also reveal to him his need of the almighty power of God's grace to save him. These truths give a rest of heart which can be obtained nowhere else. All other systems seem to me as if they trifled with man. What we need for salvation is God; and this system has God in the very forefront of it,—it makes much of God. The other system makes little of God, but exalts the creature, and cries him up as though he were everything. It needs infinite wisdom to see the right position of both God and man. My wisdom is not infinite; but if I am able to see only one thing, I had rather see the height, and depth, and length, and breadth of God's grace, than have that view in which man is the most prominent object. Since we cannot take in the infinite, if I had to make a choice, I would rather take in that which concerns God, and his glory, and the wonders of his amazing love to the undeserving and the lost.

Another reason why I believe in preaching Calvinism is *because of the consoling character of it*. If you ever have the gout, brethren, you will find that you need free grace then, that I am sure of; and if your head aches very often, and your mind is subject to dark depression, or if, as probably will be the case, you have to struggle with poverty in your future pastorates, and have times of trouble, and seasons of dismay, I know that then you will want something very solid and substantial to rest on. In your disappointments through man, you will often have to fall back upon the eternal purposes of God, and to find comfort in his unerring sovereignty. I can get comfort out of the atonement that does atone for somebody, but I could get none out of an atonement that atones for everybody, and yet really atones for nobody. I want a Gospel that stands fast, and abides for ever; not one that changes with my changing circumstances and feelings.

Perhaps someone says, 'But that does not prove a thing to be true; because it is comforting to those who believe it.' No, I know that it does not; but when we believe it to be true, we do get rich consolation out of it. I feel that the God of all comfort is pleased to make that which is true to be our comfort; and when I get comfort from that which appears to me, from a diligent study of the Word, to be God's truth, and as I know that he joins truth and comfort together, the comfort confirms the truth to me, whatever others may feel or think. I always say to the Arminian, 'My dear friend, I do not covet your doctrine. It is such a dry and bare bone that I would not take it away from you; there is no marrow in it, so I am sure I do not want it.' There is no comfort in it, so I let him have it all to himself. But I love the other system because, in it, there are wines on the lees, well refined, and fat things full of marrow; and if truth was meant to comfort us in life, and sustain us in death, that is just exactly what this doctrine does.

Just one other point, and then I have done. I like this doctrine, and hold fast to it, *because I can pray with it, and praise with it, and preach with it.* It is wonderful how difficult it is for Arminians to pray consistently with their system. They have to pray backwards if they are at all consistent with what they believe. Fancy a man, who lays it down, first of all, that God is bound to deal with all alike; he is no respecter of persons, he does not give blessings to any that he does not give to all; he does not influence the will of man in the least; or, if he does exert any influence upon any, he exerts the same influence upon all men, and therefore the doctrine of sovereign grace is false. Now listen, he is going to pray. He begins by asking God to bless the village in which he dwells. That is the first infringement of his principles. What right has he to ask God to bless that village any more than all the other villages in the land? Next, he asks God to bless the children of those that are gathered there. In his own heart, if we could read it, we should find that he is praying for his own children to be blessed. That is another infringement of his principles. If I held such erroneous notions as he does, I should never pray to God to do anything wrong; and if Arminianism is true, it must be wrong for the Lord to save one person, and not save all the rest; in fact, it is altogether wrong to pray for any man at all unless we pray for the devils as well, because they are all creatures of God, and man ought not to stand before the fallen angels. Why did God pass by angels, and set his love upon man, but that he would show his sovereignty, and prove that he does as he pleases? If you state as your doctrine that he is bound to do the same for one man as for another, and the same for all men as for any one man, then it becomes altogether invidious and wicked to pray for anybody, and especially for your own children. Do you wish to mislead God,—to lead him to do that which you believe to be wrong? I could not pray on that theory at all.

Then, how could you ask the Lord to convert multitudes by the preaching of the Gospel? That is a prayer that is prayed everywhere, and a very proper one, too, in my judgment; but it is not a proper prayer if the will of man is perfectly free, and cannot be influenced by anything that God can do. He cannot do it, in the first place, because the will of man is so strong that it can resist his power; and, as a certain eminent Arminian divine said, not long ago, 'I attribute a kind of omnipotence to the will of man;' that is to say, the will of man is so omnipotent that Omnipotence cannot master it; God has made it so strong that he has put it beyond his own power to influence it. If it be so, that it ought to be left entirely to the sinner's own choice, why do I pray that God will convert a single sinner? Is not that prayer a plea for effectual calling? It seems to me to be just the crystallization of that truth. I think, therefore, that you will have to be Calvinists before you can pray aright.

Further, when we praise God, do you not think that a great deal of the best praise that ever ascends to him is when we praise and bless him that we were ever converted by his grace? The Arminian says that it was the self-determining power of your own will that made you resolve to do what you liked, so do you not think it is wrong to praise God for that? Why should you thank him for grace, and Christ, when, according to this theory, it is your own doing entirely? On that theory of the self-determining power of the will, to yourself be the honour and the glory! But when I praise God for a renewed heart, I must still be blessing him for what he has done for me;

and I feel that I must attribute his love to himself, and not to myself, and must praise and bless him for his grace; and I call upon others to join me in praising him.

'In songs of sublime adoration and praise,
    Ye pilgrims to Zion who press,
Break forth, and extol the great Ancient of days,
    His rich and distinguishing grace.'

If you could take this doctrine away from us, you would have taken away one of the greatest blessings that God has given to his people. In fact, if you put me on the other theory, I do not know whether I shall have cause to praise God from day to day. I cannot praise him for making me his child, because I do not know whether I shall be his child tomorrow; I cannot praise him for loving me, because he may not love me tomorrow; I cannot praise him for full salvation, and the hope of Heaven; because, though I know whom I have believed, I do not know whether he is able to keep that which I have committed unto him. I do know that hitherto he has blessed me, but I do not know that he that has begun a good work in me will perfect it until the day of Jesus Christ. I am of that persuasion, namely, that he will not complete it unless I let him; my will must be concurrent with his, and must have an equal share in the work. I shall have no songs for God upon that theory. I feel like Jonathan Edwards, who said, when he had finished his great treatise upon the human will, if any man can disprove this, and disprove the whole system of grace, after he has done so, let him say within himself that he has deprived the world of that which would have afforded the greatest cause for rejoicing; if he says it is a dream, let him go and mourn for ever that it was a dream, since it would have been most glorious to God and most blessed to mankind had these things been true. Blessed be God, they *are* true, and therefore will we praise him for them world without end!

We mean to preach them, too, as well as to pray, and praise God for them. The reason why these doctrines have fallen into some disrepute is because certain brethren preach them in such a bigoted style that men recoil from them. Now, half a truth is a lie. If you take a truth, and cut it in halves, it will be two lies; and if you take a truth, and tack a piece of something else on to the end of it, it will be a lie. Take care, therefore, how you preach these doctrines. There are some, who say that we must not preach to the sinner dead in sin. Now, I hold most firmly that this is the very thing that we are to do. This I know, that God sent me not to preach life to those who are alive, and sight to those who already have good eyes, but to preach life to those who are dead, and to say to them, 'Ye dry bones, live;' and to cry to him who believes not, 'Believe on the Lord Jesus Christ, and thou shalt be saved.' If they say to us, 'It is absurd to do that,' we answer,—Yes, we know that it is absurd if God is not with us; but, as he has bidden us so to preach, we will obey his command, and expect to see sinners repenting and believing through the effectual working of the Holy Spirit upon the truth that is proclaimed to them.

Young preachers encouraged

An address at an annual meeting of the Metropolitan Tabernacle Country Mission

I HAVE made a little discovery while I have been sitting here, this evening. I could not quite make out who some of the friends were who gathered with us around the tea tables. I usually reckon that I know all my own people,—not by name, but by sight; and I can generally recollect the faces of any persons with whom I have ever spoken; so I was wondering who many of you are, and whence you have come to this anniversary meeting. But now I find that there is a little kind brotherly and sisterly contingent, from several of the places where our Country Mission brethren go to preach, come up to keep 'the Feast of Tabernacles' with us; and I am heartily glad to see you, dear friends, and I feel very thankful to you for being willing to act as pioneers in places where there are very few to labour for the Lord. In years to come, somebody will gather the fruit of your earnest service for the Master, even if you are not privileged to gather it yourselves.

You remember that Moses' prayer was, 'Let thy work appear unto thy servants, and thy glory unto their children.' When I was planting some walnut trees in my garden, the gardener said to me, 'You will never live to eat any of the fruit from them, for they will not bear anything for twenty years.' 'Well,' I replied, 'that does not matter to me in the least; yet I believe that I shall live for twenty years longer. I am not so old as I look, and I may live longer than you imagine; but even if I should not, this is my freehold ground, and my boys will eat the walnuts if I do not.' It is only ten years since the trees were planted, but I had a lot of the fruit from them last year. That is just what often happens in connection with the work we do for Christ; but even if we are not spared to see the fulness of the prosperity of our service, our children will see it; and what is far better, our God will see it. It is, however, very sweet to us when we do see any of the result of our labour for the Lord, and so prove that it is not in vain. It is also a great joy to others. If your brother is converted, or your sister is saved, or your child is brought to Jesus, at any of your services, what a rich reward it is for your kindness in having entertained the preacher, and having taken your share in the work. It may be that, long after all of us have passed away, the results of our service will be found all over the world, and that they will continue to multiply, and increase, and bring forth fruit, even to a hundred-fold. The Lord grant that it may be so!

As this is a Baptist Country Mission, I hope that you are not only Christians, but that you are out-and-out Christians, and Baptists. When a man is converted, if he does not become a Baptist, there is something lacking, of which many professing Christians do not seem to be aware. I mean that, if the ordinance of believers' baptism is according to our Lord's will,—and his Word teaches us that it is,—then, if we do not obey his will, we seem to lack one characteristic of his true disciples. Though baptism is a very small matter compared with believing in the Lord Jesus Christ, yet that is an additional reason why it ought to be observed by all the Lord's professed followers. A young lad, whom I knew, who had rather a weak intellect, but a strong love to Christ, was thought to be dying. He was very anxious to be baptized, but his sister said to him, 'Why, Isaac, baptism will not save you.' He at once replied, 'I know that; I would not wish to be baptized if I was not already saved. We have to be saved first, and baptized afterwards.' 'Well, then, Isaac,' said his sister, 'if you are saved, you will go to Heaven.' 'Yes,' he answered, 'I know that I shall. I was not thinking that baptism was going to make me fit to go to Heaven; we have no right to be baptized till we know that we are saved by grace, through faith in our Lord Jesus Christ, and that, therefore, we shall go to Heaven when we die.' 'Then, Isaac, why do you want to be baptized?' 'Because, you see, when I go to Heaven, and see the Lord Jesus Christ there, he will say to me, "Isaac, you might have done that little thing for me," and when he talks like that to me, I do not know what I shall say to him.' If it were a greater thing than it is, and our salvation depended upon it, and we should then do it, that would be sheer selfishness; but our Lord Jesus simply asks us, in this ordinance, to follow his example, and so to say to the world, 'We are dead.' Dead people ought to be buried; so we come to the baptismal pool to be buried with Christ in baptism, and thereby to say to the world, 'You will not be able to get us into your power again, for we are dead and buried with Christ, we are crucified to the world, and shall never return to it.' Baptism is, to a believer, very much the same sort of thing as happened when General Cortez landed in South America, and marched his men up into the country, where they were greatly outnumbered by the inhabitants of the country, and then sent back his principal lieutenant with orders to burn all his ships. Then he told the soldiers that they must either conquer or die, for they could not go back. In a similar fashion, in our baptism we sink our ships, and say to friends and foes alike, 'We are never going back any more.' When a man is baptized, he bears in his body one of the marks of the Lord Jesus. It is the water-mark, which can never be taken out of him. It is not a brand that can be cut out; baptized persons may disgrace their profession, but they can never be unbaptized. From head to foot, they bear the mark of Christ upon them. I would have all of you feel an intense interest in the ordinance which sets forth, so significantly, the death and burial of the believer with his Lord. If any of you say that you cannot see it, you had better buy a pair of spectacles; and if you want a little book that will tell you all about believers' baptism, I should recommend you to read the New Testament, and to ask the Holy Spirit to teach you its meaning. That is the only work on the subject that you need to study, though there are many other books that help to throw light upon the ordinance.

Now I have to say a little about these young brethren going out to preach in the country districts all round this great city. I am a great believer in our young men endeavouring to become preachers of the Gospel. I do not think that all of you would be right to attempt to preach; a large number of you would be a great deal better employed in keeping shop, or going out to day labour, rather than becoming such 'muffs' and 'sticks' of preachers as can be found without much difficulty by anybody who cares to look for them. All Christians are not called to that special and honourable work, but they should all try to be the best servants of the Lord Jesus Christ that they can be; and there are numbers of Christian young men who will never know what they can do for him until they try. In all our churches, there are numbers of godly old men, who never are heard praying in public simply because they did not begin to do so while they were young; and there are many, who will never speak well for Christ because they did not begin to do so early enough in their Christian career.

I urge all young men to try to speak for Christ, *because it is by speaking that we learn to speak*. How does a baby learn to talk? Why, by beginning to talk. It does not talk very fine language at first,—though I have heard mothers say that it is remarkably sweet to their ears;—but it gradually learns to speak more and more distinctly; and, in similar style, though in a somewhat higher sense, young men will learn to speak by speaking. You will never teach a boy or a man to swim until you take him to the water; you may talk to him about what he should do, and about what he should not do; but he will never learn to swim in that way. Throw him into the water; and then, unless he means to be drowned, he will have to swim ashore. It is very much the same with regard to public speaking. No man can possibly become eloquent by simply reading all about the laws of oratory; he must begin to speak as he has the opportunity. That is the only way to teach him to speak.

I like Christian young men to begin speaking for their Lord *because, even when they speak very imperfectly, God often blesses their message.* The polish that can be given to an address may add to its power in delivery; but I have known both addresses and sermons to be as polished as steel, and just as cold, and with no edge to them whatever. No one would be likely to be either cut to the heart or pricked in the heart by such blunt weapons. Sometimes, I think that the wild-bird notes of young beginners have a peculiar charm about them; there is something delightful in the very tremulousness of the accents, the feeble way in which you can see that the speaker puts his thoughts, yet the strong way in which you feel that he would put them if he could. You can read much 'between the lines' of his stammering, blundering address. Let the young men speak by all manner of means; they often speak best when they seem to speak worst. David said, 'Out of the mouth of babes and sucklings hast thou ordained strength;' and we may say that, out of the mouth of the most veritable suckling orator who ever attempted to speak in his Lord's name, God has oftentimes ordained strength.

I like these young men to speak *because it will do them good.* They will find out their blunders in the process of making them. Frequently, you cannot tell where your faults lie until you have developed them, just as you cannot tell what strength you have until you have tested it. There are many people, who think it is a wonderfully easy thing to preach until they try to do it themselves; after that, their opinions are considerably modified. Possibly, you have heard of the youth, who had long wanted to preach, and who thought it was, as he said, 'as easy as kissing your hand;' but when, at last, an opportunity was presented for the display of his talents in the pulpit, he delivered the following practical if not very eloquent speech, 'Now then, if any of you have conceit enough to think that you can preach, just come up here, and you will soon have it all taken out of you.' I am not certain that it is recorded whether anyone accepted the invitation or not, but I believe that other instances of the same sort of thing have been observed in other pulpits since that memorable occasion. I am firmly convinced that attempting to preach does help a young man to find out how great his weakness is; and the more he suffers in that way, the better will it be for him, for other influences, not so beneficial, will be brought to bear upon him. The young lady, whom I call 'Jemima' when I am talking to the students of the College, is delighted with him. She feels that, now, a young man has risen, who will dazzle the people; of course, she judges by the way in which she is herself dazzled by his wonderful eloquence. She tells him what glorious things will happen to the world now that he has begun to preach, and perhaps he is silly enough to believe what she says; but, as he continues speaking and preaching, he will find that there are other people beside 'Jemima' who will come to hear him, and they will not all be so struck with him as she is. Some will say that he is about the biggest fool they ever heard talk. Others will observe, possibly even in his hearing, that, if he would hold his tongue, he would be a wiser man than he is now. Some will tell him to his face, 'You had better learn a little more yourself before you try to teach others.' Some Hyper brother will say that his sermon was a mingle-mangle, and neither law nor Gospel, and will express his belief that the young man came from Spurgeon's, which is the worst thing that can be said of anybody who attempts to preach in the hearing of certain people. All that will do the young man good, it will be greatly blessed to him if he is made of the right sort of stuff. I believe that a preacher is made useful in very much the same way as a beef steak is made tender,—that is, by being well hammered. If there is really anything of value in a young man, he will have no need to ask anybody to hammer him; there will be plenty of people willing to do that without being asked. I can speak from experience upon this question, for I had, in my earlier days, my full share of this hammering. I have several volumes of pamphlets, at home, in which I find myself described in various ways, the titles ranging from 'the greatest preacher of the age' to 'a man, who, if he were conscious of the meaning of what he was saying, and not too ignorant to understand his own utterances, would be a blasphemer.' I do not suppose that any of those criticisms have ever raised or lowered my spirits to the tenth part of a degree; still, they are very excellent medicine to anyone who needs them. They are admirably adapted for cutting a young gentleman's comb, and that is one of the most useful operations that can be performed; for some of them are very, very big when they begin to preach.

Another good thing about this preaching is that *it gives the young men confidence;* it knocks it out of them, in one way, and puts it into them in another way; they have less confidence in themselves, and more confidence in God. Our young men in the College are not with us very long before they learn one most important truth, viz., that they are great fools; and, afterwards, they learn a second truth, *i.e.,* that they are not the only ones. The first truth knocks one over, but the second sets him up again. When I first came to preach in London, I imagined that all the people who came to the chapel would be wise, intelligent, and judicious;—I don't suppose that I thought they would all have their Greek Testaments with them, and read their Hebrew Bibles to see whether I gave the right meaning of the original; but when I went into the pulpit at New Park Street, the thought that crossed my mind was that I could eat the lot! You know, probably, what I mean by that expression; and I have felt a good deal like that ever since; and, in another sense, I have gone on from that day to this eating and being eaten, enjoying the very heart and soul of Christian love.

It does our young men good to get back this kind of confidence after they have learned not to put confidence in themselves. I know what a young brother says when he commences to speak. 'I will make my sentences short, so that I shall not lose myself;' but, after a little while, the nominative and the verb and the objective case get hopelessly confused, and the sentence, which was to have been so short and clear, becomes hopelessly muddled. I have seen brethren going along, like Blondin on the tight-rope, with balancing pole in hand, and looking very grand indeed; but they have not got to the end of the appointed course. It is always interesting to watch a budding orator when he is in such trepidation that he is not quite sure where his next step will be; and, presently, down he comes on all fours! He makes up his mind that he will try again, and it is very amusing to an onlooker to watch his performance, though it may not be at all amusing to him. There are some, who go through the ordeal all right, and never slip at all. I have even heard of some, who could keep on speaking without really saying anything for half an hour. They are like the Yorkshire deacon, whose mill was going, one bright Sunday morning, while the good man was at chapel. Someone pointed it out to one of his friends, but the man replied, 'The sails are going round, it is true;

but our deacon is not the man to work on Sunday, and if you go into the mill, you will see that the wheel is going Click-a-de-clack, Click-a-de-clack, but that it is not grinding anything.' So there are some speakers, whose tongues go Click-a-de-clack, Click-a-de-clack, but they are not grinding anything. That is one of the evils that will grow, in some cases, out of constant practice in speaking; a man is able to keep on talking when he has little or nothing to say. Beware, brethren, lest that should be the case with any of you.

Some of our young friends develop extraordinary talent through beginning to preach, as many of them do, in the villages and small country towns around London. I wish I could get some more of them into the College; I would give almost anything for Mr Fullerton* if I could have him, and there must be others, too, who will grow into able ministers of the Word. I am afraid that the leaders of this Mission and the Evangelists' Association must almost dread to hear of a young man getting on well in preaching, as they know that I shall be sure to want him for the College. They feel just as a mother does when her daughter begins to look so attractive, and she says to her husband, 'John, I do not think it will be very long before somebody will be after our Jemima;' yet no mother would wish to see her daughter stunted and dwarfed. So, my good brethren are right glad to see their sons reaching that excellence of beauty of speech which we have seen in those of them, who have spoken to us to-night. Long may it continue so!

Note

* 'Sword and Trowel' readers are, of course, well aware that Mr Fullerton did enter the Pastors' College, and that he is one of the most notable ministers who ever went forth from the Institution.

Christ's superlative loveliness

A communion meditation

'What is thy Beloved more than another beloved, O thou fairest among women? what is thy Beloved more than another beloved, that thou dost so charge us? My Beloved is white and ruddy, the chiefest among ten thousand. His head is as the most fine gold, his locks are bushy, and black as a raven. His eyes are as the eyes of doves by the rivers of waters, washed with milk, and fitly set. His cheeks are as a bed of spices, as sweet flowers: his lips like lilies, dropping sweet smelling myrrh. His hands are as gold rings set with the beryl: his body is as bright ivory overlaid with sapphires. His legs are as pillars of marble, set upon sockets of fine gold: his countenance is as Lebanon, excellent as the cedars. His mouth is most sweet: yea, he is altogether lovely.'—Solomon's Song 5:9–16.

WE have no time for a preface, so we will go at once to the passage which is to be the subject of this evening's meditation.

I. The text is a question repeated, and we will commence with a few remarks concerning the question.

Our first remark is this,—*it was a question asked of the spouse when she was in sadness*. She had lost the presence of her Lord, and she was seeking him in the dark. She had lost her veil, she had been beaten and wounded by the watchmen of the city, and it was at that time that she said, 'I charge you, O daughters of Jerusalem, if ye find my Beloved, that ye tell him, that I am sick of love;' and then it was that the question was asked of her, 'What is thy Beloved more than another beloved?' Learn hence, that a Christian may be useful even in his lowest spiritual condition, and that sadness and depression of spirit ought not to prevent our looking out for opportunities of magnifying our Lord. Even if he should not smile on me, yet will I trust him; and if I cannot preach with delight, I will preach all the same. If I may not myself enjoy the feast, I will spread the table for others. If Christ is not pleased to give me the dainties of communion with himself, yet will I wait at the posts of his door, and be found willing to serve him there or anywhere. As the spouse, though in distress, was made a blessing to the daughters of Jerusalem, so you, my brethren and sisters, though not always enjoying the full assurance of faith, may yet be made a blessing to those among whom you dwell.

The question in the text was also put *because those who asked it perceived a singular beauty in the spouse*. They addressed her as 'fairest among women.' If she had been an ordinary person, the object of her love would not have interested them; but when they looked upon her, and saw her to be so supremely beautiful, they then took an interest in that which interested her. Learn from this, my brethren and sisters in Christ, that if we would attract the world's attention to our holy faith, we must be renowned for holiness ourselves. If you who profess to be Christians are no better than other people, no one will want to know what your religion is. If you can be as false and as frivolous, as wicked and as worldly, as others are, then men will care nothing at all for the faith you hold, but they will suppose it to be of that worthless and useless kind which is so abundant throughout the world. A holy Christian makes an enquiring family, and by-and-by, an enquiring neighbourhood. When men see you to be more strict in your integrity than they are, they will want to know of whom you learned this virtue. If they see you more patient in suffering, more zealous in service, more generous to the poor, more careful of the sick, they will ask, 'With whom do these people consort? Who is their Lord and Master? for we would fain know him, too, and learn of him as they have done.' Oh, that each of us had this beauty! I am afraid that, oftentimes, we are so unlike what we should be, that men may be well acquainted with us, and yet never be concerned to know the motives which actuate us.

Further, the question in the text was *suggested by the evident earnestness of the person to whom it was addressed*. She came to the daughters of Jerusalem with anxious face and tearful eye, and spoke of her Beloved, and then they enquired, 'Who is he, and what is there about him that is so charming as thus to ravish thy heart?' Yes, and we also must be in earnest concerning our religion if we are ever to make the world care to know anything about it. You who play fast and loose with Christ, you who wear his holy Name, but have never felt the power of it in your souls, who were never transported with his charms, who never did give yourselves up wholly to him,—you, I say, will never lead others to him. Give me the man whose heart is full of Christ, whose eye flashes with celestial joy at the very thought of Jesus, give me the man all on fire with love to Christ, a man of zeal, and earnestness, and holy passion, and such a man will burn his way through the dull, stolid masses of this city's population, and compel men to ask, 'Why is this stir? What is it all about? Why is the man so in earnest? What is his Beloved better than any other beloved that he should so charge us?' Oh, for the sacred fire of this holy enthusiasm! It is this that we want; may the Spirit of God mightily work it in us!

Please notice also that, as the beauty and earnestness of the spouse led to enquiries being made, *she was ready at once to give an answer*. 'What is thy Beloved more than another beloved?' was the question, and there was no time lost between the query and the reply of the spouse: 'My Beloved is white and ruddy, the chiefest among ten thousand;' and then she went on to describe all the parts of his person with an infinite delight. She had the subject, as we say, 'at her fingers' ends,' or, what is much better, she had it in her heart's core. So, dear Christian friends, if you have in like manner excited enquiry concerning your holy religion, 'be ready always to give an answer to every man that asketh you a reason of the hope that is in you with meekness and fear.' There is nothing to be ashamed of in being a follower of Christ, but there is much to be ashamed of if we are ashamed of him. You will find some professors who know so little, who have so small an intelligent knowledge concerning the Saviour, that if anyone should enquire of them concerning Christ, he would get but a sorry answer. Let it not be so with you, beloved. Study his Word, for there you have a description of his many charms. Live near to him, for by close communion with him you will come to know him better, and then, though your accents should be stammering, and your cheeks should blush under the soft impeachment of being in love with Jesus, yet as you tell out the story of his matchless beauty, and magnify his peerless person, others shall be won to love him, too.

It seems that *the answer given to the question was amply blessed*. If you turn to the next chapter of the Song, you will find the daughters of Jerusalem saying to the spouse, 'Whither is thy Beloved gone, O thou fairest among women? whither is thy Beloved turned aside? that we may seek him with thee.' Oh, happy result! The question was asked, and in answering it the spouse had an opportunity of praising her Beloved so that the enquirers said to her, 'Whither is thy Beloved turned aside? that we may seek him with thee.' So, dear friends, while I am trying to talk to you about Christ, my heart longs, and pants, and thirsts that some of you may say, 'We will seek him with thee.' If that shall be the result of our meditation, my soul will be perfectly satisfied with so blessed a reward.

These, then, are my remarks respecting the origin of the question.

II. I will now speak to you CONCERNING THE QUESTION ITSELF.

If you look at it carefully, you will see in it three things. First, you will at once see that, *in every true lover of the Saviour, his love is so conspicuous that the most shallow observer will soon discover it.* These daughters of Jerusalem who asked the question were merely people whom the spouse met in the street, yet they asked her, 'What is thy Beloved more than another beloved?' We are not true Christians unless Christ is conspicuously the Beloved of our souls. I am persuaded that there are thousands of people who claim to be Christians who never really had in their souls a grain of love to Jesus. They go to their places of worship because it is proper to do so, and they would hardly be reckoned respectable if they did not go; but they wish in their hearts that they dared to stop away. As for love to Christ, or the kindling of a holy flame of ardent affection for the things of God, they are strangers to it. Dear friends, let me tell you solemnly that the religion which does not grow out of love to Christ is a religion of which you will be ashamed at the last great day. You must love Christ, ay, and love him better than kinsfolk or acquaintance, or you are none of his, for he himself has said that, unless you love him better than father, and mother, and wife, and children and brethren, and sisters, yea, and your own life also, you cannot be his disciple. Christ will either monopolize your affection or have none of it. He must be the Head of your whole being, and you must take him to be your bosom's absolute Lord for ever, or else you really know nothing of him, and are not saved by him. What say you, dear hearers,—especially those of you who are coming to the Lord's table,—do you truly love Jesus? Let each one put in his inmost soul the question,—

Chapter 17

'Do I love the Lord or no?
Am I his, or am I not?'

and let the answer be distinct and clear, 'Lord, thou knowest all things;
thou knowest that I love thee.'

'Do not I love thee, O my Lord?
  Behold my heart and see;
And turn each odious idol out
  That dares to rival thee.

'Thou know'st I love thee, dearest Lord;
  But oh, I long to soar
Far from the sphere of mortal joys,
  And learn to love thee more!'

The second thing in this question is this,—it is quite clear that, *even in
the judgment of the casual observer, a Christian who is truly in love with
Christ prefers him to all others.* We have all heard of the Pantheon which
was erected in the form of a circle in order that all the gods of the heathen
might stand looking towards one another, each one having an equal place
of honour. It is said that it was proposed to put the statue of Jesus there, that
he might have a place with all the other gods, and mere worldly professors
might agree to this. Buddhists, and Mohammedans, and idolaters of every
kind may say, 'Oh, yes! you may worship your Jesus, and we will serve
Juggernaut,' or whatever idol they may prefer; but the religion of the Lord
Jesus cannot consent to this arrangement, for it is intolerant of all others.
It is tolerant to the last degree as far as touching men with the arm of the
law is concerned, for we believe in perfect freedom for all in matters of
religion, and we hold that no government as such has any right either to
support or to condemn a religion. We believe that there is no more right
to be an established episcopal church in this land than that there should be
an established religion of fire-worshippers. Let the church stand or fall on
her own merits as judged by the Word of God; and if she cannot maintain
herself, let her perish. This is but fair and honest to all men; but, though we
preach that doctrine, and hold it firmly, and maintain that no man should

suffer in this world for his faith, let that faith be what it may, yet all are responsible to God to find out what is true, and the religion of Jesus does not say, 'You may believe as you like, and yet it will be all right at the last,' but Christ says, 'He that believeth and is baptized shall be saved; but he that believeth not shall be damned;' and there it ends. It makes no allowance for those who have not believed. When Christ comes into the Pantheon, down must go all the idols and false gods, that Christ, and Christ alone, may sit upon the throne. Our Beloved is so much more than another beloved that we claim the preference for him, and we will not have a good word for any other beloved. He must be loved, and he alone, and all the gods of the heathen and all the gods of man's base heart must be given up. I ask you, dear friends, whether your religion is the chief thing with you. If not, I am afraid you have not a religion that is worth having. Unless it is above all other things to you, I fear you have never learned it in deed and in truth.

One thing more this question teaches us, namely, that *if we stand on this high ground, we may expect many to dispute it with us.* They will ask the question, 'What is your Beloved more than another beloved, that you set him up alone, and put everyone else down?' Christ always had adversaries and gainsayers, and he always will until the brightness of his presence shall consume them. Do not the kings of the earth still stand up, and take council together against the Lord and against his Anointed? Did not Herod seek to destroy the young child Jesus, and did not wicked men hunt him all his life until on the cross they thought they had conquered him, whereas he had really vanquished them? Are not the great ones of the earth still opposed to King Jesus? Well, then, Christian, expect it to be the same with you, reckon upon having a life of warfare; but be of good cheer, for he has overcome the world, and so shall you.

III. Having spoken to you of the surroundings of the question, and of the question itself, I must now ask your attention for a few minutes to THE ANSWER TO THE QUESTION.

Is Christ better than any other object of love? Speaking experimentally, we can say that we know that he is, for some of us, after having tried other lovers, have proved him to be the best of all. There are some here present who now love the Lord, but who once loved the pleasures of sin. I know what you would say if you were to stand up and speak. Well, dear friends, were the pleasures of sin ever equal to the pleasures of the love of Christ? I know that once you could empty the flowing bowl, you enjoyed the sweet sound of the lute and the viol, you were with the giddy multitude by day, and with the wicked by night; some of you spent the earlier part of your life in such ways, but how is it with you now? 'Oh!' answers one, 'I am ashamed that it was ever true of me; I cannot look back upon it with any satisfaction; while I was in it, the mirth was loud, but it was not solid; the waters rippled, but they were shallow; now I have come to this well, the waters of which are deep and satisfying, I dare not even put in contrast Belial and Emmanuel; I would not for a moment compare the pleasures of sin with the perfections of the Lord; truly, there is none that is equal to my Beloved.' Some of you, perhaps, have tried the ways of the world in the matter of respectability and wealth. Thousands of people live only to get money,—not, perhaps, to grow immensely rich, but still to occupy in society a certain position of respectability. This is not altogether the grossest aim a man might have; still, it is living for self, and nothing more. You who have attended to your business with all your might and soul, and who thereby have made money, I know, if you now love Christ, the sweetness of love to him makes all your successes pale their fires. In all that the world can yield, you find no joy that can be compared with the love of Jesus. Is it not so? And do you not perceive that, when your substance shall vanish in the cold blast of death, Christ will then stand out as the only real wealth that you possess?

There may be some young man here who is trying hard to obtain all the learning that he can, and his head aches with his long studies. Study as hard as thou canst, my young friend, but remember that, if the attainment of learning be thine only object, if thou hast nothing higher or deeper than that, thy learning, when thou hast mastered it all, will only make thee a learned fool. It is a poor thing to live for by itself. Take up the skull of the philosopher, and the skull of the greatest dunce, when they have been dead three years, and find out the difference between them if you can; there is no more then within the one than there is within the other. He who lives only to acquire learning loses it when he dies, but he who lives wholly for Christ may take his learning with him across the stream of death into the land of immortality. Whatever else there may be that is admirable in the world, I am resolved more and more to exalt my blessed Master, arrayed in robes of glory and beauty, and to say, 'There is no beloved like my Beloved.'

This is what is to be said in praise of him. First, *our Beloved has a character such as was never heard or known of before.* The spouse says, 'My Beloved is white and ruddy.' Our Lord Jesus is perfectly pure. Infidels have read the life of Christ through and through to try to find faults in it; but, as to any truthful accusation against him, they have utterly failed, and the most of them have been subdued by its charms. That life of Christ, if it could be proved to be a fiction, would prove man himself to be infinite in having conceived so marvellous an idea,—no virtue in excess, and not the slightest taint of evil. The matchless character of Christ Jesus our Lord must strike every mind with awe, and every holy man with love. Taken in connection with his substitutionary sufferings, that life has charms indeed. He was perfect, yet despised and rejected of men, and led like a lamb to the slaughter,—'white and ruddy.' O beloved, I wish I could take you into the very heart of my subject, but I cannot! Yet my Master's sweet character, and his bitter death, ought to win your hearts to him; they ought to fasten the eyes of your soul upon him till you should be enraptured with him. Fires of holy love, vehement as the flame of the coals of juniper, should burn in the bosom of everyone who loves the Lord.

If you will, at your leisure, read the spouse's description of her Bridegroom, you will find that it is exceedingly delightful. She says of him, '*His head is as the most fine gold.*' Truly, when Christ teaches us, the thoughts that come from his marvellous head, the mighty doctrines which emanate from that wondrous brain of his, are like fine gold. The teachings of human philosophy are mere dross and alloy compared with the philosophy which Christ taught. He is the Master-Teacher, the Great Rabbi, the Divine Philosopher who has taught us to love the true wisdom: 'His head is as the most fine gold,' and further, says the spouse, '*His locks are bushy, and black as a raven.*' No age has affected him. Systems of theology and systems of philosophy have grown grey and disappeared; but the religion of Jesus Christ still has locks that are bushy and black as a raven. Christ still has 'the dew of his youth.' The longer the world exists, the more fair will be the truth as it is in Jesus. You need never fear that, in twenty years' time, the gospel will be superseded; the old-fashioned gospel of our grandsires, the gospel of the Puritans, the gospel of the Smithfield martyr-fires, the gospel of the Alpine valleys, the gospel of the Roman amphitheatre where the early Christians died, the gospel of Paul, the gospel of our Lord Jesus, still is as young and fresh and vigorous as ever.

Then the spouse says of her Bridegroom, as though she knew him well, '*His eyes are as the eyes of doves by the rivers of waters, washed with milk, and fitly set.*' When he looks upon the sons of men, his eyes are the eyes of a peaceful dove; there is no thought of cruelty in Christ, no desire to destroy. All is meekness and gentleness in him, but that gentleness is associated with purity: 'His eyes are as the eyes of doves by the rivers of waters.' These are the rivers of his tears, for his eyes poured forth floods of grief on our account. 'Washed with milk,' it is said. So pure is Christ's love to his people that he hates their sins while he loves their souls with a love unfathomed and eternal. 'And fitly set,' Christ's eyes look straight on. Wisdom governs all that he does; there are no imperfections in his judgment, no mistakes in his purpose. Those eyes of love which he fixes upon you, my Christian brother or sister, are eyes of wisdom as well as eyes of affection, eyes of purity as well as eyes of grace.

The spouse next goes on to describe her Bridegroom's cheeks: '*His cheeks are as a bed of spices, as sweet flowers.*' Christ's silent communings with his people the spouse compares to a bed of spices, and all of you who have ever had communion with Christ,—not merely in public through the Word, but alone in the privacy of your chambers,—you know how fragrant the love of the Saviour is. 'As sweet flowers,' says she, yielding their perfume to all who can perceive it. Oh, to be near Christ! There are no flowers that bloom on earth that can be compared in their best sweetness, or on the sunniest May day, with the love of our Lord Jesus. I cannot fully explain this mystery to you who know nothing of it, but the fact will never be denied by you who have proved it by happy experience.

The spouse, as she still thinks of her Beloved, says, '*His lips like lilies, dropping sweet smelling myrrh.*' Christ's promises are all pure and perfect; they are what earthly lilies are not, they are full of myrrh. A promise from Christ is richer than all the promises of a king. One word from thy blessed lips, my Master, shall more delight me than all the hallelujahs of the skies. Let me but hear thy voice, and I would not change its music for all the harps of gold that ring out their melody in the streets of Heaven.

The spouse further adds, '*His hands are as gold rings set with the beryl.*' Christ is an active Saviour, working and toiling for us, and he does such marvels for us that we see the ring of his everlasting love set with the jewels of his omnipotence, his faithfulness, his wisdom, and his immutability. Look back upon all the history of Christ, and you will see this to be true.

Then the bride passes on to the more hidden parts of her Bridegroom. She speaks of his bowels, for that is the word, the bowels of his compassion towards us, and these she compares to '*bright ivory overlaid with sapphires*' as if she did not know how to set forth all his glories.

'The love of Jesus, what it is,
None but his loved ones know;'

and neither bright ivory nor precious sapphires shall be able to describe the condescension, the gentleness, or the love of Jesus. As for his goings-forth, which were of old, and all his present movements towards his church, the spouse says, '*His legs are as pillars of marble,*' and as the strength of a pillar depends greatly upon its base, she says that they are '*set upon sockets of fine gold.*' Yes, the goings of Christ towards us are based and grounded upon his deity, his infallibility, his immutability, his truth, his faithfulness. All else stands upon a sandy foundation, but our Lord Jesus is firmly fixed for ever and ever, blessed be his holy Name!

The bride closes her description by declaring of her Bridegroom that '*his countenance*'—or rather, as the word should be, '*his whole aspect is as Lebanon, excellent as the cedars. His mouth is most sweet: yea, he is altogether lovely.*' It has been said that, if the history of all the tyrants in the world had been lost, you might paint a picture of all tyrants out of the one portrait of Henry the Eighth. Whether that is true or not, we know that, if all the pictures of loveliness in this world were lost, you might portray all true loveliness out of the single person of our Lord Jesus Christ. Oh! but you should see him! Oh, but you should get even a glimpse of him! How can we rightly talk of beauty? It is a thing to be seen; it is a matter, not so much for the tongue of the speaker as for the eye of the observer. Oh, but you should see him! Beloved, you should see Jesus in your darkest hours appearing as the Sun of Righteousness to make you glad. You should see him as some of us have seen him when we have been communing with him at his table, and he has taken us in the chariots of Ammi-nadib away from all this world's care. You should see him as some of the saints of old saw him, in their prison cells or in their private place of retirement, when they waited upon him, and he revealed himself unto them as he doth not unto the world. You should see him as the angels see him; how glad their eyes are made by looking upon him! Nothing charms them in all Heaven like a sight of Christ. The pavement of shining gold, the walls of chrysolyte and of jasper, and the gates of pearl, are as nothing to them; Jesus, *Jesus*, JESUS, he is Heaven, he is bliss, he is the very glory of glory. Ah! and you shall see him,—some of you perhaps in a very few weeks' time,—when your spirit shall be freed from the shackles of this clay; yes, you shall see him whom you have loved. It is sweet to hear of him, but what must it be to behold him!

Ah! and you ungodly ones shall see him, as we all shall see him, for he will come in the latter days upon the clouds of heaven to judge the world in righteousness. Then you who have despised him will not sing as you do now; for then shall your harps and viols give place to mournful wailings which shall never know an end. Then shall you look on him whom you have pierced,—not to trust him, but to flee from him, and to cry to the rocks and to the hills to hide you from the face of him that sitteth upon the throne.

Behold he comes; on flying clouds he comes! Ye who love him, let the prospect cheer you. You shall see him, but not afar off; for you shall fly into his bosom. You shall be like him, you shall reflect his beauty everlastingly; and this shall be your never-ending portion, to be with him where he is, and to behold his glory, the glory which his Father gave him or ever the earth was. O beloved, are you not longing to be with him? Do not your souls pine for him? If so, ask him to manifest himself to you now, for though he is not here in person, yet his Holy Spirit can so describe and depict him to you that your spirit shall be brought into sweetest fellowship with his Spirit. Say unto him, 'Sweet Lord, talk with me as thou didst with the disciples at Emmaus.' Put the preacher aside, forget his feeble words. Ay, and when you come to the table, I pray you put aside the emblems; do not think of them further than they can help you to think of him. If your eyes be defiled and dim, so that you see the signs but see not him, let this be a grief to you; cry to him,—'Saviour, I must have thee; I cannot take a stone instead of bread; I must have thyself. Sacraments and ordinances, what are these by themselves? I cannot be content with anything but thyself.'

'Come, spread thy savour on my frame,
  No sweetness is so sweet;
Till I get up to sing thy name,
  Where all thy singers meet.'

Humble and contrite spirits, you shall not be denied. Christ will bid you put your finger into the print of the nails, he will bid you thrust your hand into his side. He loves you, he is very near to you; think not that he forgets you because he is in Heaven, and you are down here. His heart is with you, and he is himself present with you according to his promise, 'Lo, I am with you alway, even unto the end of the world.' If any of you suffer, he suffers with you. If you rejoice, he rejoices in sympathy with you. Look up to him, and beseech him to look down to you, and may you have a blessed and happy time of fellowship with him at his table!

If there be any of you who wish to know him, remember that to know him you have nothing to do but to trust him, to depend upon him. May the Holy Ghost give you the power to exercise simple faith in him! The moment that you do so, you are saved. May God give you his blessing, for Christ's sake! Amen.

Chapter 18

He shall see his seed

A communion address at Mentone, delivered on Lord's-day afternoon, 4 December 1887

'When thou shalt make his soul an offering for sin, he shall see his seed."—Isaiah 53:10.

THE death of our Lord was not the death of his cause. His end upon the cross was not the end of him. He was that corn of wheat, which must fall into the ground, and die, or else 'it abideth alone; but if it die, it bringeth forth much fruit.' This verse is a most blessed prophecy of the result that is to follow from the death of Christ: 'When thou shalt make his soul an offering for sin, he shall see his seed.'

Note then, dear friends, that *the death of Christ produces a posterity to him:* 'He shall see his seed.' This posterity of Christ could not be according to the flesh, for our Saviour had no seed after the flesh. It is a spiritual seed, born in the power of his Spirit. It must be so; this is self-evident. It means, surely, that there would be born out of his energy a people who should be quickened by his life, and who should be partakers of his character; men and women who should be his children because they should be like him, because they should bear his image, because they should reproduce his likeness in themselves. 'He shall see his seed.' The Christ has a seed sown; Christians are those who spring out of him as he is sown. What a sweet satisfaction it is to remember that all those who believe in Christ are his seed! As Isaac was the seed of Abraham, so are we the seed of Jesus Christ our Lord; and it is written, 'If children, then heirs;' if the seed of Christ, then partakers of all that is his, so that all that Christ has is ours today, because we are his seed; and the covenant made with him, and with his seed, is made with us, and we are joint-heirs with Christ, partakers with Christ, one with Christ.

Someone may say that the faithful are described as born again of the Father and of the Holy Spirit. That is true, most true; and it is because of the death of Christ that the Father begetteth us; it is because of the death of Christ that the Spirit is sent down to breathe on such dry bones as we are, and make us live. But we know that, if we believe in Jesus, we are his seed, for we hear him say to his Father, 'Behold I and the children whom thou hast given me.' He regards all believers as his sons and daughters, and he is the 'Wonderful, Counsellor, the Mighty God, the Everlasting Father, the Prince of Peace.'

Note, next, that, according to this text, Jesus will always have a seed, *this seed will continue*. It is implied in the very indefiniteness of the text: 'He shall see his seed.' The prophet does not say when he shall see his seed; and when there is no note of time, it is implied that it will always be so. When he saw the few disciples who gathered about him after his resurrection, he saw his seed. When he looked down from the glory on the day of Pentecost, and saw the three thousand converts gathered in, he saw his seed. He is always seeing his seed, in every land, of every rank, and every class, among all kindreds, and nations, and people, and tribes, speaking all manner of tongues. It is still true, 'he shall see his seed,' and he will always see his seed throughout all eternity.

Besides, I find that the Hebrew is in the plural, 'he shall see his seeds,' by which is meant that he should see seed after seed, as we might say of a man, 'He shall see his children and his children's children.' Christ will always see, not only those who were immediately converted under his personal ministry, but also those who would afterwards believe on him through his disciples' word. There are some of us, whose joy it is to bring souls to the Saviour, to bring to Christ those who are our spiritual children; but who are, in a much truer sense, his spiritual children, too: 'He shall see his seed.'

In the Septuagint, which is, of course, the Greek translation of the Hebrew, the passage runs thus: 'He shall see his long-lived seed.' Although I do not think that is a correct translation, yet still it goes to strengthen this thought, that the seed of Christ shall endure for ever. It is long-lived; as long as the sun and the moon endure, and long after they pass away, there will be a people who will believe in Christ, and will love Christ, and will exhibit the likeness of Christ. There is no fear of failure for his cause; there will always be, even in the darkest days, thousands who have not bowed the knee to Baal.

This may cheer each one of us in our holy service. Our dear brother, who is labouring for the Lord in Mentone, may rest assured that he will not labour in vain, for the promise still stands, 'He shall see his seed.' And we, who labour in London and elsewhere, may rest assured that, in every place, there is a remnant according to the election of grace, and we have to find them out with this gracious promise to encourage us, 'He shall see his seed.' Let us keep on preaching Christ; for, if we do, some, who hear us, shall believe on him through our word.

There was another thought that struck me as I was reading this passage: 'When thou shalt make his soul an offering for sin, he shall see his seed.' Then it is certain that, although Jesus died, although his soul was made an offering for sin, *he still lives*. He is not dead, for 'he shall see his seed.' Oh, what a joy it is to us to have a living Christ, a living Saviour! The poor Church of Rome has only a dead Christ or a baby Christ; you never see him represented anywhere except on the cross or in the Virgin's arms; but we have a full-grown living Christ, who looks down from Heaven, and sees his seed.

We have a Christ who is not far removed from us; we cannot see him, but he can see us. He is, therefore, within eye-shot of us, and he is taking a loving interest in everything that concerns us here below. His eyes are upon us always; he looks from the battlements of glory, and beholds every penitent and believing soul, and he sees the agonies and tears, the sighs and sorrows, and the joys and triumphs of his redeemed ones. He is not dead; and he is not far removed from us.

And he is personally concerned in every conversion; for everyone, who is born to God, is his seed; and he sees that soul, hears its first cry, puts into his bottle its first tears, looks upon it with joy as the fruit of the travail of his soul.

And when we go to work for him, let us always remember that our Master is looking on all the while, beholding what we are doing, watching our exertions, perceiving our travail in birth for souls, witnessing our defeats or victories, noticing our despondencies or our joys, seeing us as we sorrowfully cry, 'Who hath believed our report?' He sees our rejoicing over every soul that is saved. He is no dead Christ, no Christ who has turned his face away from us, but he is a living, loving, observing, interested Christ: 'He shall see his seed.'

I think that, *in this truth, there are a great many comforts for us,* and I will conclude my little talk when I have just mentioned some of them.

Our Saviour sees his seed; that is, he sees the purchase of his agonies, the outcome of his passion, the result of the travail of his soul. There was not one unrewarded pang in his heart, not one tear that fell in vain, not a drop of his heart's blood that was wasted; but all had its full reward. As it was so with Christ, so it will be with us. We shall receive a full reward for all our labours;

we, too, shall see our seed. We may have to scatter seed broadcast, as men cast their bread upon the waters, but we shall find it after many days. This which is said of the Head is said of each of the members of his mystical body, 'He shall see his seed.' Work on, beloved; sow, and faint not. 'Be ye steadfast, unmoveable, always abounding in the work of the Lord, forasmuch as ye know that your labour is not in vain in the Lord.'

Then there is a further comfort that, I doubt not, we are intended to gather from this passage; that is, that Christ sees his people with intense delight. With all the rapture with which a mother looks upon her babe, with infinitely more of pleasure than that with which a father gazes upon his son, Jesus sees the children for whom he died, the new-born sons and daughters for whom he travailed in awful agony. He takes the greatest delight in every one of his people. Hath he not said, 'Thou shall no more be termed Forsaken; neither shall thy land any more be termed Desolate: but thou shalt be called Hephzi-bah, and thy land Beulah: for the Lord delighteth in thee, and thy land shall be married'? Even Heaven, with all its splendour, hath its greatest delight to Jesus because his redeemed are to be with him there for ever and for evermore. 'Father, I will, that they also, whom thou hast given me, be with me where I am; that they may behold my glory.'

And, once more, Jesus sees us with paternal care: 'He shall see his seed.' He shall look upon them with more than a father's loving solicitude. He shall have eyes for their wants, and also for the supply of those wants. What does 'providence' mean but fore-sight, providence, seeing for others? Our Lord Jesus Christ has gone before us into glory to make ready a place for us; even through the grave, he has gone to appear in the presence of God for us. His eye is on his people perpetually: 'He shall see his seed.'

At this moment, he is looking upon me; he knows what a battle* I am in for the cause of God and truth, and what guidance, and grace, and help I need. He sees you, dear sister, who may be sickly; and he knows all that you need to cheer and sustain you just now. He sees you, too, dear brother, working here in a foreign land; and he knows what sustenance your heart continually needs. We may drift hither and thither upon the sea of life; winds and waves may seem to toss us at their own wild will; but never is the eye of our Lord off us night or day. Earthquake, storm, or danger of sudden death makes no difference to him; and, under all circumstances, 'He sees his seed.' He sees that seed when it sees not him. When we are in the dark, the darkness is light to him. I love to think that, when the shadows fall at last, and we have to soar through tracks unknown, when they shovel the earth in upon our coffins, and we have to go into that viewless state where no eye of wife or child can see us, 'He shall see his seed.' He shall see our soul, and shall see our body; and, at the last great day, when he shall call us, we shall each one answer, 'Here am I,' and he will take us up to be for ever with him, ourselves for ever seeing him, and he for ever seeing us, for so it is written, 'He shall see his seed.'

Note

* This address was delivered at the very height of 'The Down-grade Controversy.'

Signs of the Saviour

A communion address at Mentone, delivered on Lord's-day afternoon, 15 December 1889

YOU know, dear friends, that 'we walk by faith, not by sight.' We do not expect here to see our Lord; we sometimes wish we could. Oh, that he would come and work a miracle among us, or that we might at least have such a vision of him as John had 'in the isle that is called Patmos'! Now, all these wishes for visions and signs come of our flesh, for the spirit walks by faith. We trust; and trust is to us instead of ears, or eyes, or feelings. We believe; firmly, steadfastly, we believe; and this is to us our one mode of communion with our Lord. We do not ask to touch him with the finger, as Thomas did; nor to behold him, as Mary Magdalene did, nor to hear his voice as she did when he said to her, 'Mary!' We wait for all that until we are in another world. Faith is our soul's sense by which we perceive our Lord.

When certain of the scribes and Pharisees asked to see a sign, our Saviour said to them:—

'An evil and adulterous generation seeketh after a sign; and there shall no sign be given to it, but the sign of the prophet Jonas; for as Jonas was three days and three nights in the whale's belly; so shall the Son of man be three days and three nights in the heart of the earth. The men of Nineveh shall rise in judgment with this generation, and shall condemn it; because they repented at the preaching of Jonas; and, behold, a greater than Jonas is here. The queen of the south shall rise up in the judgment with this generation, and shall condemn it: for she came from the uttermost parts of the earth to hear the wisdom of Solomon; and, behold, a greater than Solomon is here.'—Matthew 12:39–42.

The first sign is, JONAS; OR, THE PROPHET OF RESURRECTION.

Jonah rose again from the dead, as it were. Coming out of the very midst of the great fish, and from the bottom of the sea, and from the heart of the earth, he was like a dead man coming out of his coffin; and when he came to the shore again, and afterwards went to Nineveh, he preached almost as one who was alive from the dead. But our Lord Jesus Christ is a far more wonderful person than Jonah, for he did actually die, and he was buried, and lay in the earth three days and three nights, according to the Hebrew mode of measuring time, and then he came to life again. The resurrection of Christ is a sign to us of the truth of his doctrine. I have often, when troubled with doubts, fallen back on this great truth,—Jesus did rise again. There is no disputing that fact. He was laid in the grave; they sealed the stone over the mouth of the sepulchre, and they set a watch; yet he came out of the tomb at the time that he said he would come out of it. He did rise again, and he was seen by a number of persons who had known him most intimately, and who could not be deceived about him. One saw him, two saw him, seven saw him, 'the eleven' saw him; and, on one occasion, he was seen by 'above five hundred brethren at once.' They all knew that it was that same Jesus with whom they had consorted for three years, who had died on the cross, and had been buried in Joseph's new tomb. There is no one fact in history that is so well attested by evidence as the resurrection of Christ. The men who said that they saw him after he had risen were so sure of it that the majority of them died to prove it; they did not shrink from even the severest test. They died cruel deaths, but they maintained this truth to the last; and the belief in it was so general that multitudes came and joined them, and so perpetuated the testimony that Christ really did rise from the dead.

Well, now, think for a minute or two of Jonah going to preach at Nineveh after his wonderful deliverance. What *a strange experience* he had had,—the experience of a man who had been in the belly of the fish, and who could say, 'The waters compassed me about, even to the soul: the depth closed me round about, the weeds were wrapped about my head.' In its awful pain, the huge fish had plunged deep into the sea, so that Jonah said, 'I went down to the bottoms of the mountains; the earth with her bars was about me for ever: yet hast thou brought up my life from corruption, O Lord my God!' There must have been something strange about that man when he rose from his living tomb, and came back to the shore. It was an extraordinary tale that he had to tell; but our Lord Jesus Christ can tell a much more wondrous story than that. He did really die; he passed through all the pains, and griefs, and sinkings, and agonies of death; he passed into the dark abode of death; yet he lives. Whatever he tells me, I believe. One who has had such an experience as he has had will tell me many mysteries. He may tell me as many mysteries as he pleases, he may even tell me things that would be unbelievable if told by anyone else; but I will believe all that he tells me, and I expect wondrous instruction from a Teacher who has undergone such an experience as he has passed through in his death and resurrection.

And Jonah, when he preached in Nineveh, must have manifested *a singular enthusiasm*. A man who had been in the regions of the dead, and had come back to life again, would speak with the accent of conviction. You brethren and sisters, who are familiar with our English literature, remember how Coleridge's 'Ancient Mariner' cast a strange spell over the wedding-guest, and held him while he told his wondrous tale. And there must have been a far stranger spell about the Lord Jesus Christ when he came back from the dead. There is a singular and unique charm to us about our risen Redeemer, who, after having died for us, after having borne the wrath of God for us, after having put our sins away by the sacrifice of himself, yet lives to tell the wondrous story. Oh, I must listen to all that he says; I must give good heed to the Christ who rose again from the dead!

Then, Jonah's ministry, as that of a man risen from the dead, had *a special seal* attached to it. The Ninevites would be obliged to listen to him. There could be no doubt about his being God's messenger after such a resurrection; so they gave heed to his message. Our Lord Jesus went into the grave as the Hostage of his people; if he had not paid their debt, he would not have been released from the bands of the grave.

'If Jesus ne'er had paid the debt,
He ne'er had been at freedom set.'

But as he had discharged all the obligations of his people, he, as their Surety, was suffered to go free; and we are free, too, by virtue of our union with him. Well may we rejoice in the risen Christ, who can minister such solid comfort to us because he has God's seal upon him, which seal is also the seal of our acceptance in him.

I do not wonder that the preaching of Jonah in Nineveh was followed by *a speedy repentance*. Short was his sermon, monotonous was his message; but the king repented, and all the people proclaimed a fast, and put on sackcloth, from the greatest to the lowest in the city, and even the very cattle were made to fast; so that the howls of hungry animals mingled with the wails of penitent but hungry men. All Nineveh was smitten with sorrow and repentance through the preaching of Jonah; and, surely, beloved, you and I ought to be far more impressed with every word that Christ speaks to us. We ought to feel a double repentance for forgiven sin, and a double joy in the pardon that he gives us as the result of his shameful death and glorious resurrection.

It is a suggestive thought for us that those people in Nineveh were not Jews; they were heathen, they were Gentiles, as we are. Jesus has for ever done away with the privileges that were conferred upon the Jews, and he has brought us, the far-off Gentiles, to accept the great truth of his resurrection from the heart of the earth, and to rejoice in him as our risen Redeemer. I feel, in my heart, an indescribable love to the risen Jesus. Rutherford says that he never looks so lovely as in the red shirt of his own blood; yet, just now, there seems to me to be a brilliance about the array of the risen One that surpasses everything else. Is he not clothed in light as we see him sitting at his Father's right hand, having left the abode of the dead for ever? Hold fast, dear friends, this wondrous sign, this strangest of all signs,—Jonah, the prophet of resurrection.

The other sign mentioned by our Lord is SOLOMON; OR, THE KING OF WISDOM.

We know that Christ is true from the wisdom of his words. Only think of what he has taught us, and what he is still teaching us by his Spirit. It is more full of wisdom than anything Solomon ever thought, or wrote, or spoke. Well might 'the queen of the South' come from far to hear the wisdom of Solomon; and well may we quit everything else that we may listen to the wisdom of him who is far 'greater than Solomon.'

Perhaps, when you are at home, you will read, in the tenth chapter of the first Book of Kings, about the queen of Sheba coming to Solomon, for you will then see how wonderfully he is a type of the Lord Jesus Christ, the true King of wisdom, who has none of the folly that was in Solomon.

And, first, you will read that '*she came to prove him with hard questions.*' If you want to make sure that Christ is true, prove him with hard questions. How can God be just, and yet forgive sin? It is only Christ who can answer that hard question. How can God's wrath burn like fire, and yet his love burn still more mightily? Christ answers that. If ever you have a difficult question in your own personal experience, take it to Jesus, and you will get an answer. When you do not know what to do, the very best guide you can have is one that I saw in one of our schoolrooms at the Orphanage. On the wall there hung a large card bearing upon it these words,—'WHAT WOULD JESUS DO?' Whenever you do not know what to do, ask what Jesus would do if he were in your place, for that is the thing for you to do if you belong to him. Any hard question that you may have, you may put to Christ, for it will not be 'hard' to him. I never found him at fault yet. I never had a problem that he could not solve. I never had a difficulty in which he was unable to help me; and, therefore, I believe in him, and I will continue to believe in him.

Further on, you will read that, when the queen of Sheba came to Solomon, '*she communed with him of all that was in her heart.*' If you have learned how to commune with Christ, you have proved that he knows everything that is in your heart, and that he meets every need of your heart. Christ's truth fits the believer's experience like a key fits the wards of the lock for which it was made. I know that Christ fits me exactly, and the same is true of each of you, dear brethren and sisters; you have a Christ who could not be more suited to you if you were the only man or woman in the world. When I am lifted up with high joys, Christ suits me in my gladness; and when I am down,—and I do sometimes go down very low,—I always find him ready to meet me in my sadness. He seems to say to me, even then, 'It is all right; I am here.' I can say to him, with David, 'If I ascend up into Heaven,'—in some high spiritual ecstasy, 'thou art there;' and 'if I make my bed in hell,'—in some terrible agony of despair, 'thou art there.' 'If I take the wings of the morning, and dwell in the uttermost parts of the sea.'—in some strange experience which separates me from all my fellow-creatures, 'even there shall thy hand lead me, and thy right hand shall hold me.' This singular communion of Christ with the human heart is one of the best proofs that he is both God and man, and he will always be dear to us in that double capacity.

Then the queen of Sheba was astonished at *the buildings that Solomon had made*. When she had seen his palace, the temple, and other noble buildings, 'there was no more spirit in her.' And when you and I think of what our Lord has done, we shall be filled with amazement. There is the palace of his redemption, with the foundation laid in his wondrous sacrifice, and piled high in his glorious person right on to the splendours of his second advent. The architecture of redemption is such as never could have come from any mind that was not Divine, and yet such as could never have been found in any but One who was also in fullest fellowship with man. Christ's marvellous works prove him to be far 'greater than Solomon.'

And when the queen of Sheba saw *how Solomon judged the people,* 'the sitting of his servants,' the arrangements of his court, and the way in which he decided cases that were brought before him, she was filled with wonder; and when I see how Christ governs his Church, how he feeds his people, how he arranges Providence, and manages all things, I am filled with wonder. O thou mediatorial King, who is like unto thee? We believe in thee to the full as we see thy matchless government. The day shall come when his unsuffering Kingdom shall fully come; then shall all the earth see what a great God, and what a wondrous Man he is.

The queen of Sheba was, I suppose, most of all touched by Solomon's *royal generosity,* for he gave unto her 'all her desire, whatsoever she asked, beside that which Solomon gave her of his royal bounty.' So she felt, queen as she was, well repaid for her long journey, and she returned to her own country filled with admiration of the great king of the Jews. So you and I, who have been the recipients of Christ's bounty, have been filled with wonder at it. You pray, dear brother, and he gives you far more than you asked; you come to him full of love, and find that he loves you a hundred times more than you love him. You rejoice in him, and he carries you away, all of a sudden, with torrents of joy. He brings to you greater joy than you ever bring to him. Perhaps, throughout your life, you have had so many favours from him, that you have wondered what more he could do for you; but his next gift has been still more wonderful; and you have scarcely enjoyed that, when there has been something more marvellous still. My own path in life has been strewn with miracles of mercy. When I have lived near to my Lord, and walked closely with him, I have had to say, 'O world of wonders! I can say no less.' They who know him best love him most. People say that, if you want to know a man, you must live with him; and if you want to know Christ, you must live with him. When you live with the best of men, they may probably go down in your esteem, for you find out their foibles and failings; but you will never find out any foible or failing in your Lord, for he has none. He is a hero to his valet; he that will unloose the latchets of his shoes is the man who will think most of him. It is his surpassing wisdom that has been to us as a sign, and will be to us as a sign still. We do not want any dreams, we do not want any visions, we do not want any voices from the sky, nor sights in the air. We believe Christ because of these two sure things,—he rose from the dead, and he is infinitely, royally wise; here will we rest, and in him will we trust.

Grace for grace

A communion address at Mentone, delivered on Lord's-day afternoon, 8 December 1889

'Of his fulness have all we received, and grace for grace.'—John 1:16.

JOHN here speaks of all the saints; and of all believers he says, 'Of his fulness'—that is, of Christ's fulness, 'have all we received.' He does not say, 'We *hope* we have;' but, 'We *have*.' He does not say, 'We *shall* receive;' but, 'We *have* received.' Looking round this little assembly, this afternoon, we trust that we may say, with holy confidence, of ourselves and of each other, 'Of his fulness have all we received;' and that each one can say, 'He loved me, and gave himself for me; and I have received of his fulness, and grace for grace.'

What does that expression, 'grace for grace,' mean? It means a great deal more than I can tell you, and more than all the whole company of preachers of the Gospel can tell you. There are only three words here; but, the longer I think of them, the less I seem able to comprehend them. There is a whole sea of meaning in them, though the words are only like a few precious drops.

Chrysostom thinks, and at least in part I agree with him, that this expression means that, *in Christ, we receive all the grace that Moses set forth in the figures of the law,* since it is added,—and we must always take the connection of the text,—'for the law'—that is, the ceremonial law—'was given by Moses, but grace and truth'—that is, the grace of it, and the truth of it, 'came by Jesus Christ.' Whatever of grace there was in the law, we get the grace of that grace in Christ. If it concerned the shedding of the sacrificial blood, we get that, and more than that, in Christ; if it brought, through that blood-shedding, cleansing from sin, access to God, acceptance with God, and ten thousand things beside, we have all that in Christ: 'Of his fulness have all we received, and grace for grace,'—all the grace that Moses signified and symbolized in the whole of the ceremonial law. What a wonderful substance is this, which is the substance of all those thousands of shadows! It has been said by somebody, I forget who it was, that it would be a great puzzle indeed to invent anything that should set forth and answer to all the symbols of the law. I should like to give this task to some sceptic, to let him sit down, and try to invent a character, in whose person, life, and acts, all the symbols of the law should be brought out. This is done in Christ, without any straining of metaphors, and without doing any violence to truth. A child can see, if it be but taught of the Spirit of God, that in Christ there is everything that is set forth from the first type in the Old Testament to the last, and from the institution of the Mosaic and Aaronic economy right down to its close. We have grace for every grace that God ever revealed under the law.

But I believe that it also means something different from that; namely, that *Christ has given us grace to receive grace*. We have received his grace, for we were dead; and how can living grace dwell in dead hearts? It is true that we could be saved by believing; but we could not believe while we were dead. It is true that we could be saved by repenting; but we could not repent. We were under a moral disability which amounted to being 'without strength;' ay, and without will, and without life; but Christ came to us, and he poured into us, of his fulness, a prevenient grace, which came before saving grace, a grace that made us feel our need, a grace that made us willing to receive grace, a grace that opened our heart that grace might come in, and fill it. At the very beginning of our spiritual life, we have received from Christ the grace to make us able to receive grace.

And since then, the text has had another meaning to us, for *we have received grace in proportion to the grace given*. Whenever our Lord gives us the grace of faith, he gives us other graces with it; love, hope, patience, and so on. He gives us grace with other graces in its train; each grace is like a star with so many more graces to be its satellites, the graces that grace that grace, the many graces that go with each grace, and the whole multitude of graces that grace the heart, and make it gracious and grace-full. Christ has given us all these graces: 'Of his fulness have all we received, and grace for grace.' It is not only faith that comes through grace, but also all the breathings and longings of faith, all the realities that grow out of faith, all the acts of faith, and all the joys of faith. Christ gives us every grace in its due proportion, and all the graces in proportion to one another.

And I believe, dear friends, that *Christ gives us grace that we may get more grace*. I believe that every grace that a Christian gets is a grace looking forward to another grace; that, all the way to Heaven, every step we go is a help to the next step, and that step to another. It is with Heavenly grace as it is with trade; we have, first, a little capital to start with; with the first returns on that capital, we take a wider range; and with our increased capital we enter upon larger speculations. So it is in the great business of the soul. After our first spiritual gains, we invest all we have in our Lord's name; or to change the figure, we launch out into the deep, and let down our nets for a draught. Then, getting our nets full, we go in for filling the ship; and when that is done, we build a bigger vessel, and so go on from grace to grace. We do not reach the loftiest heights of grace at first, and many young believers fall into great trouble through measuring themselves with full-grown saints; but we begin like apprentice boys, and, at first, learn only the bare elements of our holy trade, and afterwards advance to its higher branches. We make many mistakes, but we resolve to do better next time. By and by, we shall become journeymen, and then we shall execute some very good work; and, in due time, we shall become masters of our sacred art, and shall be able to put the finishing touch upon our work; and, after that, some of us shall even become inventors, and shall devise great things to our dear Master's honour and glory. I wonder how many of you know Miss Havergal's beautiful poem, 'From glory unto glory.' It has thrilled my soul, through and through, as often as I have read it. It is a truly wonderful conception of the glory yet to be revealed; but before we ascend into that high region, we shall have to go from grace to grace; but, all the way, we shall continue to receive 'of his fulness.' If grace comes out of the old grace, it will still have to come out of Christ; and every growth or advance out of our own experience is really the result of drawing out of that deep well of the fulness of Christ.

I hope that we shall never imagine that we are, in ourselves, as good as a person, whom I once met, told me that she was. She said that it was several years since she had sinned; but, as she added that she had not prayed for months, as she had grown so perfectly acquiescent to the will of God, I said to her, 'When a soul does not need to pray, it is "dead in trespasses and sins." You will have to begin at the very bottom of the ladder of salvation, for you evidently know nothing whatever of the work of Divine grace within your soul.' She may have thought that I was harsh and rude in speaking thus faithfully to her, but I felt that she needed such a straight message as that to bring her to a sense of her true condition before God. When we can live without grace, and without prayer, whatever love we may profess to have is of a kind which is unknown to God, and which he will repudiate at the last great day.

Yet, dear friends, I think that there is still more in our text, and that it also means that *Christ has given us grace to the highest form of grace.* We have received, 'of his fulness, grace for grace,' and we shall go on receiving grace from him until we have the whole of grace; not that we shall ever exhaust the Divine treasury of grace, but we shall become full of grace to our utmost capacity. Let us not think that the small store of grace, we have already, is all that we can have; let us not imagine that we cannot, by God's grace, overcome our evil temper, or our sinful propensities, or that we cannot grow to be like Christ. We can, and we must; for he gives us grace with the view of perfecting the work of grace in us until we shall be saturated with it from head to foot, 'filled with all the fulness of God,'—a most marvellous expression, which I will not attempt to explain, but which proves that he gives us grace in its highest, weightiest, and most unbounded sense.

But even now, I am inclined to think that I have not given you the full meaning of the text: 'Of his fulness have all we received, and grace for grace;' that is, *grace according as there is grace in Christ.* As the child receives, while yet a child, the lineaments of the father's face, and some traces of the father's character, so the grace of God has been given to us in such a way as to stamp us with his own likeness. Christ is the type, we are letter-press printed from him; for we have received grace answering to the grace that is in him. It is wonderful that there should be, in each one of us who believe in him,—poor, imperfect creatures though we are,—even a faint outline of the character of Christ sketched as you may have seen a great artist drawing his sketch, and then laying on his colours until the painting is finished. We do not look much like Christ yet; but the first sketch of any picture never looks like what it is to be when it is finished. I see, in some of the saints, just a glance of Christ's eye; in others, who speak for him, I seem to see something of the very lip of the Master; and, in others, a compassionate sympathy which is like the tear-drops that glistened in the Saviour's eye. I think I see, in most of my Christian friends, a likeness to their Lord; I can certainly see more of Christ in some of them than I can see in myself; I only hope that some of the saints can see the beginnings of the likeness to Christ in me; but, whether you and I see it, or not, it is being put there. Dear friends, do you realize what, by God's grace, you are yet to be? You are to be like Christ. God has predestinated us 'to be conformed to the image of his Son;' and the full issue of his predestinating purpose is that we shall be, every one, like Christ. Did you ever stand in a hall of mirrors, and see yourself reflected hundreds of times? Christ stands in the centre of the Church; she is his mirror, in which he is to see himself reflected, his grace shining in his people's graces, his image reproduced in them. When God shall have made all his saints completely into the image of Christ, then he will see that his new creation, like the old one, is 'very good.' Then will the eternal Sabbath begin, and he shall be satisfied, his Son shall be adored, his Spirit shall be magnified, and we shall be glorified in Christ and with Christ for ever and for evermore. Amen.

Separation from the world

An address at a united communion service at the Metropolitan Tabernacle*

DEAR FRIENDS,—I believe I am expected to say a few words to you before we come to the breaking of bread. There is a passage of Scripture which has been very much upon my mind, and I should like to bring it to your remembrance, and impress it upon your hearts, for it seems to me to be a message which needs to be spoken, throughout the whole of Christendom, with a voice of thunder, yet with the utmost love and tenderness. This is the passage; it is in 2 Corinthians 6:15–18:—

And what concord hath Christ with Belial? or what part hath he that believeth with an infidel? And what agreement hath the temple of God with idols? for ye are the temple of the living God; as God hath said, I will dwell in them, and walk in them; and I will be their God, and they shall be my people. Wherefore come out from among them, and be ye separate, saith the Lord, and touch not the unclean thing; and I will receive you, and will be a Father unto you, and ye shall be my sons and daughters, saith the Lord Almighty.

I do not see the slightest use of the Church of God in the world if it be not separate from the world. What its object and design can be, if it is to be like the rest of mankind, I am unable to conceive. It must be in its separateness that it is to fulfil the purpose of God in creating it, and preserving it. Of old, the Lord chose Israel to be the type of his Church, and he laid many precepts upon them,—some of them hard to keep,—but most of them intended to emphasize their separation from the people by whom they were surrounded. So far as possible, they were not to live among the heathen, for there were habits and practices of the ungodly nations, in which they must have become, perhaps unconsciously, partakers, if they had dwelt amongst them. Their dress, their language, their religion,—in fact, everything about them made them a separate people, dwelling apart from the Gentile nations. And even in their fall and degradation, there still remain many signs and tokens of that separation; so that the Jews cannot become Poles, or Russians, or Englishmen, but they are known everywhere as German Jews, or Polish Jews, or Russian Jews; but always as Jews wherever they dwell.

It is quite clear, from the Word of God, that it was the Lord's purpose—in choosing us to be his people, quickening us by his Holy Spirit, and redeeming us with the precious blood of his dear Son,—to make us a separate people, that we might not be numbered among the nations, and might be as distinct from them, in moral and spiritual aspects, as the Jews were distinct from other men. I beseech you, as members of the Church of Jesus Christ, to keep up this distinction.

I do not ask you to make any distinction in your dress, though I wish we could always be so distinguished by the plainness and simplicity of our apparel that we should never be mistaken for the vain men and the foolish women who have their portion in this life. It is a shame when a woman, who professes to be a follower of the meek and lowly Saviour, is so tricked out as to be taken for a harlot rather than a Christian; and it is equally shameful when an avowedly Christian man can be charged with being a fop or a dandy.

Neither do I think that we need to make such distinctions in our speech as the Friends who say 'thee' and 'thou' to one another. Yet let us always take care never to let anything be mentioned among us but that which is becoming in saints.

There are other points in which we may be distinct from the ungodly among whom our lot is cast. You and I, Christian brethren and sisters, must not trade as do others, who are not actuated by Christian principles. We must not conform to any trade customs if they are not strictly right and honest. There should be, on the part of a Christian man, a resolute putting down of his foot, even if he should be the only man in his particular line of business to do what is just and right. Though all others differ from him, it does not make any difference to his course of action. There are what are called 'tricks in trade', and customs that are undoubtedly evil; but I would remind all who adopt them, that God has a custom of punishing sin, by whatever name it may be called to gloss over its real character.

Then there should be about our families a great distinction from others; not as it was in that house where the servant said, 'I am glad my mistress goes to the sacrament; for, if she did not, I should not know that she was a

Christian.' Let our households be such as we would like them to be if Christ lived there; and, indeed, he does live there if we are living in him, and living to him, and for him. I wish that things could be ordered, in our houses, as they were in the days of Cromwell, when people used to say that, if you went down Cheapside at eight o'clock in the morning, you would see the blinds down at every house, for the inmates were at family prayer. I lay down no cast-iron rules; but this I would say,—let us be distinct from the ungodly in the ordering of our households.

And, especially, let me entreat you to have nothing to do with the places where vice dares to show her brazen forehead. Be careful not to go anywhere where you cannot take Christ with you, or to be seen in any company but that in which you would wish to die. Go anywhere to do good, or to get good; but go nowhere where good cannot be found. Let nobody successfully tempt you to go there; let your life be so strict that the devil himself would know that it was no use for him to seek to lead you astray in that respect. Rise, brethren and sisters, to the dignity of the separated life; and when you have risen to it, keep to that high level.

You know that the happiness of a Christian's life consists in his walking with God; he can never be truly happy in any other condition. Think of the contrast between Abraham alone with God living the separated life, and Lot in Sodom. When the herdsmen of Abraham and Lot fell out, and they separated, Lot chose the plain of Jordan, and pitched his tent toward Sodom, while Abraham dwelt under the oak at Mamre. Abraham must have grieved over Lot when he went to live among the men of Sodom;—not altogether to become one of them, for he always was 'righteous Lot' even when he was in Sodom. But what a terrible experience he had! Abraham had to go and deliver him from captivity when the confederate kings had taken him prisoner; and there were even worse things to follow,—his wife a pillar of salt, and his family,—you know what that was like. Abraham, out there alone, is a happy man; and God appears to him, and says to him, 'Lift up now thine eyes, and look from the place where thou art, northward, and southward, and eastward, and westward: for all the land which thou seest, to thee will I give it, and to thy seed for ever. And I will make thy seed as the dust of the earth: so that if a man can number the dust of the earth, then shall thy seed also be numbered. Arise, walk through the land in the length of it and in the breadth of it; for I will give it unto thee.' He possesses all things who can, for the Lord's sake, and the truth's sake, give up all things; but he, who would cling to the world, sees the fire fall from heaven, and consume all that he has grasped.

If you, who belong to the true Church of God, really want to obtain the blessing for which we have been praying, this is the way to get it: 'Come out from among them, and be ye separate, saith the Lord, and touch not the unclean thing; and I will receive you, and will be a Father unto you, and ye shall be my sons and daughters, saith the Lord Almighty.' You cannot expect to be treated as the Lord's children unless you do this; unless, indeed, you should be whipped for being disobedient children. Do, I beseech you, be determined to be separate from the world; and if it does find fault with you, count that an honour rather than a disgrace. 'You are very precise,' said one to a Puritan minister. 'Yes,' he replied, 'I am, for I serve a very precise God.' The Lord our God is a jealous God, and hates all iniquity. So, with this thought upon our mind, let us draw near to his table, and draw near to himself; with true separateness of heart, let us come near to him who is 'holy, harmless, undefiled, and separate from sinners.'

Note

* This is probably the address 'upon the separateness of believers from the world' mentioned in a note in *The Sword and the Trowel*, December 1880, and delivered on Monday evening, 15 November 1880, at 'the annual communion in connection with The London Baptist Association.'

At the Lord's Table

An address before the communion service at the Metropolitan Tabernacle, Monday evening, 12 February 1866

WHEN we meet together to break bread it is well for us to examine ourselves as to whether we be in the faith. Remember, my dear friends, that your coming tonight to the Lord's Table is, if you be not indeed believers in Jesus Christ, a great and grievous sin against God, so much so that by so doing you eat and drink damnation to yourselves, not discerning the Lord's body. If any man who is unconverted shall come, either to baptism or to the Lord's Supper, he takes that which is not his, and which he has, therefore, no right to; he ventures to the King's Table uninvited, and he brings wrath upon his soul. So far are these outward ordinances from being of any service whatever to the unconverted, that they will even do them mischief instead of good. We do not ask you to come to the Table as if that were coming to Christ. We know that you must come to Christ first, and know him, and rest on him, and then, but not till then, you may take the outward symbol. Of old they took the symbol and then looked for the substance, but under the new covenant you must get the substance and then you may take the symbol.

Beloved believers in Christ, it will be a source of great comfort to us if we shall be able tonight to get close to Christ. May I say to you—what you know already—that the only proper frame of mind in which to come here is one made up of humiliation for sin, faith in the Saviour's blood, love for his precious person, and a desire to enjoy nearness to him. You have nothing to do just now with your business cares, with the sick child at home, with the troubles you anticipate on the morrow. Cast your burden on Christ, and leave it there, and just now look at your Saviour's burdens, your Saviour's griefs, your Saviour's wounds, your Saviour's death. That is the point to which all your thoughts must now come. May the Lord enable you to be in such a happy and hallowed state that Christ may be manifestly amongst us.

But may I ask you, if it shall be well with you and if you have an audience with the King, to whisper in his ear that there are some whom he has bought with his blood who are here tonight, but who do not know that he has bought them. Tell him that there are some here whom his Father gave him, but who are not yet brought out of the world—some who have been redeemed by blood, but who have not yet been redeemed by power. Remember, it was once said by one, 'Think on me when it shall be well with you.' There are times when some of you have special power with Jesus Christ, and I might ask you that you would then speak for me to the King, even to the Captain of the Host. But I will waive that if you will speak to him for unconverted ones, for those who are only looking on tonight. You may tell him—I do not suppose that it is true of all of them—but you may tell him that some of them want him. Tell him that there are many of them who are longing after him. If you do get an interview with him do pray that he would now manifest himself to them. I know there are some among them who are saying. 'Ye daughters of Jerusalem, if ye find your Beloved tell him that we are sick of love, that we want him too.' They cannot find him. They have been saying, 'O that we knew where we might find him.' It has been your privilege to lay hold on him; now bring him to your mother's house that others may see and find him too. 'We have a little sister,' said the Church of old, but that little sister was not grown as yet, and therefore the elder sister thought of her. So we tonight have a little sister not yet brought out, not yet full-grown and developed. Let us pray that these little ones of the family may be brought out and recognised, and be divinely married unto Christ. It will be well for you believers, I say, to think of these.

And now I would say a word or two to the friends who are looking on tonight. There may be many of you who are believers in Christ, but if it is so I am very sorry that you are not downstairs with us. Allow me to say, dear friends, that it is the duty of many who constitute part of this congregation to unite either with this or with some other church. Every believer should be baptized. Remember Christ's word, 'He that believeth and is baptized shall be saved.' I am not going to argue this point with you now. It seems very clear to me. There is a little book which you can buy for twopence, called *The New Testament,* and it is the clearest book upon the subject that I know. If you want to understand the doctrine of believers' baptism read that. If you are a believer and do not keep this command, then you are a disobedient believer. I counsel thee to keep the King's commandment. There is one passage I heard quoted yesterday, and I will quote it again tonight. It is said of those who are in heaven that they 'follow the Lamb whithersoever he goeth.' Now you know that he went down into Jordan, do you not; you know that he descended into the stream, and that the Holy Ghost did rest upon him. Think of that word 'whithersoever he goeth,' and do not neglect even that which seems to you to be so unimportant, but may you be among those virgin souls who,—

'Wheresoe'er the Lamb doth lead
From his footsteps ne'er depart.'

Again, dear friends, I think you ought to belong to the Christian Church because you would bring so much strength to it. If you are really converted, your addition to our numbers would encourage everyone of us, for we should say that another soldier had joined our ranks. If I may compare small things just now with the greatest of all matters, I will remind you of the story of Napoleon's coming back from Elba. When he landed in Europe he had but a handful of men who were escorting the old Emperor back. There was a workman going to his work early in the morning, and he recognised the old familiar face, and at once joined him. 'Here is the first recruit!' said Napoleon. A little band of soldiers in the neighbourhood came to meet him, but instead of fighting him they all turned round to his side. By and by the ranks began to swell; banners were lifted high; a formidable army was formed who all followed the Emperor, and so they marched on and entered the capital of the empire victoriously. Now it seems to me that our Master's progress amongst us has been something of that sort, but there are some of you who say, 'We wish the Master well, but we will not wear the cockade, and we will not enter his service.' Well, but wherefore? Is it a bad cause? Are you ashamed of the Prince Immanuel? Are you ashamed of the company gathered round him? I am afraid that if you will not join an imperfect church on earth the Master will take it as an affront that you think so little of his Bride. Come with us and we will do you good, and I am sure you will make us happy, and if you be indeed a Christian you will come to help us, and to throw your strength into our ranks.

But there are some of you—God knows how many—who are not converted. You do not profess to be, and it is well you do not, because it would be atrocious treason against God if you professed to be what you are not. To you I would say two or three words.

We have come hither tonight to break bread in your presence principally with the view of setting before you, in these two outward symbols—this bread and this wine—that upon which we rest our only hope. You will understand that we have no trust whatever in this bread nor in this wine. This is nothing but common bread; this is nothing but common wine, but—I speak now for all believers present—our hope is built upon the fact that God was made flesh; that, in order to redeem poor fallen bodies, God took upon himself a body, and in that body was broken as we shall break this bread—broken with pangs and griefs unutterable. We rest on that. We believe, also, that the Lord Jesus Christ, the Son of God, poured out his blood that it might be an atonement for sin—not to make God love us, for God is love essentially—but in order to clear away the slur which must have been cast upon the justice of God if he had allowed sin to go unpunished. The sinner is not punished for sin when he believes in Jesus, but still God is strictly just, for he punishes the Substitute instead of the sinner.

Now you may have some other hope than this, but we avow before you that we have no hope but in the body and blood of Jesus Christ our Redeemer. Go, you who rest in ceremonies, sacraments, good works, prayers, charities, and the like, go and rest on them if you dare, but they will prove too rotten a plank to bear the weight of your soul at last. But as for us, at the foot of that cross where the Saviour poured out his soul unto death we must abide.

I will make a confession of my faith just now, and you who are members of this church, if you really believe in it, will say Amen:

'My hope is built on nothing less
Than Jesu's blood and righteousness.'

and in token of this I do now, with you, say '*Amen.*'

I pray God that all here, before the sun rises on another morrow, may be able to say the same, and to rest simply, wholly, only there.

The sabbatic year in the olive garden

A Mentone Meditation

'And six years thou shalt sow thy land, and shalt gather in the fruits thereof: but the seventh year thou shalt let it rest and lie still; that the poor of thy people may eat: and what they leave the beasts of the field shall eat. In like manner thou shalt deal with thy vineyard, and with thy olive yard.'—Exodus 23:10–11.

THE regulation that one year in seven the land should lie fallow, was manifestly wise in reference to arable ground; and even the man who studied his own interest might see convincing reason for obeying this command. In the case of fruit-bearing trees the matter is different: they would yield fruit all the same, and no after increase would come to them through the year of fallow; and therefore none but he who really obeyed the Lord would see the propriety of leaving the clusters upon the vine, and the olives upon the tree. If Israel had universally obeyed the precept, it would certainly have been distinguished from all other nations in a manner the most conspicuous, since it would be sure to become the theme of wonder among other peoples. Strange to the last degree would it seem that, for an entire year, a nation should cease from all the labours of husbandry, and even decline to gather the spontaneous fruits of their trees. No doubt it was this separation unto himself which the Lord aimed at by this regulation; he would have all people know that Canaan was a peculiar land, that he was the Lord of it in a special manner, and that his Israel was unlike all the rest of mankind. In these days, when the Church has become so like the world, it is profitable to be reminded by the type that the Lord's ideal is not so; he still would have his chosen a peculiar people, and still doth he cry to them, 'Come out from among them, and be ye separate.'

I. In further meditating upon this precept with regard to the olive-yard, we are led to feel that this Sabbatic-year observance was A STRIKING ACT OF FAITH. Reason said, 'Gather the fruit, seeing it is upon the tree;' but faith said, 'Let it alone, for so hath the Lord commanded.' Many weighty arguments against waste could have been adduced by prudence; but it was enough for faith that infinite wisdom ordained that there should be neither gathering nor storing of the produce of that year. Outward circumstances evidently argued for the basket and the press; and only the man who would obey God thoroughly would be able to put aside the suggestions of sense, and walk by the divine rule. Why has God given the olives? If he meant us to leave them, why does he load the boughs with them? Surely he would not teach us to despise his gifts, and to practise an idle improvidence? Such would be the natural questions of ordinary unbelief, and they would be difficult to answer, if not impossible, except by faith's one reply, '*So has the Lord commanded.*'

This is an all-sufficient answer to every objection, and yet few would think it so; in fact, the man who thus reasoned would be regarded as insane by mockers, and looked upon as Pharisaical and rigid in his religion by the bulk of religious professors. 'That is carrying the thing too far,' would be the remark of many a decent man who was observant of other and less expensive precepts of the law. As for the heathen, they would probably make the neglect to gather the olives the theme of the drunkard's song, a very proverb for stupid waste, to be quoted against every imprudent fool. Yet to obey Jehovah was the Israelites' highest wisdom, and in keeping the commandment there would be great reward. The Lord could readily enough increase the produce of the previous and succeeding year, and cause six crops to be far more profitable than seven; and we can well believe that he did so, as a rule, where the mandate was obeyed; and if in his highest wisdom he did not thus immediately recompense his servant, there would be such an inward satisfaction to the obedient soul that the smaller ingathering would yield larger content than a greater store. No one will ever be a real loser by God in the long run; and when he seems to be so, the true-hearted man rejoices thus to prove his loyalty to his Lord.

Still, to leave the berries on the olive-tree, must have been a trial of faith: if the crop was small, it would seem a small offence to gather them; and if large, it would be all the more difficult to avarice to leave them all for any beggar to collect. To the good man, whose store of oil was low, it would be a strong temptation to fill the oil-vessels, for fear his stock should be quite exhausted by waiting two years for more,—for two years it would be, since one year's produce was to be left ungathered, and another year would elapse before the second growth would be ready. He who kept the ordinance of God in this matter would thus be walking by faith in God as to temporal things; and this is more than many Christians are actually doing. Faith is regarded by many as having to do with spiritual things, and not with temporal matters; in their case, it deals with heavenly joys and soul difficulties, but not with corn, and wine, and olives. It seems to us that the reality of a man's faith may be tested by his bringing it to bear upon everyday life; in fact, that the faith which can let the olives go is more surely true than that which only sings psalms, and wears phylacteries. How say you, reader, can you trust God as to your fields and their crops, your business and its profits, your children and their sicknesses? Can you lose for Christ, not only the smile of worldlings, but hard cash? Can you cheerfully forego the gains of a forbidden trade, the profit of a questionable transaction? If you can only sing hymns and offer prayers, but draw back when it comes to leaving the olives, or renouncing the pelf, where is your boasted faith?

The elevated faith which led the Israelite to keep the Sabbatic year, and leave his fruit upon the trees, had respect to the word of the Lord by his servant Moses, 'Man doth not live by bread only, but by every word that proceedeth out of the mouth of the Lord doth man live.' This, in after ages, was our Lord's reply to the devil when he tempted him to turn stones into bread. Life is not sustained by outward food in and of itself, but by the power of God; therefore, if he pleases, we can live without the corn and the olives; at any rate, we will leave that matter to him, and by no means touch the forbidden thing. It seems to be necessary to gather the year's produce, but it cannot be really so: God, who fed his people in the wilderness without harvests for forty years, can surely supply them for one year if they are led by his express order to refuse the fruits of the ground. Thus faith learned to look beyond the second cause, and to cast itself upon the great First Cause, the Creator who gives to the olive its fatness, and could, if he so pleased, give to man all the nourishment and refreshment which the olive ordinarily conveys, even if no drop of oil passed his lip, or anointed his face. The Infinite God is independent of means; and when he chooses, he can bless us without them; it is ours to pass over what appears to our reason to be a needful channel of benefit, and cast ourselves immediately upon the Lord himself. It is true that he usually feeds us by means of bread, but he is not tied to this means; he usually comforts men with oil, but he is able to produce the same cheering result upon them without it. When obedience, therefore, necessitates the foregoing of the creature, we must, in unstaggering confidence, look to the bare arm of God, and send out our expectations to himself alone. 'My soul, wait thou only upon God, for my expectation is from him.' Can we do this, can we, at the call of duty, withdraw our hand from that which is doubtful, even though others freely partake? We do not here mean to enquire whether we can forego that which is actually and evidently sinful in itself, for many can do this who have no spiritual faith; but can we decline that which to others would be allowable, when we perceive that God would be more glorified by our so doing? There would have been no sin in a Philistine gathering his olives in the seventh year; and we fear that very few Israelites ever made a case of conscience of it; but the true servant of God perceives a higher law, and cheerfully obeys where others know no law. 'So did not I, because of the fear of God,' was spoken by Nehemiah in reference to the receipt of support to which he was as much entitled as any former governor of Jerusalem; for he felt himself not only bound to abstain from that which was in itself evil, but even from that which was allowable, if by such abstinence he could the better serve the Lord. Paul acted upon the same rule when he was not chargeable to the churches. Have we the grace which would enable us to trust in the Lord, and leave the olives, when according to all natural laws we have a perfect right to gather them, and even need them? If we perceive that the way of the Lord leads us to live above the ordinary rule of human prudence, can we do it? Perhaps the best reply will be, 'Lord, help us to do so! We believe, help thou our unbelief!'

To neglect means, as a rule, would be absurd and presumptuous; but there are occasions when, for the glory of God, and the instruction of our fellow-men, we may feel bound to refuse the usual means, and by prayer and supplication leave the matter entirely and specially in the hands of God. We ought, in fact, to leave all things there, even when we employ means, and this is our proper course in most cases; but we allude to peculiar positions in which we are dealing with sceptical minds, or with ignorant persons. In such cases, if we perceive that by using means we shall make them set down the Lord's work as a mere coincidence or natural result, we may feel moved to refuse altogether to stir a finger or say a word, in order that the answer to our prayer may, even to the most blinded heart, be indisputably seen to be of the Lord. There is really a command for us to do this, since it is a law of the Spirit of life in Christ Jesus that we should in all things seek the highest glory of God; but there are not many who are able so to act. They cannot leave the Sabbatic olives in order to show that God can and will supply them with oil without them. It is true there are sluggards, who make faith the pack-horse for their sloth, and are quite willing to leave the olives on the trees all the seven years; but these come not into the secret of the Lord, and deserve to starve for their wicked presumption: the men we are speaking of are diligent in business, wise in planning, energetic in managing, economical in spending; and yet, when a precept or a desire for God's glory directs them, they can sit as still as the idler, act as simply as a child, wait as patiently as a watcher for the morning, and be as profuse as a spendthrift. The act of folly and the deed of faith may seem much the same upon the surface; but, in fact, they are as widely different as light and darkness. It was no sloth which made the Israelite leave his olive-yard to itself for twelve months; it was faith at work with her greatest energy which enabled him to stand still and see the salvation of God.

The more we think of it, the more sure are we that the non-gathering of the olives during the seventh year was a remarkable display of faith, and has in it a deep spiritual lesson for all those who are born into the family of believers.

II. In the second place, it was A GRAND LESSON OF CHARITY; for the fields, the vineyards, and the olive-yards were to be left for the poor during the seventh year. It was a large liberality which left the needy a whole year's produce of the fruit trees: many would loudly complain if, one year in seven, their gains in business or their earnings in labour were to be thus disposed of. The seventh year was intended to be a sort of quit-rent to the superior Owner, even to the Lord to whom the land of Canaan belonged; and this rent was paid to the poor by his command. Corn which had shaled out in cartage took root, and sprang up, and this spontaneous harvest no proprietor of land might appropriate; he was bound to leave it that the poor might eat. Nor was the grant to stay there; the poor man was to have a taste of luxuries as well as of necessaries, and was by no means to be debarred a little wine and a little oil now that his own year was come. Some would make pauper's fare as hard as possible, and when they relieve the wants of the needy they do it with a pinching economy, as if they feared that they might make the lot of the poor too pleasant, and over-indulge the sons and daughters of penury; for our part, we are not admirers of that uncharitable charity which begrudges every penny it bestows, and is always on the watch to find a reason for withholding. God save us from many of our philanthropists, whose choicest gift to the poor is a heap of stones, or a coil of old rope to be picked into oakum! Their remedy for poverty lies in the drying up of compassion. God's political economy, as embodied in the laws of Canaan, was generous to the needy; it aimed at producing a condition in which there should be no poor; and, meanwhile, it devised liberal things for those who were driven to necessity, and among them was this arrangement that they should enjoy the spontaneous harvests of one year in seven, and should appropriate the grapes and the olives without let or hindrance. Doubtless many would refuse to yield the boon; but he who truly honoured the God of love would cheerfully admit his poor neighbours to his olive-yard, and wish them a hearty welcome. We have no such custom in our day; we are too well acquainted with political economy to do anything of the sort, for we have learned that 'the Wealth of Nations' lies in following iron rules, and allowing laws of supply and demand to grind our fellow-creatures as if they were only so much grist for our mill. While it may be admitted that indiscriminate almsgiving is an evil, we are even more sure that indiscriminate alms-refusing is a far greater one. The poor may be spoiled by unwise doles; but, in some neighbourhoods, they would seem to be more in danger of dying of starvation while the local Solomons are organizing charity! We grant the evil against which our wise men are contending, but we fear a greater which they are unwittingly propagating.

The generous-hearted Israelite would wish prosperity to the poor man's year, and pray that, as the needy might gather the olives, there might be an abundance to rejoice their hearts. On the other hand, the niggard would be glad to see a scant produce if he obeyed the command; and if the Lord sent plenty, he would break the rule, and collect the berries himself. Yet how happy must such an one as Boaz have been, if, enjoying the Sabbatic rest himself, and living on his former stores, he walked in the olive-groves, and heard the merry songs of his poor neighbours while they beat the trees, and gathered up the fruit. His own ease would be the sweeter as he saw their happiness, and his God would vouchsafe also the light of his countenance, and a peace of conscience, while he thus freely parted with the year's produce, and cheerfully said to the gleaners, 'The Lord be with you,' and received their grateful response, 'The Lord bless thee.' The picture has an air of romance about it to sordid minds, and even those who are by no means churlish, may think it drawn by an artist from Utopia; but the man who is filled with the Spirit of Jesus will revel in its beauties, and long to repeat in a manner appropriate to our own age and clime the generosities of the land of promise. Is there any joy which excels that of open-handed benevolence? Is any feast so enjoyable as that to which we invite the poor, the halt, and the blind? Are any dainties so sweet as those which are sent from the table of self-denial to the bedside of the languishing? Speak we of luxury? Commend us to the luxury of giving. Speak we of political economy? There is none so wise as being prudently liberal to the necessitous.

III. Perhaps the most charming view of the olives left unpruned and ungathered during the seventh year, is that which sees in it A DELIGHTFUL TYPE OF SPIRITUAL REST. For six years men toiled with the sweat on their faces; on the seventh, this was wiped away, and all labour was unknown. The plough no more tore up the furrow, the knife no longer bereaved the vines, and the axe struck off no boughs from the olive; the twelve months were one long, restful, and hallowed day of the Lord. Israel was favoured with her weekly Sabbath, and her frequent festivals; but the seventh year, as far as rest was concerned, was the crown of all. What would our weary nations give if it were an ordinance that they should rest during every seventh year? Alas! they are not fit to receive the boon, nor would they accept it if it were placed in their way unless they might spend it in riot and folly. We fear that very seldom, if at all, were the Jewish people observant of the institution, neither were they, as a people, worthy of it; for the same unbelief and selfishness, which led them to neglect the ordinance, rendered them unfit to enjoy the remarkable repose which they refused. Had they been spiritual, believing men, how much of benefit would they have found in keeping the commandment! That Sabbatic year might have been a little heaven to them; a foretaste, earnest, and image of the rest which remaineth for the people of God. We can form in our minds an ideal picture of a man of God walking among the olives, praising and adoring the Lord from day to day, making his whole farm a temple, wherein he himself hourly offered the sacrifice of praise for the sweet rest which he enjoyed, and for the luxury of seeing his poor neighbours gathering with delight the fruits of his garden. Then was fulfilled that glorious promise, 'Strangers shall stand and feed your flocks, and the sons of the alien shall be your plowmen and your vine-dressers; but ye shall be named the Priests of the Lord; men shall call you the Ministers of our God.'

Alas! we fear the ideal was never realized; and by disobedience the people turned the law of liberty into a yoke of bondage; yet it is pleasant to see how fair a rest was within their reach, though they entered not into it because of unbelief. Earth would have become the vestibule of heaven if they would have walked in the statutes of the Lord, not one of which was grievous. The highest and most distinctive of the Mosaic precepts were those which brought the amplest rewards, for in this case the Sabbatic rest, if truly observed, would have been in itself a delight, and would have made the Israelites' life the envy of all other races.

It is not in our power to practise literally the liberality and rest of the seventh year, but the spirit of the command is ours, and we shall do well to grasp the privilege to the full. Ceasing not only upon certain occasions, but altogether, from all servile work, let us rest in the perfect work of our Lord Jesus. Casting all our care upon him who careth for us, let us labour as though we laboured not, gather as though we gathered not; and, though working, let us not live by working, but by faith in the God of Providence and Grace. Let us sit loose by visible possessions, being willing to part with them to the poor, or to the Lord's cause, regarding them indeed as only ours upon lease, and even in that respect not as the true food of our life so that we could not do without them. Be it ours to live upon the Lord himself, looking for him to supply our needs, and viewing temporal goods as the outward husks which only contain and embody the essential sustenance of our lives, which is the divine power and love. Happy is the man who has slain anxiety by faith, who has ended care by trust. He is not his own, and lives not for himself; he looks to his Master for support, and as for himself, he is only concerned to please his Lord in all things. While others slave for outward wealth, he rejoices in the true riches; while they weary themselves with sore labour and travail, his heart is restful before the Lord. He works with his hands that he may have to give to him that needeth; and it has become his business, as a steward of the Lord, to bring forth things new and old for the nourishment of his fellow-servants. God takes care of him, and he takes care of others; resting, and as far as possible giving rest and joy to those around him. May his olive-tree be loaded with fruit, since by his abundance the poor are made rich!

The gleanings of the olives

A Mentone meditation

'When thou beatest thine olive tree, thou shalt not go over the boughs again: it shall be for the stranger, for the fatherless, and for the widow.'—Deuteronomy 24:20.

WHEN resting in the olive-groves of Mentone, I have continually heard the sound of the long cane with which the villagers were beating down the olives. I have also heard them shaking the tree at the same time, and thus I have noticed both the processes which are referred to in Scripture, namely, *beating*, as in the text; and *shaking*, as in Isaiah 24:13. The use of the stick would appear to be almost universal in olive-producing countries, although it is stated by some authorities that it has an injurious effect upon the trees; probably the natives overlook this small damage, and are swayed by the greater ease and expedition with which they obtain their fruit. The Abbot Fortis complains of the Neapolitans, that they use what he calls the absurd mode of beating the branches with long poles in order to make the olives fall; and he says, 'This foolish method, beside hurting the tree, and spoiling many branches that would bear the year following, makes the ripe and unripe fruit fall indiscriminately, and bruises a great deal of both kinds, whereby they become rancid in the heaps, and give an ill flavour to the oil.' No great importance may be attached to this remark, since the oil made at Mentone is considered to be the best in the world, and to our own taste it certainly excels every other.

Yet, while preparing this paper for the press, we met with an observation, in *The Times*, which confirms the Abbot's opinion, for a correspondent writes of the Spanish peasant:—'He complains that, of two crops, one is almost invariably a failure, and he knows that the fault lies with his barbarous method of gathering the olives by savagely threshing or tearing the branches, by which, together with this year's fruit, there falls also the pod that contains the germ for next year; yet he goes on threshing and tearing, because the civilized plan of picking the fruit one by one would give too much trouble, and "would not pay." Surely, a yearly harvest instead of an alternative yield would be compensation for much toil, and even a Spaniard is not so blind as not to see it; but he goes on gathering his olives as his father and grandfather have always done before him, and when driven hard for arguments, and convinced against his wish, he declares that his own way suits him best, and he will have none of the fiddle-faddle innovations, none of the *tonterias Inglesas* [Spanish, nonsense] about his house or property.' Let that be as it may, we have seen the method of beating in full swing, and have heard the stick going all day long.

The generous law of Moses forbade that the olive tree should be beaten twice by its owner. The fruit which fell at the first beating, if the operation was carefully performed, would be almost the whole of the crop; and the Israelites were not to be so penurious as to look with covetous eyes for every single berry, as if they were hunting for choice jewels, and could not afford to overlook the smallest. On the contrary, they were to leave what remained, to be gathered by the poor, who are described under three characters as 'the stranger', or foreigner, who possessed no land of his own, the 'fatherless', who had no paternal guardian to provide for them, and 'the widow', who, in addition to her sorrowful bereavement, suffered the straitness of poverty. This precept, like the law of the Sabbatic year,* made another opening for the display of holy charity, and would be obeyed by godly proprietors, whose trust in God enabled them to answer those arguments of economy which are so dear to miserly worldlings. They were to beat the trees, and collect the precious fruits, for this was the reward of their toil; but they were not to do this in a niggardly fashion, so as to gather the wages of covetousness. The God who gave them the land, and under whose Theocratic government they were life-tenants, made a reserve of the gleanings of the corn, and the oil, and the wine. It was a kind of rent which was to be received by the Lord's deputies; the orphans and widows had a lien upon the land, and the gleanings were their due. No doubt, the ordinary Israelite would obey the letter of the precept, but take care, with microscopic eyes, to spy out all the fruit, so that only a few scanty berries would remain. These, in missing the spirit of the command, would lose the reward which is promised to 'the liberal soul', that he 'shall be made fat': they would get the olives, but they would miss the fatness. Others would enter into the generous spirit of the precept, and leave a larger portion for their poverty-stricken neighbours; they would be sure to find a joy in the deed, and they would likewise receive a blessing upon the produce of their trees. The ordinance of gleaning was meant to suggest and promote generosity. The glorious Jehovah did not wish to be King of a nation of niggards. Labans and Nabals are not to his mind. 'God loveth a cheerful giver.' He hath said, 'Thou shalt surely give to thy poor brother, and thine heart shall not be grieved when thou givest unto him: because that for this thing the Lord thy God shall bless thee in all thy works, and in all that thou puttest thine hand unto:' and, on the other hand, he hath made it a proverb of his kingdom that 'There is that withholdeth more than is meet, but it tendeth to poverty.'

We judge that it would be Christlike if our farmers would literally keep the Mosaic command with regard to gleanings: 'When ye reap the harvest of your land, thou shalt not wholly reap the corners of thy field, neither shalt thou gather the gleanings of thy harvest.' It is pleaded that the horse-rake must be used, or that too much corn would remain in the stubble. Upon this we will not pronounce a judgment; but we do urge that something should be left that the poor of the land may gather it, especially when it is considered that, at the very utmost, the wages of the agricultural labourer are nonc too great. We feel the more at liberty to argue this point in reference to corn because we have neither olives nor vines, and therefore, if, from the nature of our climate, there is but one kind of fruit of the earth which can be gleaned, the precept should certainly be observed in reference to that one. Let Christian farmers think of this matter in the light of that text, 'He that hath pity upon the poor lendeth unto the Lord; and that which he hath given will he pay him again;' and that other word spoken by the prophet, 'The liberal deviseth liberal things; and by liberal things shall he stand.'

'Be not too narrow, husbandman! but fling
From the full sheaf, with charitable stealth,
The liberal handful. Think, oh! grateful think,
How good the God of harvest is to you,
Who pours abundance o'er your flowing fields,
While these unhappy partners of your kind

Wide-hover round you, like the fowls of heaven,
And ask their humble dole.'
(From James Thompson's *Autumn*)

There were, doubtless, many churls who would say, 'We do not object to the poor gleaning the corn, for they have need of bread, and must eat; but why should we leave the grapes for them? Are the poor to be furnished with luxuries? Must they needs have fruit and wine at our expense? As to the olives, they can eat their bread dry; why need we give them a relish with their food, of which they will, no doubt, eat quite enough without the aid of oil?' It would be idle to answer such persons, for their real argument lies in their penurious nature; but to generous minds, it is sufficient to remark that God has given to the poor the same tastes as ourselves, he has given them a palate, and a capacity to relish the sweetness of the grape, and the fatness of the olive, and these tastes and appetites are no more sinful in them than in ourselves. Are the desires which are natural to poor men and women never to be satisfied? Are they given to them to become sources of misery by never being gratified? Is a human being to be condemned perpetually to the barest fare? It is a sad heart indeed which never rejoices, but lives like a prisoner throughout all its life. If dry bread be all or even more than the miser's charity can accord, it is not so much as the ever-merciful God awards to the needy. He would have the stranger, the fatherless, and the widow refreshed, like the rest of his creatures, with corn, and wine, and oil; and our Lord Jesus not only bids us give to the poor, but he commands us to feast them when we are having special times of rejoicing in our houses.

After all, the olive gleanings were no great luxury, for the berries left for the poor would probably be of a kind of which only a small proportion would yield such oil as would be fit for food; the bulk would be mainly used for light and fuel. The widow would thus be able to trim her little lamp during the dismal nights of winter, and to cook her mess of pottage and bitter herbs when no fire burned on the hearth. The Lord knows and cares for the wants of the needy, and those who are truly like him have the same considerate heart. The great God finds a sweetness in benevolence, and he will cause the generous to participate in his happiness, for he has said, 'If thou draw out thy soul to the hungry, and satisfy the afflicted soul; then shall thy light rise in obscurity, and thy darkness be as the noon day: and the Lord shall guide thee continually, and satisfy thy soul in drought, and make fat thy bones: and thou shalt be like a watered garden, and like a spring of water, whose waters fail not.' (Isaiah 58:10–11.) Let us not be slow to secure the blessings of this promise by fulfilling its conditions.

It is worthy of observation that the owner of the olive trees was not commanded carefully to gather all the fruit, and then make a judicious distribution of it. The probability is that, in that case, his judiciousness would have led him to the conclusion that it was best to keep it all for himself. The command was that he should leave the berries ungathered, and then permit the poor to enter the olive-garden, and gather for themselves. This did not render the charity altogether indiscriminate, since there was a degree of labour involved in the beating down of the berries by the poor; and, consequently, the more industrious would be likely to obtain the larger portion of the spoils; but still, there could not, in the nature of things, be any rigid scrutiny; those who first came were first served, and all who would might partake. If a man saw a wealthy neighbour base enough to mingle with the poor, so as to filch from them their portion, he would probably warn him off; or more likely still, the clamours of the needy would sufficiently protect that which was left for their gleaning: but, with this exception, all might come. We feel very jealous for the freedom of almsgiving. Of course, we have no objection to the 'organization' of charity; but we have our suspicions that, with some, organization of charity means the extermination of charity. We fear that, in some cases, the net result of their organic arrangement has been the shutting up of their bowels of compassion, and the fabrication of a plausible excuse for so doing. Matthew Henry has wisely commented upon the precept thus, 'Say not, "What I give, I will give, and know to whom I give it. Why should I leave it to be gathered by I know not whom, that will never thank me?" But trust God's providence with the disposal of thy charity; perhaps that will direct it to the most necessitous.' To encourage imposition by the almsgiving which is utterly indiscriminate, is censurable, for it turns virtue into a vice, and causes our good to be evil spoken of; but, on the other hand, to spend more time and money in sifting out the unworthy than in helping the unfortunate, is a folly and a crime, and the tendency of the present age is much in that direction. It were better that the undeserving should filch our alms than that suffering virtue should be left to pine in wretched want. Open the gate, and let the stranger, the fatherless, and the widow come in, and take their portion. God wills it; let us will it, too.

Let no one object that our text is a command of the old law, for in spirit it is worthy of the New Testament, and is consonant with the words of our Master, who said, 'Give, and it shall be given unto you; good measure, pressed down, and shaken together, and running over, shall men give into your bosom:' 'Give alms of such things as ye have; and, behold, all things are clean unto you:' 'When thou makest a feast, call the poor, the maimed, the lame, the blind: and thou shalt be blessed; for they cannot recompense thee: for thou shalt be recompensed at the resurrection of the just.' The great apostle of the Gentiles pressed upon us the same duty when he said, 'Charge them that are rich in this world … that they do good, that they be rich in good works, ready to distribute, willing to communicate; laying up in store for themselves a good foundation against the time to come, that they may lay hold on eternal life:' and again, 'He which soweth sparingly shall reap also sparingly; and he which soweth bountifully shall reap also bountifully … God loveth a cheerful giver.'

The moral and spiritual teachings of this gracious precept are not far to find. It teaches us, first, *a generous remembrance of the needy at all times;* but especially when we ourselves are gathering the fruit of our labours, or in other words, when we are receiving supplies from the bounteous Giver of all good. If we are ourselves prospering, it should be our desire that others should be partakers of the benefit. It would be unseemly that, when harvests are bountiful, the labourer should be none the better off. If we may not muzzle the mouth of the ox, much less may we close the mouth of the man. When business succeeds, and brings in larger profits than usual, workmen and clerks should be remembered promptly and cheerfully. The distribution of a *bonus* is a happy and commendable practice, and we are pleased to see that some of our largest firms attend to it. It is true that, in these hard days of political economy, the workers usually remember themselves quite soon enough, and are at times unreasonable in their demands for higher wages; if this be wrong on their part, it must not be balanced by another wrong, namely, by harshness and niggardliness on the part of the employer. We are simple-minded enough to hope that generosity displayed by the masters would at least have a tendency to mitigate the rigour of the unkind relations which now exist between two mutually dependent classes; at any rate, let it be tried, and tried again, and let it be shown that the love of Christ in the heart of godly business men is not to be quenched by all the cold water which ingratitude can throw upon it. In all transactions, it is better to err on the side of generosity to the poor than to earn the name of 'a hard man.' There are little perquisites and minute discounts, which excessively prudent men take care to sweep into their own pockets, eagerly hunting up every solitary farthing which might perchance find its way into another man's purse; but we have no admiration for such beggarly economy. Bargains are often so hardly driven that there is scarcely a margin of profit, even though it must be within the knowledge of the trader that the person whom he thus tightly presses will be driven to the verge of starvation.

How can this be justified in men who profess to be under the law of love? We need not mention instances; but the spirit of the precept is capable of very wide application. When we are travelling, we prefer to pay a little more rather than a little less to the numerous persons whose acts of courtesy and kindness are needful to make the journey pleasant. If we are anxious to save, let us stop at home; but if we go on a pleasure-trip, let us give pleasure as well as receive it. We have observed fellow-travellers, who appear to lose the rest and enjoyment of their sojourn abroad by continually meditating, from morning to night, and probably through the night, upon the all-important question of how they can save half a franc, or by some means rescue a *centime* from the hand of a poor waiter or servant. Both in getting and spending there is such a thing as going over the boughs of the olive trees again with a very thick stick, with very heavy blows, and plenty of them. We have no desire to learn the secret joy which lies in the skinflint's bosom. We suggest that Christians should never exact all that they have a right to, when the contract bears hardly on the other party; nor should they be content to supply just what bare justice demands, but give a little more than is strictly due. Customary gifts to servants, who call with parcels, or who attend us in a friend's house, should not be forgotten, lest religion should get a bad name through our omissions. We must never be of the Gradgrind family, nor act upon the rule of the bare knife-board; it is our privilege to be good to all, yea, even to the unthankful and the evil, that so we may prove that we are the children of our Father who is in heaven.

The divine command may also suggest to us *the beauty of a kind consideration of those who are poor and needy in spiritual things*. When we are preaching the gospel, we beat down from the olive tree the rich ripe fruit of the doctrines of grace; but we should remember that there are some who, through their weakness in the faith, are not able to participate with us in the higher truths; we ought therefore to remember them, and permit them to share in other portions of the Divine Word more suited to their capacities. There should be handfuls let fall on purpose for the trembling and the desponding; we should not be so strict in the description of character as to hand over every cluster of the spiritual vine to a small company of rich saints, but we should leave bunches of the grapes of Eshcol for those whose evidences are dim, whose faith is feeble, and who but for our thoughtfulness concerning them would exclude themselves from all heavenly comfort. It is true that the comfort of the text may chiefly belong to a certain character; but be not so rigid as to shut out the humble souls who dare not put in their claim for a share in it. Leave some olives on the tree. Do not beat the text too closely.

Nor is the lesson for the preacher only; it ill becomes the hearer of the Word to be always clamorous to be himself fed under every sermon, especially if he is well instructed in the faith, and if a relish for the mysteries of the kingdom has been given to him. He must not be so selfish as to complain when the more elementary truths are preached again and again. What if they do not feed him? Are the olive trees of the Word to be so beaten for him that nothing shall remain for others? Are there not feebler folk who need spiritual sustenance? What if he be no longer a babe in grace, and having grown to ripe manhood, is able to digest the strong meat? Yet let him not demand of his Master's steward that he should always set strong meat, and nothing else, on the table. Let the babes be fed with milk even if the man of perfect stature cares not to partake of it. Let the humble soul have his portion; yea, let even the stranger who is within the gates of the Lord's house have a share in the produce of Emmanuel's land. We have known some who appeared to be utterly thoughtless of everybody but themselves: their one test of a sermon is their own profiting by it, and they never think that other classes beside instructed believers are to be considered by the true pastor. They demand that we shall beat the olive trees scores of times to get every berry for them alone: they even want us to extort more from our texts than they truly yield, by beating them with the rod of spiritualizing; and, meanwhile, the poor in spirit are to be left to shift for themselves, that these 'dear people of God' may be surfeited. We scorn to be subservient to their unchristian greed. Misers who hoard their gold are rightly despised; but what shall we say of those who would monopolize the Word of God? Our heart is not in the slightest sympathy with them; we hope ever to leave large gleanings for the poor of the kingdom, and never to gather all the olives for those who are in their own opinion rich and increased in goods.

In preaching, of what is thought to be a high order, there is too frequently a forgetfulness of the uninstructed. Words are used which are only understood by the cultured, and phrases are employed which are like another tongue to the common people. Where such preaching is natural, we will not indulge a censure upon it; but we earnestly maintain that at least some portions of every religious discourse ought to be so simple that the most illiterate should be able to understand them, and profit by them. There should be some gleanings even for the children, a bunch of grapes for the eager mouth of the hopeful boy, a few olives for the poor aged widow, a handful of corn for the weary labourer, a portion for seven, and also for eight. To forget the lowlier classes in our ministrations, will be to sin against the Lord. It is the glory of the dispensation of Christ that 'the poor have the gospel preached unto them,' and yet it would seem, in the judgment of too many, to be the glory of the pulpit if its teaching is only suited to the *élite,* and if the pews around it are never occupied by the peasant or the artizan. We would far sooner use such 'great plainness of speech' as to appear to neglect the refined classes, than that we would be chargeable with the 'wisdom of words', or with casting a veil over the truth so that the multitude are unable to perceive it. O ye masters of Israel, think of this, and in the largeness of your hearts act accordingly!

Another bearing of the same precept would lead us, in our arrangements for public teaching and evangelization, largely to *consider them that are without, in the depths of spiritual poverty.* Provision must certainly be made for Christian people, for their families, and for those who attach themselves to our congregations; yet, when this is done, all is not accomplished. Let the olives be well beaten for the household, and let the children have their portion in due season; but we must also think of the stranger, and lay ourselves out for the neglected classes. The City of God is not a close borough, imprisoned within gateless walls, within which provender is to be hoarded, while the famine rages without. No, the leaves of the tree of life are for the healing of the nations, and the gospel is a feast for those who lie in the highways and hedges. By some means, the careless crowds must be brought under the sound of the truth; and if they will not come to us, we must go to them, and preach Christ in the marketplace, or even in the theatre and the music-hall. No single class should be forgotten, and the poorest and most degraded should lie heaviest upon our hearts. They need the light, and they must have their share of the oil, and of the olives. Some churches appear to beat their trees only for their seat-holders; but it must not be so among us, we must gather together the outcasts of Israel, and have it said of us as it was of our great Exemplar, 'Then drew near unto him all the publicans and sinners for to hear him.'

The subject grows upon our consideration when we remember the teeming millions of the heathen world, for whom but few olives are left when the Christian Church is gathering her fruit. Alas! the money spent upon heathendom is far too little even in proportion to that which is spent at home, and that is none too great. When we are ourselves being fed with the finest of the wheat, can we not spare a sheaf for China? When our faces are made to shine with the anointing oil, have we no oil for India and Japan? And when we are gathering the clusters of Eshcol, and satisfying our mouths with the good things of the Lord's vineyard, have we no grapes for the parched lips of Africa, no draught of the wine of consolation for the dying millions of South America? Surely, there is no need to press the point; but, henceforth, Israelites indeed will not plead home claims as a reason for stinting missionary contributions. Leave a fair share of olives for the stranger; and may the Lord therefore send a blessing on the whole olive-yard, according to his wont!

Note

* See *The Sword and the Trowel,* January, 1893 (i.e. the previous chapter of this volume).

Chapter 25

A land of oil olive

An address delivered and revised at Mentone

'A land of wheat, and barley, and vines, and fig trees, and pomegranates; a land of oil olive, and honey.'—Deuteronomy 8:8.

TO the grateful mind, it is very pleasant to observe what a variety of fruits God has prepared for the delectation of man. He has not only commanded the earth to bring forth wheat and barley that men may eat bread without scarceness, but also fruits sweet and pleasant to the appetite, and other products which serve for divers uses according to man's multiplied necessities. God's thoughts towards us are full of liberality; he not only supplies his creatures with necessaries, but he gives them luxuries in abundance. He indulges their sense of beauty, and their longing for variety; and does not bind them down to workhouse fare, or Spartan diet. How thoughtful has God been that his creatures may be rendered happy! He is 'the happy God' himself, and he delights to rule a happy empire.

The wisdom and power of God are also admirably illustrated by the production of such a variety of fruits from the same soil, by the same sun and showers. It must always remain one of the marvels of nature that from one common plot of ground should spring such different fruits as the fig, the olive, and the pomegranate; and that such a profusion of flowers of varied hues and forms and properties should be produced out of the same garden. What a marvel, too, that so vast a variety of blossoms should all combine for the creation of honey by the agency of such tiny creatures as bees, who in the East produce it in such abundance that the land literally flows with it! We need not lift our eyes to heaven to discover proofs of the goodness and greatness of God in the sun, moon, and stars; but we may even see them at our own table, when we sit down to partake of the fruits of the earth. If in revelation there are great marvels which exercise our faith, there are certainly equal wonders in nature which we see with our eyes. We believe the witness of our senses, but the witness of God is greater: will we reject it because of the difficulties caused by the limitation of our powers? Nay, rather, as we do not permit the mysteries of nature to prevent our partaking of its blessings, so we will not be hindered by the mysteries of grace from accepting its diviner benefits. When the infidel shall have explained how the same country yields from a like soil such a variety of distinct substances as corn, fruit, oil, and honey, he may then refuse to believe in the miracles of Scripture, and in the wonders wrought by the Holy Spirit; but not till then.

Canaan appears to have been a country rich beneath its surface with various minerals, and equally wealthy above ground in all kinds of precious fruits. It was a symbol of that happy condition into which the Lord brings his believing people, a type indeed of our Lord Jesus Christ, in whom we dwell, and in whom we discover all manner of goodness. 'We which have believed do enter into rest,' and that rest is found in Christ. Better than Canaan is the inheritance of the faithful. In our Lord we find food more nourishing than bread; he is as sweet to us as the fig, and as refreshing as the pomegranate; we find in him our anointing, for he is the true olive; and he is as delicious as the virgin honey. 'The name of Jesus,' says Bernard, 'is not only light, but food; it is likewise oil; without it, all the food of the soul is dry; it is salt, unseasoned by which whatever is presented to us is insipid; it is honey in the mouth, melody in the ear, joy in the heart, and medicine in the soul, and there are no charms in any discourse in which his name is not heard.'

We need not go abroad to find dainties, for sitting at home we discover everything in the Lord Jesus. The Israelites were so richly supplied that they were able to export oil to Egypt where none was produced, and even to supply Tyre and Sidon, which 'country was nourished by the king's country;' so, believers send forth great stores of rich things to all the nations of the earth, but they need not borrow from any one of them. Neither the philosophy of Greece, nor the power of Rome, nor the magnificence of India, is a subject of envy to us who possess the all-sufficiency of the spiritual Canaan, for Christ is all to us. The Israelites had all the common blessings of life, and in addition the supreme benediction of heaven; and in Christ Jesus we have things present and things to come, and we are complete in him.

All the various orders and grades of Christians may find in their Lord all that they desire. While they are yet children, he feeds them with butter and honey; and when they become men fit for contests and labours, he refreshes them and strengthens them as with the anointing of oil. The subject is a very tempting one to linger upon; we will only say that, the more by experience we know of Christ Jesus, the more shall we be filled with grateful wonder at the boundless variety and infinite all-sufficiency of blessedness which is stored up in him. 'It pleased the Father that in him should all fulness dwell,' 'and of his fulness have all we received, and grace for grace.'

'All things are ours; the gift of God,
The purchase of a Saviour's blood;
While the good Spirit shows us how
To use and to improve them too.'

While we admire the many blessings which our heavenly Canaan yields us, we must not forget that in any one of the many mercies there will be found a multitude of mercies compacted and condensed. There are many good things in any one good thing which is bestowed upon us by the covenant of grace; each of them is what George Herbert calls—

'A box where sweets compacted lie.'

We take the 'oil olive' as an apt illustration of this; for it was useful in so many ways. It was *eaten* by the people in their repasts, and the olives of Judæa were highly esteemed as the most delicate of their kind. It was used by the natives in the same manner as our own countrymen use butter and other animal fats. Bread and oil were regarded as quite sufficient for an ordinary meal; and those of us who have learned to enjoy it can speak highly in its praise. Thus is Christ Jesus the rich food of the soul.

'E'en as with marrow, and with fat,
    My soul shall fillèd be;
Then shall my mouth, with joyful lips,
    Sing praises unto thee.'

The Orientals also used olive oil for *anointing*, to relieve weariness, and to give increased strength. In the wrestlings and journeyings of our daily conflict and pilgrimage, we find the most delightful refreshment in communion with Christ. He prevents our being weary of life, and worn down with its sorrows; and in fellowship with him our youth is renewed, and our strength is increased. The Easterns used oil, when saturated with sweet perfumes, to add the pleasure of fragrance to their feasts. Olive oil having a peculiar power of preserving odours, it was the vehicle in which they were ordinarily contained; and when poured upon the heads of the guests, the whole room was filled with the aroma. Verily, the name of Jesus is like ointment poured forth, therefore do the virgins love him. The most exquisite delight of the senses is but a poor figure of the rapturous joys of believers when Jesus manifests himself to them as he does not unto the world. One drop of his love is enough, not only to perfume all the earth, but even heaven itself.

Olive oil was, moreover, used as *medicine*. It was thought to possess a suppling and healing virtue, and the opinion is justified by the apostolic prescription, 'Is any sick among you?' says James, 'let him call for the elders of the church; and let them pray over him, anointing him with oil in the name of the Lord.' The good Samaritan poured oil and wine into the wounds of the man who had been almost killed by the robbers on the road to Jericho. Probably there is far more medical virtue about oil than is believed in by the bulk of modern physicians, although they also speak of it in its outward use as an emollient vehicle for liniments and other external applications, and of its service in burns and scalds to protect the injured surface from the action of the air. It is also employed as an antidote in cases of poisoning. It acts by enveloping the virus, and sheathing the living surface, thus mechanically obstructing absorption.

Externally applied, it is sometimes useful in preventing, or at least relieving, the ill effects produced by the stings of insects. Dr F. J. Farre says that 'the obstruction which it causes to the absorption of poison is often very serviceable, and is sometimes sufficient to prevent any bad effects from following. I have often applied oil to the recent sting of a wasp or bee even after the pain has extended from the wounded finger to the entire arm, and have always found the pain cease after a few minutes. It has sometimes returned for a day or two, immediately after washing the hands, until oil was again applied to the wound.' We might readily enlarge this testimony; but it will suffice to spiritualize it by the remark that Jesus Christ is a 'cure-all.' When we are anointed by his grace, evils are prevented, wounds are healed, and the sting of sin is removed. In all times of soul-sorrow, we may fly to him, and find immediate relief. It has been asserted that oil, when freely used internally and externally, is a preservative against the plague. Mr Jackson relates that the coolies who are employed in the oil-stores at Tunis smear themselves all over with oil, and are seldom afflicted with the plague when it rages in that city. Experiments were made at Morocco, in the year 1819, which proved the efficacy of oil as a plague preventive when taken internally. Assuredly, the deadly plague of reigning sin cannot come near the man who receives the grace of our Lord Jesus Christ in its fulness.

Once again, olive oil was continually used by the peasantry of Palestine for *lighting* their houses. When we read in the Scriptures of candles and candlesticks, we must not imagine that the people used animal fat as we do; but they burnt olive oil. Need we say that our glorious Lord is our light? 'In him was life; and the life was the light of men.' He said of himself, 'I am the Light of the world.' Blessed and happy are they who find all the light for their minds and hearts in him!

Thus have we, in a very cursory manner, shown how varied are the blessings contained in one blessing of our gracious God. Be it ours, by a happy experimental acquaintance with divine truth, to be continually making new discoveries of how the all-sufficiency of Christ may be turned to account in all the phases of our trials, weaknesses, sins, and necessities! We know but in part as yet, but every day should add to our knowledge; meanwhile, we are lost in admiration of the marvellous preciousness of the Lord Jesus to them that believe in him.

* = NOT REPRESENTED ELSEWHERE IN SPURGEON'S SERMONS

(expanded & corrected)

An asterisk (*) after a sermon number indicates explanatory material at the end of the chronological index. Entries *in italics* identify weekdays other than Thursday evenings; references to S&T give the month and year of other dated sermons published in *The Sword and the Trowel*. References to BV63 are to *C H Spurgeon's Sermons Beyond Volume 63*. On a few occasions only the text of a sermon is known from contemporary accounts. N/A indicates that another preached.

1853

	Sunday a.m. p.m.	Weekday
18 Dec:	2 in autobiography	
	(incl. BV63 no.41)	

1854

	Sunday a.m. p.m.	Weekday
28 Apr:	COMMENCED PASTORATE	
		20 Jul: S&T 2/02
		27 Jul: S&T 3/02
20 Aug:	2896*	
27 Aug:	2875*	
03 Sep:	3108	
17 Sep:	3120*	
15 Oct:	3114*	
05 Nov:	2908	
24 Dec:	2392	2915

1855

	Sunday a.m.	p.m.	Weekday
07 Jan:	1	2	*10 Jan: BV63 no.40*
14 Jan:	3		
21 Jan:	4	5	
28 Jan:	10		
04 Feb:	6		
11 Feb:	7–8		
18 Feb:	9		

25 Feb:	11		
04 Mar:	12		
11 Mar:	13		
18 Mar:	14	15	
25 Mar:	16		
01 Apr:	17		*03 Apr: 3139*
08 Apr:	18		
15 Apr:	19		*18 Apr: S&T 10/89*
22 Apr:	20		
29 Apr:	21		
13 May:	22	23	
20 May:	24	25	
27 May:	26	27	
03 Jun:	28		
10 Jun:	29		
17 Jun:	30		*18 Jun: 3126*
24 Jun:	31		
01 Jul:	32		
08 Jul:	33		
TOUR OF NORTH & SCOTLAND (including GLASGOW:			
29 Jul: *Penny Pulpit*	no.2402	no.2403)	
05 Aug:	34		
12 Aug:	35		
19 Aug:	36		
26 Aug:	37		*29 Aug: 3133*
02 Sep:	41–42		*04 Sep: 39–40*
09 Sep:	43		
16 Sep:	38		20 Sep: 2581*
23 Sep:	44	2651*	
07 Oct:	45		
14 Oct:	46		
21 Oct:	47		
28 Oct:	48		
04 Nov:		49	
11 Nov:	53		
18 Nov:	50	2554	

25 Nov:	51	2563	
02 Dec:	52	54	
09 Dec:	55		
16 Dec:	56		
23 Dec:	57		
30 Dec:	58	2602	*31 Dec: 59*

| Undated Sunday p.m. | S&T 1/96 |
| Late Thursday | 2703* |

1856

	Sunday a.m.	p.m.	Weekday
06 Jan:	60	2567	
HONEYMOON IN PARIS			
20 Jan:	61–62		
27 Jan:	63		
03 Feb:	64		
10 Feb:	65		
17 Feb:	66–67	3042	*20 Feb: S&T 3/97*
24 Feb:	68		
02 Mar:	69		*14 Mar: S&T 11/99*
16 Mar:	70		
23 Mar:	71		
30 Mar:	72*	Ps. 126:1–2	03 Apr: N/A
06 Apr:	73 (*-dated 30 Mar a.m.)		
13 Apr:	74		
20 Apr:	75		*23 Apr: S&T 8/96 (BRIGHTON)*
27 Apr:	76		
04 May:	77		
11 May:	79		
18 May:	80		22 May: 78
25 May:	81–82		
01 Jun:	83		
08 Jun:		84	
15 Jun:	86	85	

22 Jun:	87	88	
29 Jun:	89	90	
06 Jul:	91	92	
VISIT TO SCOTLAND			
03 Aug:	93		
10 Aug:	95	96	
17 Aug:	97	98	
24 Aug:	100	102	*25 Aug: 94*
31 Aug:	103	108	*03 Sep: S&T 9/97*
07 Sep:	117		11 Sep: S&T 7/93
14 Sep:	3093	219	18 Sep: S&T 8/93
21 Sep:		221	25 Sep: 99
28 Sep:		367	16 Oct: S&T 9/93
19 Oct:	3036	Proverbs 3:33	
IN SHOCK AFTER MUSIC HALL DISASTER			
02 Nov:	101	2562	
09 Nov:	284		*11 Nov: 2598*
			13 Nov: S&T 10/93
16 Nov:	220	S&T 1/94	
23 Nov:	104		
30 Nov:	105		
07 Dec:	106		11 Dec: S&T 5/94
14 Dec:	107		
21 Dec:	109		
28 Dec:	110		

Untimed	BV63 no.42 (=S&T 10/99); S&T 3/95, 3/96, 2–3/00
Undated Sunday a.m.	2589, 3048*
Undated Sunday p.m.	2594; S&T 1/95
Undated weekday	S&T 5/96
Early untimed	2572
Early Thursday	2576
Autumn evening	2585

1857

Sunday a.m.   p.m.   Weekday

04 Jan:	111		
11 Jan:	112		
18 Jan:	113		
25 Jan:	114		
01 Feb:	115		
08 Feb:	116		
15 Feb:	VOICE FAILED		
22 Feb:	118		*24 Feb: Brighton Pulpit no.116 (WORTHING)*
01 Mar:	119		
08 Mar:	120	121	
15 Mar:	122		
22 Mar:	123	125	
29 Mar:	124		
05 Apr:	126		
12 Apr:	127		
19 Apr:	128		
26 Apr:	129		*29 Apr: 2625*
03 May:	130		
10 May:	131		*11 May: S&T 7/94 14 May: S&T 9/94*
17 May:	132		
24 May:	133		
31 May:	134	147	
07 Jun:	135		*8 Jun: S&T 11/94*
14 Jun:	136		
21 Jun:	137		
28 Jun:	138		
05 Jul:	139		
12 Jul:	140		
19 Jul:	141–142		
26 Jul:	143		
02 Aug:	144	2634	
09 Aug:	145		
16 Aug:	146		

23 Aug:	148		
30 Aug:	149		03 Sep: S&T 7–8/99
			(ROSS-ON-WYE)
06 Sep:	150		
13 Sep:	151		
20 Sep:	152		
27 Sep:	153		
04 Oct:	156	157	*07 Oct: 154–155*
11 Oct:	158		
18 Oct:	159		
25 Oct:	160		
01 Nov:	161		05 Nov: 178
08 Nov:	162	174	
15 Nov:	163		
22 Nov:	164		*24 Nov: 2836**
29 Nov:	165		
06 Dec:	166		
13 Dec:	167		
20 Dec:	168		
27 Dec:	169		

Undated Sunday p.m.	2639
Early untimed	2607, 2615
Early Thursday	2611
Early Sunday p.m.	2616, 2621
Summer Sunday p.m.	2629
Autumn Sunday p.m.	2642, 2647
Winter Sunday p.m.	2656

1858

	Sunday a.m.	p.m.	Weekday
03 Jan:	170	2660	
10 Jan:	171		
17 Jan:	172		
24 Jan:	173		
31 Jan:	175	2664*	*05 Feb: S&T 7–8/00*

07 Feb:	176	
14 Feb:	177	
21 Feb:	179	180
28 Feb:	181	
07 Mar:	182	
14 Mar:	183	
21 Mar:	184	
28 Mar:	185	
04 Apr:	186	*07 Apr: S&T 3/98*
		07 Apr: S&T 11/98
		(BOTH HALIFAX)
11 Apr:	187	
18 Apr:	188	
25 Apr:	189	*28 Apr: 190*
02 May:	191	*04 May: 192*
09 May:	193	
16 May:	194	
23 May:	195	
30 May:	196	
06 Jun:	197	*11 Jun: 198+199*
13 Jun:	200	
20 Jun:	201	
27 Jun:	202	
04 Jul:	203	
11 Jul:	204	
18 Jul:	205	
25 Jul:	206	
01 Aug:	207	
08 Aug:	208	
15 Aug:	209	
22 Aug:	210	
29 Aug:	211	
05 Sep:	212	
12 Sep:	213	
19 Sep:	214	
26 Sep:	215	217

03 Oct:	216	
10 Oct:	218	
SICKNESS		
07 Nov:	222	
14 Nov:	223	
21 Nov:	224	
28 Nov:	225	226
05 Dec:	227	
12 Dec:	228	
19 Dec:	229	
26 Dec:	230	

Early Sunday p.m.	2673
Early Thursday	2668, 2677
Summer Thursday	2681, 2686, 2690, 2759
August untimed	S&T 9/95* (BELFAST)
Autumn Sunday p.m.	2695, 2700
Winter Thursday	2707

Winter 1858–1859

Thursday	2711

1859

	Sunday a.m.	p.m.	Weekday
02 Jan:	231	232	
09 Jan:	233	244	
16 Jan:	234	239	
23 Jan:	235	282	
30 Jan:	236	254	
06 Feb:	237	262	
13 Feb:	238		
TOUR OF SCOTLAND			
27 Feb:	240		
06 Mar:	241		
13 Mar:	242		
20 Mar:	243		

27 Mar:	245	
03 Apr:	246	
10 Apr:	247	
17 Apr:	248	
24 Apr:	249	
01 May:	250	
08 May:	251	
15 May:	252	
22 May:	253	
29 May:	255	
05 Jun:	256	
12 Jun:	257	
19 Jun:	258	
26 Jun:	259	
03 Jul:	260	
10 Jul:	261	Afternoon: S&T 5/97 (CLAPHAM COMMON)
17 Jul:	263	*20 Jul: S&T 9/98 (CASTLETON)*
24 Jul:	264	
31 Jul:	265	
07 Aug:	266	
14 Aug:	267	*16 Aug: 268–270*
21 Aug:	271	
28 Aug:	272	
04 Sep:	273	
11 Sep:	274	
18 Sep:	275	
25 Sep:	276	
02 Oct:	277	
09 Oct:	278	
16 Oct:	279	
23 Oct:	280	
30 Oct:	281	
06 Nov:	288	
13 Nov:	283	

20 Nov:	285	
27 Nov:	286	
04 Dec:	287	
11 Dec:	289	
18 Dec:	290	
25 Dec:	291	

Untimed	S&T 5/95
Early Thursday:	2715, 2720, 2724, 2728
Summer Sunday p.m.	2733
Summer Thursday	2737, 2741
August undated	BV63 no.43 (=S&T 1/02)*
Autumn Sunday p.m.	2754
Autumn Thursday	2746, 2750
Winter Thursday	2763, 2766

Winter 1859–1860

Sunday p.m.	2772

1860

	Sunday a.m.	p.m.	Weekday
01 Jan:	292		
08 Jan:	293		
15 Jan:	294	319	
22 Jan:	295		
29 Jan:	296		
05 Feb:	297–298		09 Feb: PARIS
12 Feb:	299		
19 Feb:	300		
26 Feb:	301		
04 Mar:	302		
11 Mar:	303		
18 Mar:	304		
25 Mar:	305	320	
01 Apr:	306		
08 Apr:	307	321	*12 Apr: Penny*

			Pulpit no.3289
15 Apr:	308	310	
22 Apr:	309	322	
		324(?)	
29 Apr:	311		03 May: 312
06 May:	313		*09 May: 314*
13 May:	315		
20 May:	316		
27 May:	317	323	
03 Jun:	318	325	
HOLIDAY ON CONTINENT			
29 Jul:	326	337	
05 Aug:	327		
12 Aug:	328		
19 Aug:	329		*21 Aug: 331–332*
26 Aug:	330		
02 Sep:	333		06 Sep: HOLYHEAD
09 Sep:	334		
16 Sep:	335		
23 Sep:	336		
30 Sep:	338		
07 Oct:	339		
14 Oct:	340		
21 Oct:	341		
28 Oct:	343		
04 Nov:	344		
11 Nov:	345		
18 Nov:	346		
25 Nov:	347		
02 Dec:	348		
09 Dec:	349		
16 Dec:	350		
23 Dec:	352		
30 Dec:	353		*31 Dec: JOSHUA 5:12*
Spring Sunday p.m.	2776, 2780		

Summer Sunday p.m.   2789
Summer Thursday   2785
Winter Sunday p.m.   2794, 2798

Winter 1860–1861
Sunday p.m.   2802, 2807

1861

	Sunday a.m.	p.m.	Weekday
			01 Jan: S&T 1–2/99
06 Jan:	354		
13 Jan:	355		
20 Jan:	356		
27 Jan:	357		
03 Feb:	358		
10 Feb:	359		
17 Feb:	361	362	21 Feb: 3434*
24 Feb:	363	364	
TOUR OF NORTH & SCOTLAND			
17 Mar:	365	2815*	
24 Mar:	366	2811	*25 Mar: 369*
			29 Mar: 373+374
31 Mar:	368	375	04 Apr: N/A
07 Apr:	379		11 Apr: CHAIRED
14 Apr:	382		
21 Apr:	383		
28 Apr:	384		
05 May:	391		
12 May:	392		
19 May:	393		
26 May:	394		
02 Jun:	395		
REST IN THE COUNTRY			
16 Jun:	396		
23 Jun:	397		*25 Jun: S&T 11/95*
			(SWANSEA)

30 Jun:	398		
07 Jul:	399		
14 Jul:	400		
21 Jul:	401		
28 Jul:	402		
04 Aug:	403		
11 Aug:	404	413	
18 Aug:	405		
25 Aug:	406		29 Aug: S&T 10/98
01 Sep:	407		
08 Sep:	408		
15 Sep:	409		
22 Sep:	410		
29 Sep:	411		
06 Oct:	412		
20 Oct:	414	415	
27 Oct:	416		
03 Nov:	417		
10 Nov:	418		
17 Nov:	419		
24 Nov:	420		
01 Dec:	421		
08 Dec:	422	423	
15 Dec:	424	425	
22 Dec:	430	426	

Apr-Dec Sunday p.m.	3068
Early Sunday p.m.	2819
Summer Sunday p.m.	2828, 2833
Summer Thursday	2823, 2841
Autumn Sunday p.m.	2872

Winter 1861–1862

Sunday p.m.	2880, 2885, 2889, 2894, 2898
Thursday	2868

1862

	Sunday a.m.	p.m.	Weekday
05 Jan:	427		
12 Jan:	428		
19 Jan:	429		
26 Jan:	431	440	30 Jan: 432
02 Feb:	433		
09 Feb:	434		
16 Feb:	435		
23 Feb:	436		
02 Mar:	437		
09 Mar:	438		
16 Mar:	439		
23 Mar:	441		
30 Mar:	442	446	
06 Apr:	443		
13 Apr:	444		
20 Apr:	445		
27 Apr:	447	452	
04 May:	448		
11 May:	449		
18 May:	450		
25 May:	451	456	
01 Jun:	453		
15 Jun:	454		*18 Jun: 455*
22 Jun:	457		
29 Jun:	458	2924*	
06 Jul:	459		
13 Jul:	460	2929*	
20 Jul:	461		
27 Jul:	462		
03 Aug:	463		
10 Aug:	464		
17 Aug:	465		
24 Aug:	466		
31 Aug:	467		

	Sunday a.m.	p.m.
07 Sep:	468	470
14 Sep:	469	
21 Sep:	471	
28 Sep:	472	
05 Oct:	473	
12 Oct:	474	476
19 Oct:	475	3202
26 Oct:	477	491
02 Nov:	478	3204
09 Nov:	479	
16 Nov:	480	
23 Nov:	481	488
30 Nov:	482	3206
07 Dec:	483	616*
14 Dec:	484	
21 Dec:	485	3221
28 Dec:	486	496

Untimed	2920, 2934, 2938, 2988
Undated Sunday p.m.	2902
Early Sunday p.m.	2911

1863

	Sunday a.m.	p.m.	Weekday
			01 Jan: 3283*
04 Jan:	487		
18 Jan:	489		
25 Jan:	490		
01 Feb:	492		
08 Feb:	493		
15 Feb:	494	2835	
22 Feb:	495		
01 Mar:	497	2393	
08 Mar:	498	2993	
15 Mar:	500		
22 Mar:	501		

29 Mar:	502		
05 Apr:	503		
12 Apr:	504	505	
19 Apr:	506		
TOUR OF HOLLAND			
03 May:	507		
10 May:	508	2996	
17 May:	509		
24 May:	511		
31 May:	512		
07 Jun:	513		
14 Jun:	514		
21 Jun:	515	2972	
28 Jun:	517		
05 Jul:	518	2391	
12 Jul:	519	3210	
19 Jul:	520	3212	
26 Jul:	521	523	30 Jul: 3214
02 Aug:	522		
TOUR OF SCOTLAND			
16 Aug:	524	3216	
23 Aug:	525	3218	
30 Aug:	527		
06 Sep:	528	3220	
13 Sep:	529	3232	
20 Sep:	531	3236	
27 Sep:	532		
04 Oct:	533	3238	
11 Oct:	534	535	
18 Oct:	537	548	
25 Oct:	536		
01 Nov:	538		05 Nov: 3234
08 Nov:	539	550	12 Nov: 3240
15 Nov:	540		*17 Nov: 3242**
22 Nov:	541		
29 Nov:	542		

06 Dec:	543		
13 Dec:	544		
20 Dec:	545		
27 Dec:	546		31 Dec: S&T 1/11

Untimed	2943, 2947, 2952, 2955, 2960, 2963, 2967, 2974, 2979, 2984
Wrong year (see 1865)	3050*

1864

	Sunday a.m.	p.m.	Weekday
03 Jan:	547	3282	
10 Jan:	549		
24 Jan:	551	3250	
31 Jan:	552		
07 Feb:	553	3252	
14 Feb:	554		
21 Feb:	555	3256	
28 Feb:	557		
06 Mar:	558	3258	17 Mar: 3260
20 Mar:	560		*22 Mar: 569*
27 Mar:	562	3262	
03 Apr:	563		07 Apr: 3264
10 Apr:	564		
17 Apr:	565		
24 Apr:	566		28 Apr: 3266
01 May:	567		
08 May:	568		
15 May:	570		
22 May:	571		
29 May:	572		
05 Jun:	573		
12 Jun:	574		16 Jun: 582
19 Jun:	575		
26 Jun:	577		
03 Jul:	578		

10 Jul:	579		
17 Jul:	580		
24 Jul:	581		
31 Jul:	583	584	
07 Aug:	585		
28 Aug:	587		
04 Sep:	588		
11 Sep:	589		
18 Sep:	590		
25 Sep:	591		
02 Oct:	592		
09 Oct:	593	3268	
16 Oct:	595		
23 Oct:	596		
30 Oct:	597		
06 Nov:	598		
13 Nov:	599	3270	17 Nov: 3003
20 Nov:	601	602	
VISIT TO GLASGOW (incl.			*25 Nov: S&T 7/95**)
04 Dec:	603		
11 Dec:	604		
18 Dec:	605		
25 Dec:	606	3072	

Undated Sunday p.m.	3013, 3026
Untimed	2992, 2997, 3001, 3005, 3009, 3018, 3023, 3030
Wrongly dated	2497 (27 Dec Sunday p.m.)

1865

	Sunday a.m.	p.m.	Weekday
01 Jan:	607	3073	
08 Jan:	608	3056	
15 Jan:	609		
22 Jan:	611		
29 Jan:	612	3079	
05 Feb:	613		

12 Feb:	614		
19 Feb:	615		
26 Feb:	617		
05 Mar:	618		
12 Mar:	619		
19 Mar:	620		*22 Mar: 624*
26 Mar:	621		
02 Apr:	622		
09 Apr:	623		
16 Apr:	625		
23 Apr:	626	3062	
30 Apr:	627		
07 May:	628		
HOLIDAY ON CONTINENT			
02 Jul:	637		
09 Jul:	638		
16 Jul:	639		
23 Jul:	641		
30 Jul:	642		
06 Aug:	643		
13 Aug:	644		
20 Aug:	645	3274	
27 Aug:	647		
03 Sep:	648		
10 Sep:	649		
17 Sep:	650	3272	
24 Sep:	651		
01 Oct:	652	3276	
08 Oct:	653	3116	12 Oct: BRADFORD
15 Oct:	654		
22 Oct:	655		
29 Oct:	657		
05 Nov:	658		
12 Nov:	660		
26 Nov:	662		
03 Dec:	663		

10 Dec:	664	
17 Dec:	665	669
24 Dec:	666	
31 Dec:	667	

Undated evening	3050*, 3137*
Undated Thursday	3044
Early undated evening	3038
Harvest undated	3058

1866

	Sunday a.m.	p.m.	Weekday
07 Jan:	668		11 Jan: 3278
14 Jan:	670	672	18 Jan: 3280
21 Jan:	671		25 Jan: 3286
28 Jan:	673		
04 Feb:	674	3284	
11 Feb:	675	3288	*12 Feb: S&T 12/10*
			15 Feb: 3290
18 Feb:	676	3292	22 Feb: 3294*
25 Feb:	678	3296(?)	
		3457*	
04 Mar:	679	3298	*05 Mar: S&T 11/06*
11 Mar:	680		*12 Mar: S&T 3/09*
18 Mar:	681		*20 Mar: 3122*
25 Mar:	682		*26 Mar: S&T 10/10*
01 Apr:	683		05 Apr: 3300*
08 Apr:	684	3167*	12 Apr: 3302
15 Apr:	685	3304	*16 Apr: S&T 7–8/10*
			19 Apr: 3306
22 Apr:	687		*23 Apr: S&T 12/11*
			& 1/12
29 Apr:	688	3308	
06 May:	689		
13 May:	690	691	17 May: 3310
20 May:	692	3312	

VISIT TO SCOTLAND

10 Jun:	694	2469	*11 Jun: S&T 5–6/11*
			14 Jun: 3314
17 Jun:	695	3316	21 Jun: 3318
24 Jun:	697	3320	
01 Jul:	698		
08 Jul:	699		
15 Jul:	700		19 Jul: 3322
22 Jul:	701	3324	*23 Jul: S&T 6/06*
29 Jul:	703	706	
		3327(?)	02 Aug: 3333
05 Aug:	704	3004	09 Aug: 3329
12 Aug:	705	710	16 Aug: 3353
19 Aug:	707		
02 Sep:	708	3185*	06 Sep: 3454
09 Sep:	709		*10 Sep: S&T 11/10*
			13 Sep: 3339
16 Sep:	711	3337	*17 Sep: S&T 2/11*
			20 Sep: 3344
23 Sep:	712	3425	27 Sep: 3471
30 Sep:	713	3331	04 Oct: 3369*
07 Oct:	714	716	
14 Oct:	715		*16 Oct: 3006*
			18 Oct: BV63 no.32
21 Oct:	717		*22 Oct: S&T 4/07*
28 Oct:	718		
04 Nov:	719	3378	
11 Nov:	720	3172	
18 Nov:	721		
25 Nov:	722	3513	29 Nov: 3366
02 Dec:	723	3382	
09 Dec:	724		13 Dec: 750
16 Dec:	725		
23 Dec:	727		

VISIT TO PARIS

Undated Sunday p.m.   3151
Untimed   3163; S&T 10/96

1867

	Sunday a.m.	p.m.	Weekday
06 Jan:	728		
13 Jan:	729	3008	17 Jan: 862
20 Jan:	730		
27 Jan:	732		*28 Jan: S&T 3/67*
			31 Jan: 3375
03 Feb:	733		*04 Feb: S&T 4/10*
10 Feb:	734		14 Feb: 3380
17 Feb:	735		
24 Feb:	737		
03 Mar:	738		07 Mar: 3364
10 Mar:	739	SICK	*12 Mar: 3197*
17 Mar:	740		21 Mar: 756
24 Mar:	742	none	
31 Mar:	743	none	04 Apr: S&T 3–4/99
07 Apr:	744	none	
14 Apr:	745	none	
21 Apr:	746	none	
28 Apr:	747	3392	*01 May: S&T 1/98*
05 May:	748		09 May: 3335
12 May:	749	3373	16 May: 3355
19 May:	751		*20 May: S&T 9/06*
			23 May: 3356
26 May:	752		
02 Jun:	753		
09 Jun:	754	3397*	
16 Jun:	755	3010	
23 Jun:	757		
30 Jun:	758		04 Jul: 3011
07 Jul:	759		*08 Jul: S&T 1/09*
			11 Jul: 3012
14 Jul:	760	3015	

21 Jul:	761	3027	
28 Jul:	763	766*	01 Aug: 3017
04 Aug:	764		*05 Aug: S&T 5–6/10*
HOLIDAY ON CONTINENT			
08 Sep:	769		19 Sep: 773
SICKNESS			
06 Oct:	774		10 Oct: 776
13 Oct:	775	778	
SICKNESS			
03 Nov:	779		
10 Nov:	780		
17 Nov:	781		*18 Nov: S&T 9/10*
			21 Nov: 3170*
24 Nov:	782		
01 Dec:	783	3401	
08 Dec:	784	3351	12 Dec: 3384
15 Dec:	785	3362	
22 Dec:	786		26 Dec: 3371
29 Dec:	787	790	
Mar/Apr Thursday	767*, 768*		

1868

	Sunday a.m.	p.m.	Weekday
			02 Jan: 3412*
05 Jan:	788	3275	
12 Jan:	789	802	
19 Jan:	791	3386	
26 Jan:	792		
02 Feb:	793		*03 Feb: S&T 1/06*
			06 Feb: 3358
09 Feb:	794	3458	
16 Feb:	795	3390	*17 Feb: S&T 5/07*
23 Feb:	797		
01 Mar:	798		05 Mar: 823
08 Mar:	799		

15 Mar:	800		19 Mar: 3246
22 Mar:	801	826	
29 Mar:	803	3465	
05 Apr:	804		
12 Apr:	805		16 Apr: 806
19 Apr:	807	808	
SICKNESS			
03 May:	N/A	809	
10 May:	810		*13 May: 811*
17 May:	812		
31 May:	813	816	04 Jun: 3346
07 Jun:	814		
14 Jun:	815		18 Jun: 3460
21 Jun:	817		
28 Jun:	818		02 Jul: 3376
05 Jul:	819	3451	
12 Jul:	820		
19 Jul:	821		
26 Jul:	822		
09 Aug:	824		
16 Aug:	825		
23 Aug:	827	3357	27 Aug: 835
30 Aug:	828	3421	03 Sep: 3387
06 Sep:	829		
13 Sep:	830		
20 Sep:	831	3348	
27 Sep:	833	3398(?)	
04 Oct:	834		
11 Oct:	836	3463	15 Oct: BRISTOL
18 Oct:	837		22 Oct: 3022
25 Oct:	838		
01 Nov:	839		
08 Nov:	840		
15 Nov:	841		19 Nov: 3429
22 Nov:	842		*23 Nov: S&T 6/93*
			26 Nov: 3439

29 Nov:	843		
06 Dec:	844		
13 Dec:	845		
20 Dec:	846		
27 Dec:	847	857	31 Dec: 3323* (or 03 Jan)

Wrongly dated	3405 (21 Mar Sunday p.m.) 3415 & 3509 (both 27 Jun Sunday p.m.)

1869

	Sunday a.m.	p.m.	Weekday
03 Jan:	848		
10 Jan:	849		
17 Jan:	851		
24 Jan:	852		
31 Jan:	853	S&T 2/96	04 Feb: 3436
07 Feb:	854		11 Feb: 3025
14 Feb:	855	3024	
21 Feb:	856		25 Feb: 3019
28 Feb:	858		*02 Mar: 3271*
07 Mar:	859		
14 Mar:	860		
21 Mar:	861		
28 Mar:	863		
04 Apr:	864		08 Apr: 3409
11 Apr:	865	882	15 Apr: 876
18 Apr:	866		
25 Apr:	867		
02 May:	868	869	
09 May:	870	3400	
16 May:	871		
23 May:	872	3029	27 May: 3396
30 May:	873		
06 Jun:	874		10 Jun: 3407
13 Jun:	875		

20 Jun:	877		
27 Jun:	878		
04 Jul:	879		08 Jul: 886(?)
11 Jul:	880		
18 Jul:	881	3031	
01 Aug:	883	2478	
08 Aug:	884	3535	12 Aug: 3032
15 Aug:	885		19 Aug: 3394
22 Aug:	887		
29 Aug:	888		
05 Sep:	889		09 Sep: 3443*
12 Sep:	890		
SICKNESS			
26 Sep:	893		30 Sep: 3419
03 Oct:	894		
10 Oct:	895		
17 Oct:	896	3389*	
24 Oct:	897	3411	
31 Oct:	898		
07 Nov:	899		
SICKNESS			
26 Dec:	907	2445	

January undated evening	2448*
Jan-Mar undated evening	3360*
Undated Sunday p.m.	3014
Wrongly dated	3431 (18 Jun Sunday p.m.)

1870

	Sunday a.m.	p.m.	Weekday
02 Jan:	908		
09 Jan:	909	3035	13 Jan: 3037
16 Jan:	911	962	
		3039(?)	
23 Jan:	912		
30 Jan:	913	3041	

06 Feb:	914		10 Feb: 3413
13 Feb:	915		
20 Feb:	917	3222	24 Feb: 3417
27 Feb:	918		
06 Mar:	919	922	
13 Mar:	920		
20 Mar:	921		
27 Mar:	923	3444	
03 Apr:	924		
10 Apr:	925	930	14 Apr: 929
17 Apr:	926	3224	21 Apr: 977
24 Apr:	927		
01 May:	928	933	
08 May:	931	932	
TOUR OF SCOTLAND			
05 Jun:	934		
12 Jun:	935	936	16 Jun: 3466
19 Jun:	937	946	
26 Jun:	938	3449	
03 Jul:	939		
10 Jul:	940		14 Jul: 3423
17 Jul:	941		21 Jul: 3427
24 Jul:	942	3475	
31 Jul:	943	3557	
07 Aug:	944		11 Aug: 3486
14 Aug:	945		
21 Aug:	947	3225	25 Aug: 3442
28 Aug:	948	2858	01 Sep: 3464
04 Sep:	949		
11 Sep:	950	3437	15 Sep: 3452
18 Sep:	951	952	
25 Sep:	953	3484	29 Sep: 3244
02 Oct:	957		
09 Oct:	954	3488	13 Oct: 3473
16 Oct:	955		
23 Oct:	956		

30 Oct:	958		
06 Nov:	959		10 Nov: 3468
13 Nov:	960		
20 Nov:	961	972	
27 Nov:	963	3492	
04 Dec:	964		
11 Dec:	965		
18 Dec:	966	3506	
25 Dec:	967	2288*	

Wrongly dated	3483 (28 Sep Thursday p.m.)

1871

	Sunday a.m.	p.m.	Weekday
01 Jan:	968	2342	
08 Jan:	969		
15 Jan:	970		
22 Jan:	971		
29 Jan:	973	3558	
05 Feb:	974		
12 Feb:	975		16 Feb: 3328*
19 Feb:	976		
26 Feb:	978	3490(?)	
		3497(?)	
05 Mar:	979	3476	
12 Mar:	980		
19 Mar:	981	Afternoon: WIMBLEDON	
26 Mar:	982		
SICKNESS			
23 Apr:	987		27 Apr: 991
SICKNESS			
02 Jul:	998	none	
09 Jul:	999	none	13 Jul: 3478
16 Jul:	1000	none	
23 Jul:	1001	none	
30 Jul:	1003	3503	

06 Aug:	1004	3501	
13 Aug:	1005	3499	
20 Aug:	1006		
27 Aug:	1008	3489	
03 Sep:	1009	3496	07 Sep: Num. 10:1–10
10 Sep:	1010	3498	
17 Sep:	1011	3512	21 Sep: 3493
24 Sep:	1012	3539	
01 Oct:	1013	3481	
08 Oct:	1014	3043	12 Oct: 3045
15 Oct:	1015	3047	
22 Oct:	1017	1037*	
29 Oct:	1018		
05 Nov:	1019		09 Nov: 3049
12 Nov:	1020		
19 Nov:	1024		
SICKNESS & ON CONTINENT			
24 Dec:	1026		
31 Dec:	1027		

Mar/Apr undated	993*
Summer undated	3064
Oct/Nov undated evening	1022*
Late undated evening	3441*
Wrongly dated	3525 (22 Feb Sunday p.m.)

1872

	Sunday a.m.	p.m.	Weekday
			04 Jan: 3545
07 Jan:	1028	3517	11 Jan: 3548
14 Jan:	1029	1032	18 Jan: 3521
21 Jan:	1031	3515	
28 Jan:	1033	3554	01 Feb: 3229
04 Feb:	1034		
11 Feb:	1035	3518	
18 Feb:	1036	3531(?)	22 Feb: 3361

25 Feb:	1040		29 Feb: 1042
03 Mar:	1038		07 Mar: 1056
10 Mar:	1039	2860	14 Mar: 1062
17 Mar:	1041		
24 Mar:	1043	3051	28 Mar: 2862
31 Mar:	1044	3544	
07 Apr:	1045	3507	
14 Apr:	1046	3527	
21 Apr:	1047	3540	25 Apr: 1054
28 Apr:	1048	3551	02 May: 3227
05 May:	1049	ATTU4*	
12 May:	1050		
19 May:	1051		
26 May:	1052		
02 Jun:	1053	2459	06 Jun: 2466
09 Jun:	1055	1070	
23 Jun:	1057	3223	
30 Jun:	1058		
07 Jul:	1059	3228	
14 Jul:	1060		
21 Jul:	1061		
28 Jul:	1063		
04 Aug:	1064		
11 Aug:	1065		
18 Aug:	1066		
25 Aug:	1067	1076	
01 Sep:	1068		
08 Sep:	1069		
15 Sep:	1071		
22 Sep:	1072		26 Sep: 1077
29 Sep:	1073		
06 Oct:	1074		10 Oct: MANCHESTER
13 Oct:	1075		
20 Oct:	1078		
SICKNESS & ON CONTINENT			
08 Dec:	1084		

SICKNESS   19 Dec: 1086
22 Dec: 1087
29 Dec: 1088

Early undated evening   3129
*05 May 'Able to the Uttermost' no.4

1873

	Sunday a.m.	p.m.	Weekday
05 Jan:	1089	3130	
12 Jan:	1090		
19 Jan:	1091	3053	23 Jan: 3134
26 Jan:	1093		30 Jan: 3136
02 Feb:	1094	3146	
09 Feb:	1095		13 Feb: 3140
16 Feb:	1096		20 Feb: 3142
23 Feb:	1098	3144	27 Feb: 3148
02 Mar:	1099		
09 Mar:	1100		
16 Mar:	1101	3150	
23 Mar:	1103	3152	
30 Mar:	1104	3055	
06 Apr:	1105		
13 Apr:	1106		
20 Apr:	1107	3154	
27 Apr:	1109	3159	01 May: 3160
04 May:	1110		08 May: 3164
11 May:	1111	3057	
18 May:	1112	1117*	
25 May:	1114	3162	29 May: 3166
01 Jun:	1115	3138	
08 Jun:	1116	3059	
TOUR OF SOUTHERN ENGLAND			
06 Jul:	1120	3169	
13 Jul:	1121		
20 Jul:	1122		

27 Jul:	1124		31 Jul: 3171
03 Aug:	1125	3173	07 Aug: 3178
10 Aug:	1126		
17 Aug:	1127	3061	
24 Aug:	1128		28 Aug: 3063
31 Aug:	1129		
07 Sep:	1130	3180	
14 Sep:	1132	3182	
21 Sep:	1133		25 Sep: 3184
28 Sep:	1134		02 Oct: 3186
05 Oct:	1135	3192	
12 Oct:	1136	3194	
19 Oct:	1137	3196	23 Oct: 3198
02 Nov:	1139		
09 Nov:	1141	3200	
16 Nov:	1143		
23 Nov:	1144		
30 Nov:	1145		
07 Dec:	1146		11 Dec: 3065
14 Dec:	1147	3157	
21 Dec:	1148	3158	
28 Dec:	1149	3230	

Early undated evening	3112
Mar-Jul undated	1123*
November undated?	3155*, 3156*

1874

	Sunday a.m.	p.m.	Weekday
			01 Jan: 3231*
04 Jan:	1150	3127	08 Jan: 3074
11 Jan:	1151		
SICKNESS & ON CONTINENT			
22 Feb:	1159		
01 Mar:	1160	3067	
08 Mar:	1161	1163	12 Mar: 3076

15 Mar:	1162	3078	19 Mar: 1164
22 Mar:	1165		
29 Mar:	1166	3080	
05 Apr:	1167		
12 Apr:	1168	3502*	
19 Apr:	1169	3082	
26 Apr:	1170	3084	
03 May:	1171	1174*	07 May: 3086
10 May:	1172	3090	
17 May:	1173	3092	
24 May:	1175	3096	
31 May:	1176	3069	
07 Jun:	1177		11 Jun: 3098
14 Jun:	1179		
05 Jul:	1181	3099	
12 Jul:	1182		16 Jul: 3102
19 Jul:	1183	3104	
26 Jul:	1185		
02 Aug:	1186	3106	06 Aug: 1193
09 Aug:	1187	3132	
16 Aug:	1188	3109	
23 Aug:	1189		
30 Aug:	1190		
06 Sep:	1191	3071	
13 Sep:	1192	3111	17 Sep: 1212*
20 Sep:	1194	1213(? or 24 Sep?)*	
27 Sep:	1195		
11 Oct:	1197		
18 Oct:	1199		
25 Oct:	1200		29 Oct: 3113
01 Nov:	1201	3115	05 Nov: 3117
08 Nov:	1202		12 Nov: 3094
15 Nov:	1203		
22 Nov:	1204		26 Nov: 3119
29 Nov:	1205	3121	03 Dec: 3088
06 Dec:	1206	3123	

13 Dec:	1207	1265*	17 Dec: 3125
20 Dec:	1208		
27 Dec:	1209	1217	

1875

	Sunday a.m.	p.m.	Weekday
03 Jan:	1215	2935	
SICKNESS—AT SOUTH COAST & IN FRANCE			
28 Mar:	1226		
04 Apr:	1227	2936	08 Apr: 2937
11 Apr:	1228	2939	15 Apr: 2850*
18 Apr:	1229	2940	22 Apr: 2941
25 Apr:	1231	2944	29 Apr: 2945
02 May:	1232	2946	
09 May:	1233		13 May: 2948
16 May:	1235	1239*	20 May: 2949
23 May:	1236	2950	
30 May:	1237	2951	03 Jun: 2953
06 Jun:	1238	2954	
13 Jun:	1240	2956	
20 Jun:	1241	S&T 4–5/00	24 Jun: 2957
27 Jun:	1242	2958	
11 Jul:	1243	2959	
18 Jul:	1244		22 Jul: 2961
25 Jul:	1247	2998	
01 Aug:	1248	2962	05 Aug: 2964
08 Aug:	1249	2965	12 Aug: 2966
15 Aug:	1250	2968	19 Aug: 3000
22 Aug:	1251	2969	
29 Aug:	1252		02 Sep: 2971
05 Sep:	1253	2973	09 Sep: 2975
12 Sep:	1254	2977	16 Sep: 2978
19 Sep:	1255	2980	23 Sep: 2981
26 Sep:	1256	1259*	
03 Oct:	1257	2983	*05 Oct: S&T 4/98 (PLYMOUTH)*

			07 Oct: PLYMOUTH
10 Oct:	1258	2985	14 Oct: 2986
17 Oct:	1260	2987	
24 Oct:	1261	2989	28 Oct: 2991
31 Oct:	1264	3002	
07 Nov:	1266	2994	
AT MENTONE			
26 Dec:	1270		
Undated evening	3161		
Untimed	3165		

1876

	Sunday a.m.	p.m.	Weekday
02 Jan:	1271	2865	06 Jan: 2866
09 Jan:	1272	2867	13 Jan: 3181*
16 Jan:	1273	2869	20 Jan: 1292
23 Jan:	1275	2870	27 Jan: 2871
30 Jan:	1276		03 Feb: 2873
06 Feb:	1277		
13 Feb:	1278	2874	
27 Feb:	1281		
05 Mar:	1282	2876	09 Mar: 1310
12 Mar:	1283	2877	16 Mar: 2878
19 Mar:	1284	2881	
26 Mar:	1286	2882	30 Mar: 1297
02 Apr:	1287	2883	07 Apr: 2879
09 Apr:	1288	2884	
SICKNESS			
14 May:	1293		
21 May:	1294	2886	
28 May:	1296	2887	
04 Jun:	1298	2888	08 Jun: 2890
11 Jun:	1299	2891	15 Jun: 1302
18 Jun:	1300	2892	22 Jun: 2893
25 Jun:	1301	1308	

02 Jul:	1303	2895	06 Jul: 2897
09 Jul:	1304	2899	13 Jul: 2900
16 Jul:	1305	1315	
23 Jul:	1306	2901	27 Jul: 2903
30 Jul:	1307		
06 Aug:	1309	2933	
VISIT TO SCOTLAND			
27 Aug:	1311	2904	
03 Sep:	1312	2905	07 Sep: 2906
10 Sep:	1313	2909	
17 Sep:	1314	2910	21 Sep: 2912
24 Sep:	1316	2917	28 Sep: 2918
01 Oct:	1319	2919	05 Oct: BIRMINGHAM
08 Oct:	1317	2486	12 Oct: 2864
15 Oct:	1318	2932	
22 Oct:	1320	1322	26 Oct: 1336*
29 Oct:	1321	2921	02 Nov: 1324
SICKNESS			
12 Nov:	1323	2922	
19 Nov:	1325		23 Nov: 2923
26 Nov:	1326	2925	30 Nov: 2926
03 Dec:	1327	2927	
10 Dec:	1328	2928	14 Dec: 2930
17 Dec:	1329	2931	
24 Dec:	1330	3309(?)*	
31 Dec:	1331	2863	

1877

	Sunday a.m.	p.m.	Weekday
07 Jan:	1332	2803	
14 Jan:	1333	2804	
21 Jan:	1337		
SICKNESS—IN PARIS & AT MENTONE			
18 Mar:	1343		22 Mar: 2805
25 Mar:	1345	1346	
01 Apr:	1347	2806	

08 Apr:	1348		13 Apr: 3211
15 Apr:	1349		
22 Apr:	1351	2808	
29 Apr:	1352		
06 May:	1353		*08 May: 3095*
			09 May: 1358
			10 May: 2809
13 May:	1354	1355	
27 May:	1356		
03 Jun:	1357	2810	07 Jun: 2812
10 Jun:	1359	2813	14 Jun: 2814
17 Jun:	1360	2816	21 Jun: 2817
24 Jun:	1361	2818	28 Jun: 2821
01 Jul:	1362	2827	05 Jul: 2834
08 Jul:	1363	2837	
15 Jul:	1367	2838	
TOUR OF SCOTLAND			
05 Aug:	1368	2839	
12 Aug:	1369	2840	
19 Aug:	1370	1389	
26 Aug:	1371		
02 Sep:	1372	2942	
09 Sep:	1373	1390	
16 Sep:	1374	2847	
23 Sep:	1375	2848	*27 Sep: 1697**
30 Sep:	1376		04 Oct: 2849
07 Oct:	1377	2485	
14 Oct:	1378	2851	18 Oct: 2852
21 Oct:	1379	2853	
28 Oct:	1381		01 Nov: 1400
04 Nov:	1382	2855	08 Nov: 1383
11 Nov:	1384	2856	
18 Nov:	1385	2857	
25 Nov:	1386		
02 Dec:	1387	2061	
09 Dec:	1388	1393*	

SICKNESS

30 Dec:	1391	SICK

Undated Sunday p.m.	2914
Untimed	3237b

1878

	Sunday a.m.	p.m.	Weekday
06 Jan:	1392	1397	
13 Jan:	1394	1396	
SICKNESS—AT MENTONE			
17 Mar:	1403		
24 Mar:	1404	2773	*26 Mar: S&T 1/05*
			28 Mar: 2777
31 Mar:	1406	2778	
07 Apr:	1408	2779	
14 Apr:	1409	2781	
21 Apr:	1410		
28 Apr:	1411	2782	
05 May:	1412	2783	09 May: 3243
12 May:	1413	1414	16 May: 2784
19 May:	1415		
26 May:	1416	1506*	
02 Jun:	1417		
09 Jun:	1418		13 Jun: 2786
16 Jun:	1419	2787	20 Jun: 2788
23 Jun:	1420	2790	27 Jun: 2791
30 Jun:	1422		
14 Jul:	1426		
VISIT TO SCOTLAND			
04 Aug:	1427		
11 Aug:	1428	1466*	
18 Aug:	1429		
01 Sep:	1431		05 Sep: 1433
08 Sep:	1432	2792	
15 Sep:	1434	2793	

22 Sep:	1435	2795	26 Sep: 2796
29 Sep:	1436		
06 Oct:	1437		10 Oct: LEEDS
13 Oct:	1438	2797	
20 Oct:	1439	1520*	
27 Oct:	1441	2799	
03 Nov:	1442	2800	07 Nov: 2801
SICKNESS			
22 Dec:	1450		
SICKNESS			

Wrongly dated	3456 (02 Oct Sunday p.m.)

1879

	Sunday a.m.	p.m.	Weekday
SICKNESS			
12 Jan:	1452a (from sickroom)		
SICKNESS & AT MENTONE			
13 Apr:	1468	2742	17 Apr: 3176
20 Apr:	1469	2743	24 Apr: 2744
27 Apr:	1471	2745	01 May: 2747
04 May:	1472	2748	
11 May:	1473	2749	
18 May:	1474	1475	22 May: 1485
25 May:	1476	2751	29 May: 3208
01 Jun:	1477	3190	
08 Jun:	1478	2066	
15 Jun:	1479	2752	
22 Jun:	1480		26 Jun: 3248
29 Jun:	1481	1508	
06 Jul:	1482		
13 Jul:	1483	3188	
20 Jul:	1484	2753	
27 Jul:	1486	2755	
03 Aug:	1487		
10 Aug:	1488	1489	

17 Aug:	1490	2756	
24 Aug:	1491	2757	
31 Aug:	1492		04 Sep: 1496
07 Sep:	1493	2758	11 Sep: 3226
14 Sep:	1494	2760	18 Sep: 1515*
21 Sep:	1495	2761	25 Sep: 1583*
28 Sep:	1497	1511*	
05 Oct:	1498	2762	
12 Oct:	1499	2764	
19 Oct:	1500		
26 Oct:	1501	2765	
02 Nov:	1502		
09 Nov:	1505		
SICKNESS & AT MENTONE			

Late undated evening	1577*	

1880

	Sunday a.m.	p.m.	Weekday
SICKNESS & AT MENTONE			
15 Feb:	1523		
22 Feb:	1524		
29 Feb:	1525	2663	
07 Mar:	1526	2709	*09 Mar: 1533*
14 Mar:	1528		
21 Mar:	1529	2710	
28 Mar:	1530	2712	
04 Apr:	1531	2713	
11 Apr:	1532	2714	
18 Apr:	1534	2716	
25 Apr:	1535	2717	
02 May:	1536		06 May: 3291*
09 May:	1537	2000*	13 May: 2718
16 May:	1538		20 May: 2719
23 May:	1539		
30 May:	1540		

06 Jun:	1541	2721	10 Jun: 2722
13 Jun:	1542		17 Jun: 1629
20 Jun:	1544		
27 Jun:	1545	2723	01 Jul: 2725
04 Jul:	1549	2726	
VISIT TO SCOTLAND?			
25 Jul:	1550	2727	
01 Aug:	1551	2729	05 Aug: 2479
08 Aug:	1552	2480	12 Aug: 1595
15 Aug:	1553	2730	
22 Aug:	1554	2731	
29 Aug:	1555		
12 Sep:	1557		
SICKNESS			
10 Oct:	1561		
17 Oct:	1562	2732	21 Oct: 2734
24 Oct:	1564	2735	28 Oct: 1566
14 Nov:	1567		*15 Nov: S&T 9/04**
21 Nov:	1568	2736	
28 Nov:	1570	2738	*29 Nov: S&T 1/81*
05 Dec:	1571	2708	09 Dec: 2739
12 Dec:	1572	2740	
SICKNESS			

January undated	3255 (Afternoon - MENTONE)
Jan/early Feb undated	3267 (MENTONE)
Late February evening	S&T 4/02*
Jul-Sep undated evening	1652*
Late Oct/Nov undated	1574*

1881

	Sunday a.m.	p.m.	Weekday
SICKNESS			
30 Jan:	1581	2676	03 Feb: 1630
06 Feb:	1582	1600	
20 Feb:	1584		

27 Feb:	1586		03 Mar: 1588
06 Mar:	1587	2767	
SICKNESS			
27 Mar:	1590		
03 Apr:	1591	2774	07 Apr: 2678
10 Apr:	1592	2679	14 Apr: 1693*
17 Apr:	1593		21 Apr: 2680
24 Apr:	1594		*27 Apr: 1596*
			28 Apr: 1633
01 May:	1597	2682	12 May: 2683
15 May:	1598		19 May: 2472
22 May:	1599		
29 May:	1601	2684	02 Jun: 1605
05 Jun:	1602	2769	09 Jun: 1632
12 Jun:	1603	1691	
19 Jun:	1604		
26 Jun:	1606	1635	
03 Jul:	1607		07 Jul: 1872
10 Jul:	1608	2685	
17 Jul:	1609	2687	21 Jul: 2688
24 Jul:	1610	2689	
31 Jul:	1611	2691	04 Aug: 1634
07 Aug:	1612		11 Aug: 1615
14 Aug:	1613		18 Aug: 2692
21 Aug:	1614		25 Aug: 1626
28 Aug:	1616	2693	01 Sep: 2694
04 Sep:	1617	1871	08 Sep: 2696
11 Sep:	1618	1620	
18 Sep:	1619		
25 Sep:	1621	2697	29 Sep: 2775
02 Oct:	1622	2699	06 Oct: 1686
09 Oct:	1623	2698	
16 Oct:	1624	2701	20 Oct: 2702
23 Oct:	1625	2704	27 Oct: SOUTHAMPTON
30 Oct:	1627	2705	
06 Nov:	1631	2706	

HOLIDAY AT MENTONE

25 Dec:	1636	2340

Summer undated	3273

1882

	Sunday a.m.	p.m.	Weekday
01 Jan:	1637	2617	
08 Jan:	1638	1640	
15 Jan:	1639	2618	19 Jan: 2619
22 Jan:	1641	2620	26 Jan: 2622
29 Jan:	1642	2659	02 Feb: 2623
05 Feb:	1643	1646	
12 Feb:	1644	2624	16 Feb: 1649
19 Feb:	1645	2626	23 Feb: 2627
26 Feb:	1647	1657	02 Mar: 1650
05 Mar:	1648	2628	
SICKNESS			
09 Apr:	1653		
16 Apr:	1654	2630	*21 Apr: S&T 10/82**
23 Apr:	1655	2631	
07 May:	1658		
14 May:	1659	2632	18 May: 2633
21 May:	1660	2635	
28 May:	1662	2636	01 Jun: 2637
04 Jun:	1663	2638	08 Jun: 1670
11 Jun:	1664	1717*	15 Jun: 2640
18 Jun:	1665	2641	22 Jun: 2643
25 Jun:	1666	2644	29 Jun: 2645
02 Jul:	1667	2646	
09 Jul:	1668	2648	13 Jul: 2649
16 Jul:	1669	2650	20 Jul: 2475
23 Jul:	1672	2652	
06 Aug:	1673	2653	10 Aug: 1680
13 Aug:	1674	2654	
20 Aug:	1675	2655	

27 Aug:	1676	1688	31 Aug: 2657
03 Sep:	1677	2658	07 Sep: 2661
10 Sep:	1678	2662	
17 Sep:	1679	1712	
24 Sep:	1681		28 Sep: 1690
01 Oct:	1682	2665	
08 Oct:	1683	2666	12 Oct: 2667
15 Oct:	1684	2669	19 Oct: 2670
22 Oct:	1685	2771	26 Oct: 2820
29 Oct:	1687	2671	02 Nov: 2822
05 Nov:	1689	2672	
AT MENTONE			
24 Dec:	1698	2674	
31 Dec:	1699	2675	

Early undated	1656*
Mid to late Thursday	1694*
December 03, 10 or 17	3295 (Afternoon—MENTONE)

1883

	Sunday a.m.	p.m.	Weekday
07 Jan	1700		11 Jan: 2555
14 Jan:	1701		18 Jan: 2556
21 Jan:	1702	2557	25 Jan: 2559
28 Jan:	1703		01 Feb: 2560
04 Feb:	1704	2561	08 Feb: 2564
11 Feb:	1705	2565	15 Feb: 2566
18 Feb:	1707	2568	22 Feb: 2569
25 Feb:	1708	2570	01 Mar: 2571
04 Mar:	1709	2573	08 Mar: 2574
11 Mar:	1710	2575	15 Mar: 2577
18 Mar:	1711	2578	22 Mar: 2579
25 Mar:	1713	2065	29 Mar: 2580
01 Apr:	1714	2582	05 Apr: 2583
08 Apr:	1715	2584	
15 Apr:	1716	2586	

SICKNESS

06 May:	1719		10 May: 1722
13 May:	1720	2587	17 May: 1732
20 May:	1721	2588	24 May: 2590
27 May:	1723	2591	
03 Jun:	1724	2824	07 Jun: 2592
10 Jun:	1725	1746	14 Jun: 1729
17 Jun:	1726	2593	
24 Jun:	1727	2596	
01 Jul:	1728	2595	05 Jul: 1730
15 Jul:	1731		

VISIT TO SCOTLAND?

12 Aug:	1734	1754	
19 Aug:	1735		23 Aug: 2597
26 Aug:	1736		30 Aug: 2599
02 Sep:	1737	1740	06 Sep: 2600
09 Sep:	1738	3313	13 Sep: 2768
16 Sep:	1739	2601	
23 Sep:	1741	2770	27 Sep: 2603
30 Sep:	1742		04 Oct: 1761
07 Oct:	1743	2825	11 Oct: 2604
14 Oct:	1744	2605	
21 Oct:	1745	2606	25 Oct: 1755
28 Oct:	1747	2608	01 Nov: 2609
04 Nov:	1748	2610	08 Nov: 2612
11 Nov:	1749	1750	15 Nov: 2613
18 Nov:	1751	2614	
25 Nov:	1752	1830	
02 Dec:	1753	1760	

TO FRANCE

16 Dec:	1757 (Afternoon—MENTONE)

AT MENTONE

19 or 26 Aug Sunday p.m.	1762*

1884

	Sunday a.m.	p.m.	Weekday
HOLIDAY AT MENTONE			
03 Feb:	1764	1768	07 Feb: 1829
10 Feb:	1765	2525	14 Feb: 1769
17 Feb:	1766	1770	
SICKNESS			
16 Mar:	1771		20 Mar: 2526
23 Mar:	1772	1826	27 Mar: 2527
30 Mar:	1773	2528	03 Apr: 2529
06 Apr:	1774	2530	10 Apr: 2531
13 Apr:	1775	2532	17 Apr: 2533
20 Apr:	1776	2534	
27 Apr:	1777	2535	*30 Apr: 1778*
			01 May: 2071
04 May:	1779	2826	*07 May: 1785*
			08 May: 1825
11 May:	1780	1792	15 May: 2536
18 May:	1781		
25 May:	1782	2537	
01 Jun:	1783	1831	
08 Jun:	1784		
15 Jun:	1786	2541	
22 Jun:	1787		
29 Jun:	1788	1851	03 Jul: 1823
06 Jul:	1789	2542	
13 Jul:	1790		17 Jul: 1824
20 Jul:	1791	2543	31 Jul: 1797
03 Aug:	1793	2544	
10 Aug:	1794	2545	14 Aug: 1798
17 Aug:	1795	2546	
SICKNESS			
14 Sep:	1799		18 Sep: 1805
21 Sep:	1800	2547	25 Sep: 1810
28 Sep:	1801	2548	02 Oct: 2550
05 Oct:	1802		09 Oct: 1828

12 Oct:	1803	1811	16 Oct: 1833
19 Oct:	1804	2551	23 Oct: 2552
26 Oct:	1806	2553	30 Oct: 1822
02 Nov:	1807	1834	06 Nov: 1809
09 Nov:	1808	1832	
SICKNESS			
07 Dec:	1812		
14 Dec:	1813	1821	18 Dec: 1819
21 Dec:	1815	1827	
28 Dec:	1817	2549	

June(?) evening	undated series 2538, 2539, 2237, 2540
Summer Thursday	1796
Wrongly dated	1837 (02 Jun evening)

1885

	Sunday a.m.	p.m.	Weekday
			01 Jan: 1816
04 Jan:	1818		
SICKNESS & HOLIDAY AT MENTONE			
12 Apr:	1835	2493	16 Apr: 2494
19 Apr:	1836	2495	23 Apr: 2496
26 Apr:	1838	2498	30 Apr: 2499
03 May:	1839	2501	
10 May:	1840		14 May: 3303
17 May:	1841	2502	21 May: 2500
24 May:	1842	2503	28 May: 2524
31 May:	1843		
07 Jun:	1844	1850	11 Jun: 2504
14 Jun:	1845		
21 Jun:	1846	2505	25 Jun: 1861
28 Jun:	1847	2506	02 Jul: 2507
05 Jul:	1848	2508	
12 Jul:	1849	2509	16 Jul: 2510
19 Jul:	1852	1934	
VISIT TO SCOTLAND			

02 Aug:	1853	1874	06 Aug: 2511
09 Aug:	1854	2512	
16 Aug:	1855	1878	20 Aug: 2513
23 Aug:	1856	1881	
30 Aug:	1857	1876	
06 Sep:	1858	2514	10 Sep: 1933
13 Sep:	1859	1870	
20 Sep:	1860	2068	
27 Sep:	1862	2515	*28 Sep: 1864*
04 Oct:	1863	2516	
11 Oct:	1865	2517	
18 Oct:	1866	2518	22 Oct: 2519
25 Oct:	1867	2520	29 Oct: 2521
01 Nov:	1868	2522	
08 Nov:	1869	2523	12 Nov: 1880
22 Nov:	1873		26 Nov: 1877
29 Nov:	1875		
SICKNESS & AT MENTONE			

1886

	Sunday a.m.	p.m.	Weekday
SICKNESS & AT MENTONE			
07 Feb:	1885	2451	
14 Feb:	1886	2452	18 Feb: 2453
21 Feb:	1887		25 Feb: 2454
28 Feb:	1888	1889	04 Mar: 2455
07 Mar:	1890	2456	11 Mar: 2457
14 Mar:	1891	2458	
21 Mar:	1892		25 Mar: 2916
28 Mar:	1893	2460	
04 Apr:	1894	2461	08 Apr: 2462
11 Apr:	1895	2463	
18 Apr:	1896		22 Apr: 2464
25 Apr:	1898		29 Apr: 2465
SICKNESS			
23 May:	1901	1938	

30 May:	1902	2081	
06 Jun:	1903		10 Jun: 2467
13 Jun:	1904	2468	17 Jun: 2345
20 Jun:	1905	2470	24 Jun: 2471
27 Jun:	1907		
SICKNESS			
11 Jul:	1909	2473	
18 Jul:	1910	2474	22 Jul: 2476
25 Jul:	1911	2481	
01 Aug:	1912	2477	05 Aug: 1916
08 Aug:	1913	2482	12 Aug: 2829
15 Aug:	1914	2483	19 Aug: 2830
22 Aug:	1915	2484	26 Aug: 2831
29 Aug:	1917	2487	02 Sep: 2832
05 Sep:	1918	2488	09 Sep: 1944
12 Sep:	1919	1930	
19 Sep:	1920	1936	
26 Sep:	1922	1939	30 Sep: 1932
03 Oct:	1923	2489	07 Oct: 1935
10 Oct:	1924	2490	
17 Oct:	1925		
24 Oct:	1926	1997*	28 Oct: 1940
31 Oct:	1927	2491	
07 Nov:	1928	2492	
14 Nov:	1931		
HOLIDAY AT MENTONE			

Undated Thursday	2050	
Wrong year (see 1866)	3294*, 3300*, 3369*	

1887

	Sunday a.m.	p.m.	Weekday
02 Jan:	1941 (Afternoon—MENTONE)		
09 Jan:	1943 (Afternoon—MENTONE)		
SICK AT MENTONE			
30 Jan:	1945	2394	03 Feb: 2395

06 Feb:	1946	2396	10 Feb: 2064
13 Feb:	1947	2397	17 Feb: 2398
20 Feb:	1949	2399	24 Feb: 2401
27 Feb:	1950	2400	03 Mar: 2402
06 Mar:	1951	2403	
13 Mar:	1952	2404	
20 Mar:	1954	2405	24 Mar: 1979
27 Mar:	1955	2406	31 Mar: 1994
03 Apr:	1956	2407	07 Apr: 1998
10 Apr:	1958	2408	14 Apr: 2440
17 Apr:	1959	2409	*19 Apr: 3350**
24 Apr:	1960		
01 May:	1961	2410	
08 May:	1962	2411	12 May: 2412
15 May:	1963	2413	19 May: 2414
22 May:	1964	2415	26 May: 2416
29 May:	1965	1991	02 Jun: 2417
05 Jun:	1966	2418	
12 Jun:	1967	2419	16 Jun: 2420
19 Jun:	1968	2421	23 Jun: 2422
26 Jun:	1970		30 Jun: 2441
03 Jul:	1971		
10 Jul:	1972	2423	14 Jul: 2058
17 Jul:	1973	2424	
31 Jul:	1975		
07 Aug:	1976		11 Aug: 2425
14 Aug:	1977	2426	18 Aug: 2427
21 Aug:	1978	2428	25 Aug: 2054
28 Aug:	1980		
04 Sep:	1981	2429	08 Sep: Romans 8:9
11 Sep:	1982	2442	15 Sep: 2430
18 Sep:	1983	2431	22 Sep: 2432
25 Sep:	1985	2433	
02 Oct:	1986	2434	06 Oct: 2435
16 Oct:	1987		
23 Oct:	1988	2436	27 Oct: 2437

30 Oct:	1990	2438	03 Nov: 1993
06 Nov:	1992	2439	
HOLIDAY AT MENTONE			
04 Dec:	S&T 10/03 (Afternoon—MENTONE)		

Wrongly dated	2010 (17 May Thursday)

1888

	Sunday a.m.	p.m.	Weekday
HOLIDAY AT MENTONE			
08 Jan:	2002	2350	12 Jan: 2351
15 Jan:	2003		
22 Jan:	2004	2352	26 Jan: 2353
29 Jan:	2006	2354	02 Feb: 2067
05 Feb:	2007	2355	
12 Feb:	2008		16 Feb: 2356
19 Feb:	2009	2357	23 Feb: 2358
26 Feb:	2011	2359	
04 Mar:	2012	2360	08 Mar: 2361
11 Mar:	2013	2362	15 Mar: 2363
18 Mar:	2014		22 Mar: 2364
25 Mar:	2015	2365	29 Mar: 2062
01 Apr:	2016	2059	05 Apr: 2366
08 Apr:	2018	2367	
15 Apr:	2019	2368	
22 Apr:	2020		
06 May:	2022	2369	10 May: 2370
13 May:	2023	2371	17 May: 2372
20 May:	2024	2373	24 May: 2374
SICKNESS			
17 Jun:	2029		
24 Jun:	2030	2375	
01 Jul:	2031	2376	05 Jul: 2377
08 Jul:	2032	2378	12 Jul: 2049
15 Jul:	2033	2379	19 Jul: 2380
22 Jul:	2034	2381	26 Jul: 2382

29 Jul:	2036	2383	02 Aug: 2057
05 Aug:	2037	2060	
12 Aug:	2039	2384	
19 Aug:	2040	2385	23 Aug: 2053
26 Aug:	2041	2386	30 Aug: 2210*
02 Sep:	2042	2051	06 Sep: 2842
09 Sep:	2043	2387	13 Sep: 2843
16 Sep:	2044	2844	20 Sep: 2845
23 Sep:	2045	2846	27 Sep: 2056
30 Sep:	2046	2388	04 Oct: 2389
07 Oct:	2047	2390	11 Oct: 2082
14 Oct:	2048		

SICKNESS & IN SOUTH OF FRANCE

April undated evening	2021*

1889

	Sunday a.m.	p.m.	Weekday
SICKNESS & IN SOUTH OF FRANCE			
24 Feb:	2072		28 Feb: 2300
03 Mar:	2073		07 Mar: 2121
10 Mar:	2074		
17 Mar:	2075	2447	
24 Mar:	2076		
31 Mar:	2077	2304	04 Apr: 2301
07 Apr:	2078	2302	11 Apr: 2305
14 Apr:	2079	2306	18 Apr: 2085
21 Apr:	2080	2308	25 Apr: 2303
28 Apr:	2083	2310	
05 May:	2084	2307	
12 May:	2086	2309	
19 May:	2087	2122	23 May: 2313
26 May:	2093	2111	30 May: 2315
02 Jun:	2088	2312	06 Jun: 3321*
09 Jun:	2089	2311	13 Jun: 2317
16 Jun:	2090	2314	

23 Jun:	2091	2319	27 Jun: 2449
30 Jun:	2092	2316	
07 Jul:	2094	2320	
14 Jul:	2095	2321	18 Jul: 2164
21 Jul:	2096	2322	
28 Jul:	2097	2318	01 Aug: 2323
04 Aug:	2098	2324	08 Aug: 2106
11 Aug:	2099	2325	15 Aug: 2326
18 Aug:	2100	2327	22 Aug: 2328
25 Aug:	2101	2329	29 Aug: 2330
01 Sep:	2102	2331	05 Sep: 2120
08 Sep:	2103		12 Sep: 2332
15 Sep:	2104	2333	19 Sep: 2334
22 Sep:	2105	2335	
29 Sep:	2107	2336	03 Oct: 2337
06 Oct:	2108	2338	
13 Oct:	2109	2339	17 Oct: 2343
20 Oct:	2110	2341	24 Oct: 2119
27 Oct:	2112		31 Oct: 2118
03 Nov:	2113	2344	07 Nov: 2346
10 Nov:	2115	2347	14 Nov: 2348
17 Nov:	2117	2349	21 Nov: 2177*
HOLIDAY AT MENTONE			
08 Dec:	S&T 12/03 (Afternoon—MENTONE)		
15 Dec:	S&T 11/03 (Afternoon—MENTONE)		
Wrongly dated	3504 (22 Aug Sunday p.m.)		

1890

	Sunday a.m.	p.m.	Weekday
HOLIDAY AT MENTONE			
02 Feb:	2128		06 Feb: 2181
09 Feb:	2129	2275	
16 Feb:	2130	2269	20 Feb: 2287
23 Feb:	2132	2180	
02 Mar:	2133	2271	06 Mar: 2259

09 Mar:	2134	2260	13 Mar: 2267
16 Mar:	2135	2270	20 Mar: 2446
23 Mar:	2136	2138	27 Mar: 2273
30 Mar:	2137	2178	03 Apr: 2251
06 Apr:	2139		10 Apr: 2276
13 Apr:	2140	2277	
20 Apr:	2141		*25 Apr: 2185*
27 Apr:	2142	2262	
04 May:	2143	2286	08 May: 2278
11 May:	2144		15 May: 2246
18 May:	2145	2282	22 May: 2285
25 May:	2146	2279	
01 Jun:	2147	2268	05 Jun: 2281
08 Jun:	2148		
15 Jun:	2149		
22 Jun:	2150	2152	*26 Jun: 3370**
29 Jun:	2151	2283	03 Jul: 2264
06 Jul:	2153	2265	
13 Jul:	2154	2257	
20 Jul:	2155	2284	24 Jul: 2254
27 Jul:	2156	2247	31 Jul: 2241
03 Aug:	2157	2256	07 Aug: 2280
10 Aug:	2158	2171	14 Aug: 2261
17 Aug:	2159		21 Aug: 2195
24 Aug:	2160	2240	28 Aug: 2172
31 Aug:	2161	2255	04 Sep: 2258
07 Sep:	2162	2248	11 Sep: 2174
14 Sep:	2163	2272	18 Sep: 2250
21 Sep:	2165	2188	25 Sep: 2252
28 Sep:	2166		
05 Oct:	2167	2263	09 Oct: 2184
12 Oct:	2168	2175	16 Oct: 2242
19 Oct:	2169	2243	*22 Oct: 2245*
			23 Oct: 2244
26 Oct:	2170	2266	30 Oct: 2253
02 Nov:	2173	2294	

SICKNESS AT MENTONE

28 Dec: Deuteronomy 32:10 (p.m.—MENTONE)

1891

	Sunday a.m.	p.m.	Weekday
SICKNESS AT MENTONE			
18 Jan:	Psalm 32:9 (Afternoon—MENTONE)		
08 Feb:	2189	2249	12 Feb: 2223
15 Feb:	2190	2229	19 Feb: 2274
22 Feb:	2191	2230	26 Feb: 2218
01 Mar:	2192	2228	
08 Mar:	2193	2220	12 Mar: 2221
15 Mar:	2194		19 Mar: 2226
22 Mar:	2196	2227	26 Mar: 2212
29 Mar:	2197	2236	02 Apr: 2225
05 Apr:	2198	2234	09 Apr: 2239
12 Apr:	2200	2907	
19 Apr:	2201	2235	*24 Apr: 2213*
26 Apr:	2202	SICK	
03 May:	2203	2238	07 May: 2206
10 May:	2204	2231	14 May: 2233
17 May:	2205	SICK	
SICKNESS			
07 Jun:	2208		
FINAL SICKNESS			
26 Oct:	TO CALAIS THEN TO MENTONE		
31 Dec:	S&T 2/92 (Evening—MENTONE)		

1892

1 Jan: *S&T 2/92 (Morning—MENTONE)*

31 Jan: DEATH AT MENTONE

Completely undated sermons showing year of publication

New Park Street Period (1854-March 1861)

1856: 3446* (in advertisements)

1860: 342
1861: 351, 360 (a.m.)

Republished posthumously (sometimes with new or modified titles):

(a) Previously in *The Baptist Messenger*
1855: 3105
1856: 2558
1857: 2443
1870: BV63 no.44 (a.m.)*

(b) Previously in *The Pulpit Library* Vol.2
1858: 3054, 3060, 3066, 3077, 3081 (a.m.), 3087 (a.m.), 3100
Also: 3254? (preached 'more than half a century' before 15 Jun 1911)

Metropolitan Tabernacle Period (March 1861–1891)
1863: 499, 510, 516, 526, 530
1864: 556, 559, 561, 576, 586, 594, 600
1865: 610, 629–636, 640, 646, 656, 659 (originally issued 'some years ago', i.e. in a 24 page booklet in **1861**), 661
1866: 677, 686, 693, 696, 702, 726
1867: 731, 736, 741, 762, 765, 770–772, 777
1868: 796, 832
1869: 850, 891, 892, 900–906
1870: 910, 916
1871: 983–986, 988–990, 992, 994–997, 1002, 1007, 1016, 1021, 1023, 1025
1872: 1030, 1079–1083, 1085
1873: 1092, 1097, 1102, 1108, 1113, 1118, 1119, 1131, 1138, 1140, 1142
1874: 1152–1158, 1178, 1180, 1184, 1196, 1198
1875: 1210, 1211, 1214, 1216, 1218–1225, 1230, 1234, 1245, 1246, 1262, 1263, 1267–1269
1876: 1274, 1279, 1280, 1285, 1289–1291, 1295
1877: 1334, 1338–1342, 1344, 1350, 1364–1366, 1380
1878: 1395, 1398, 1399, 1401, 1402, 1405, 1407, 1421, 1423–1425, 1430, 1440, 1443–1449
1879: 1451, 1452b, 1453–1465, 1467, 1470, 1503, 1504, 1507, 1509–1510

1880: 1512–1514, 1516–1519, 1521, 1522, 1527, 1543, 1546–1548, 1556, 1558–1560, 1563, 1565, 1569, 1573
1881: 1575, 1576, 1578–1580, 1585, 1589, 1628, 1634b
1882: 1651, 1661, 1671, 1692, 1695, 1696, 2027 (in *Farm Sermons*)
1883: 1706, 1718, 1733, 1756
1884: 1758, 1759, 1763, 1767, 1814
1885: 1820
1886: 1879, 1882–1884, 1897, 1899, 1900, 1906, 1908, 1921, 1929, 1937
1887: 1942, 1948, 1953, 1957, 1969, 1974, 1984, 1989, 1995, 1996, 1999
1888: 2001, 2005, 2017, 2025, 2026, 2028, 2035, 2038, 2052, 2055
1889: 2063, 2069, 2070, 2114, 2116
1890: 2123–2127, 2131, 2176, 2179
1891: 2182, 2183, 2186, 2187, 2199, 2207, 2209, 2211, 2214–2217, 2219, 2222, 2224, 2232

Republished posthumously (sometimes with new or modified titles):

(a) Previously in *The Sword and the Trowel*
1866: 2970
1867: 2982
1869: 2976, 2999, 3028
1870: 2990, 2995, 3007, 3021, 3034
1871: 3040, 3046, 3052, 3070
1872: 3075, 3083, 3089, 3101
1873: 3107, 3118, 3124, 3135
1874: 3143, 3149
1875: 3168
1876: 3174, 3187, 3193, 3199
1877: 3205, 3217, 3237a
1879: 3249
1880: 3261
1881: 3153
1882: 3279
1883: 3289, 3301, 3307, 3319
1884: 3330, 3340
1885: 3345

1887: 3479
1891: 3175

(b) Previously in *The Baptist Messenger*
1865: 3085, 3091
1866: 2444, 3097, 3103, 3110, 3131, 3147
1867: 2450, 3141, 3179, 3191, 3203, 3209, 3215, 3233, 3239
1868: 3245, 3251, 3257, 3263, 3269, 3281, 3287, 3293, 3299, 3305, 3311
1869: 3317, 3326, 3338, 3343, 3347, 3352, 3365, 3368, 3374, 3379
1870: 3332, 3334, 3385, 3391, 3395, 3399, 3404, (BV63 no.45)
1871: 3402, 3403, 3406, 3410, 3414, 3418, 3422, 3424, 3426, 3432, 3445
1872: 3408, 3416, 3420, 3428, 3430, 3433, 3435, 3438, 3440, 3447, 3448
1873: 3450, 3453, 3455, 3459, 3461, 3462, 3467, 3469, 3470, 3472, 3480
1874: 3474, 3477, 3482, 3485, 3487, 3491, 3494, 3495, 3500, 3505
1875: 3508, 3510, 3511, 3514, 3516, 3519, 3520, 3522, 3523, 3524, 3526, 3528
1875: 3508, 3510, 3511, 3514, 3516, 3519, 3520, 3522, 3523, 3524, 3526, 3528
1876: 3529, 3530, 3534, 3537, 3538, 3541, 3542, 3546, 3547, 3552, 3553, 3559
1877: 3532, 3533, 3536, 3543, 3549, 3550, 3555, 3556, 3560, 3561, (BV63 nos. 1–2)
1878: 3562, 3563, (BV63 nos. 3–12)
1879: (BV63 nos. 13–24)
1880: (BV63 nos. 25–31, 33–36)
1881: (BV63 nos. 37–39)

(c) Previously in books of Sunday and Thursday evening sermons:

In *Types and emblems*
1873: 2913, 3297

In *Trumpet calls to Christian energy*
1875: 2854

In *Storm Signals*
1885: 2859

(d) Previously in *Spurgeon's Shilling Series*:

In *Seven wonders of grace*:
1877: 3354, 3359, 3363, 3367, 3372, 3377

In *The Mourner's Comforter*:
1878: 3325, 3336, 3341, 3349

In *Be of good cheer*:
1881: 3016, 3020, 3128, 3145, 3153, 3277, 3285

(e) Previously in *Farm Sermons*
1882: 3315, 3381, 3383, 3388, 3393

Published posthumously (# = first published in *Grace Triumphant*, 1904):
2289–2293, 2295–2299, 2861, 3033, 3177#, 3183#, 3189#, 3195#, 3201#,
3207#, 3213#, 3219#, 3235#, 3241#, 3247#, 3253#, 3259#, 3265#, 3342
Able to the Uttermost 1–3, 5–20

Dating of undated sermons etc. (revised and expanded)

72–73: Both of these sermons are dated Sunday morning 30 March 1856 and
contain internal references to being preached in the morning. G.H. Pike, *The life
and work of Charles Haddon Spurgeon*, vol. 2, pp. 223–6 preserves an eye-witness
account which confirms that **72** is correctly dated; the evening sermon on that day
was not **73**. Possibly this was preached on the next Sunday morning 6 April 1856
which is unusually unrepresented.

616: This evening sermon indicates that the sermon preached in the morning
considered God's calling to receive Christ and to walk in him, which was the theme
of **483**, the sermon on Colossians 2:6 preached on the morning of 7 December
1862.

766: A footnote to **3017**, preached on Thursday 1 August 1867, identifies **766** as
the sermon preached on the previous Sunday evening, thus dating it to 28 July
1867.

767–768: G.H. Pike, *The life and work of Charles Haddon Spurgeon*, vol. 4 pp.
200–1 records that, during the renovations carried out at the Metropolitan
Tabernacle in March and April 1867 when the Agricultural Hall was used instead on
Sunday mornings, an offer of Surrey Chapel for the weekday meetings was gladly
accepted. **756**, preached at Surrey Chapel on 21 March 1867, would have been

the first of the Thursday sermons and the undated evening sermons **767–8**, also preached there, must have been on subsequent Thursday evenings. The sermon preached at Surrey Chapel on Thursday 4 April 1867 appears in *The Sword and the Trowel*, March 1899.

993: A footnote identifies **980**, preached on 12 March 1871, as the other sermon about Jeremiah mentioned as having been preached recently. Spurgeon's absence through sickness for most of April and the whole of May and June means that **993** must have been preached in late March or early April 1871.

1022: In this undated sermon published in 1871 Spurgeon indicates that he had spoken on the words 'Ye shall die in your sins' (John 8:21,24) 'the other Sunday night'. This clearly relates to the striking last section of **3043**, the Sunday evening sermon of 8 October 1871. **1022** must have been preached between mid October and late November 1871 when Spurgeon left for the continent.

1037: In this undated sermon published in 1872 Spurgeon indicates that on the previous Sunday evening he had spoken on the fact that Christians are saved with great difficulty. This appears to relate to **3047**, the sermon on 1 Peter 4:18 preached on the evening of 15 October 1871. **1037** seems to be the evening sermon of 22 October 1871.

1117: This evening sermon includes a reference to a hymn quoted earlier that day in the morning sermon; the same hymn is quoted in **1112**, preached on the morning of 18 May 1873.

1123: A suggestion that Luke 19:10 was considered 'not long ago' appears to refer back to **1100** preached on 9 March 1873. **1123** was published in July 1873 and would seem to have been preached in the period between.

1174: This evening sermon is said by Spurgeon to be exactly 24 years since his baptism which was on 3 May 1850, thus dating it to 3 May 1874.

1212–1213: A footnote to **1213** indicates that **1212** was preached on the previous Thursday evening, thus dating **1213** to either the following Sunday evening or Thursday evening. **1212** also contains a reference to the likeness of a child to its father being in some points a caricature, a point mentioned in **1194** (Sunday morning 20 September 1874) as also having been made on the previous Thursday. Thus **1212** was preached on Thursday 17 September 1874 and **1213** on the evening of either Sunday 20 or Thursday 24 September 1874, no other sermons of Spurgeon being allocated to either of these. However, a newspaper report on 23 September 1874, quoted by G.H. Pike, *The life and work of Charles Haddon*

Spurgeon, vol.5 pp. 138–139, would appear to rule out the sermon preached on the evening of Sunday 20 September.

1239: G.H. Pike, *The life and work of Charles Haddon Spurgeon,* vol. 5 p. 154 dates this sermon to the evening of Sunday 16 May 1875.

1259: This evening sermon includes a reference to a point made in the morning sermon of the same day to the effect that that 'the more grace a man has the lower he lies before God'. The same point is found in **1256** (Sunday morning 26 September 1875) where Spurgeon likens good men to ships—'the fuller these are the lower they sink'.

1265: A footnote to this evening sermon links it to **1207**, the sermon preached that morning (Sunday 13 December 1874).

1336: A reference to a sermon preached on Matthew 11:28 'the other night' appears to point back to **1322** preached Sunday evening 22 October 1876. **1336** was probably preached on Thursday 26 October 1876, no other sermon being attributed to that evening.

1393: A footnote to this evening sermon links it to **1388**, the sermon preached that morning (Sunday 9 December 1877).

1466: This sermon, published early in 1879 and preached on an occasion when the Tabernacle was vacated by the regular hearers, probably relates to such an occasion on the evening of 11 August 1878, as noted in *The Sword and the Trowel*, September 1878.

1506: A footnote to this evening sermon links it to **1416**, the sermon preached that morning (Sunday 26 May 1878).

1511: This short evening sermon published at the very beginning of 1880 was followed by a farewell address by Spurgeon's son Thomas. Such a valedictory address appears in *The Sword and the Trowel,* January 1896 and was delivered on 28 September 1879 just before Thomas Spurgeon's second voyage to Australia. Thomas Spurgeon referred to his father's morning sermon, identified by a footnote as **1497**, preached earlier that Sunday.

1515: According to T. Hancocks in *The Sword and the Trowel*, February 1900, pp. 75–77, this Thursday evening sermon 'was preached on the night following the medical decision that "Son Tom" could not possibly continue to reside in England, but must return to the sunny Antipodes.' This probably dates it to 18 September 1879 (see **1511** above).

1520: Footnotes to this evening sermon link it to **1439**, the sermon preached that morning (Sunday 20 October 1878).

1574: In this sermon published at the end of 1880 Spurgeon says 'almost the last time I stood here' he 'spoke of Peter from the words—"When he thought thereon, he wept"'. This refers to Mark 14:72, the text of **2735**, preached on the evening of Sunday 24 October 1880. **1574** would appear to have been preached at the end of October or early in November 1880.

1577: Spurgeon had 'lately' spoken on the words 'Who forgiveth all thine iniquities', the theme of **1492**, preached on 31 August 1879.

1583: A description by W. J. Harris in *The Sword and the Trowel*, December 1900, pp.628–9, identifies this sermon on Exodus 33:14 as that preached on the evening of the last Thursday (25th) of September 1879.

1652: During this undated evening sermon published in 1882 Spurgeon remarks, 'I cannot get at any of my books, for they are all packed away', probably identifying this as one of the evening sermons unaccounted for at or around the time of his move to Norwood in the first half of August 1880.

1656: This undated sermon, published at about the end of April 1882, contains a reference to the gospel still being true 'in the year "eighteen hundred and eighty-two"', thus dating it to early 1882.

1693: In this undated Thursday evening sermon published in 1882 Spurgeon refers to the difficulties householders had been experiencing while completing their census forms; he also describes his reading of Colossians 3 on the previous Sunday morning. However, his description of his reading of Colossians 3:15 aptly reflects the exposition of that chapter attached to **2679**, preached on Sunday evening 10 April 1881, which was a week after the taking of the 1881 census. Allowing for a slight editorial lapse some twenty months after the event, **1693** would seem to be the missing sermon preached on Thursday 14 April 1881.

1694: In this Thursday evening sermon, published at the end of 1882, reference is made back to the prayerful response to the 'fearful assassinations in Ireland.' G.H. Pike, *The life and work of Charles Haddon Spurgeon* vol. 6 p. 262 indicates that on Sunday 14 May 1882 Spurgeon prayed for Ireland in the wake of the murders of Lord Cavendish, the new Chief Secretary to the Lord-Lieutenant of Ireland, and of Burke, the permanent Irish Undersecretary, in Phoenix Park, Dublin. This sermon was therefore preached on one of the unrepresented Thursdays between late May and November 1882.

1697: This sermon was preached at the opening of the original Trinity Road Chapel on the afternoon of Thursday 27 September 1877.

1717: This sermon, for which 'the regular hearers left their seats to be occupied by strangers', was published in 1883 and seems to relate to such an occasion on the evening of 11 June 1882. *The Sword and the Trowel*, July 1882 notes that the event gave 'proof that when Christ is lifted up, men are drawn to him', a clear vindication of the text of **1717** (John 12:32–33).

1762: This undated evening sermon was preached at Exeter Hall. From 12 August to 2 September 1883 Sunday services were held at Exeter Hall during repairs to the Metropolitan Tabernacle. The four morning sermons (**1734–7**) are all dated, as are two of the evening ones—**1754** (12 August 1883) and **1740** (2 September 1883). **1762** appears to be the evening sermon of either 19 or 26 August 1883. The Thursday meetings seem to have been held at Christ Church, Westminster Bridge Road where **2597** and **2599** were preached on Thursdays 23 and 30 August respectively. **2600** (Thursday 6 September 1883) marked the reopening of the Metropolitan Tabernacle.

1997: A footnote to **2492**, preached on 7 November 1886, indicates that **1997** (dated Autumn 1886) was the sermon mentioned as having been preached in the evening two weeks previously, thus dating it to Sunday evening 24 October 1886.

2000: The 'two thousandth published sermon' is dated 9 May 1880 in C.H. Spurgeon, *Messages to the multitude,* and was the evening sermon on that day.

2021: This undated evening sermon is identified in a footnote to the exposition attached to **2375**, preached on 24 June 1888, as another sermon on Nathanael preached 'a short time ago'. It was published about the end of April 1888 and probably relates to one of the unrepresented dates in that month.

2177: This undated sermon, published after the death of William Olney in October 1890, is said to have been preached on a Thursday evening before Spurgeon left for his winter's rest. Internal references indicate that William Olney was present and that Spurgeon had known the congregation for 36 years. He first preached at New Park Street Chapel in December 1853 and the various factors would seem to date **2177** to Thursday 21 November 1889 just before his winter holiday at Mentone. A letter attached to **2117** and dated Mentone, Nov. 28 1889 announced his safe arrival. However, G.H. Pike, *The life and work of Charles Haddon Spurgeon,* vol. 6 p. 312 states 'On November 17 he preached for the last time before going to his winter retreat'.

2210: This sermon on Ephesians 2:9–10 contrasts 'not of works' with 'created in Christ Jesus unto good works', and can be dated to Thursday 30 August 1888 by a reference at the start of **2042**, preached on 2 September 1888, to the effect that this theme had been dealt with 'last Thursday evening'. Spurgeon had discussed the supposed difference between the doctrines of faith and of the new birth 'not long ago', in fact only the previous Sunday evening, 26 August 1888 (no.**2386**)!

2288: This sermon was preached 'On a Christmas Day Evening' and is described internally as being 'on this last Sabbath night of another year'. All but one of the relevant years in which Christmas Day fell on a Sunday can be ruled out: 1859 by a reminiscence of the New Park Street days, 1864 and 1881 by already being accounted for, 1887 by Spurgeon's absence abroad. By process of elimination **2288** seems to have been preached on the evening of Christmas Day 1870.

2448: Spurgeon's description of a funeral at Abney Park Cemetery the previous day matches that of Mrs Orsman, as described by G.H. Pike, *The life and work of Charles Haddon Spurgeon,* vol. 4 p. 305. Mrs Orsman died in mid-January 1869 and the sermon appeared in *The Baptist Messenger* in 1870.

2581: Spurgeon had seen the Queen's plate on the morning of the Thursday on which he preached this '1856' sermon, so dated because it appeared in the 1856 *Baptist Messenger*. In **71**, preached on 23 March 1856, he mentioned having seen it at Windsor. By means of a reference in **2651**, preached on Sunday evening 23 September 1855, a visit to Windsor Castle can be dated to the previous Thursday 20 September 1855.

2651: Though dated Autumn 1857, due to its appearance in the 1857 *Baptist Messenger*, this sermon had been added to an editorial leader in the *Patriot Newspaper* and there dated Sunday evening 23 September 1855.

2664: In this evening sermon preached 'early in the year 1858' Spurgeon reports that on the next Sunday a place with disreputable connections would be opened for a Sabbath concert in connection with the preaching of the gospel and that 'The Messiah will be performed as the great inducement for attracting them.' A footnote identifies the venue as the 'Alhambra Palace' and adds that the experiment was abandoned after one attempt as being likely to do more harm than good. The Alhambra Palace had once been used for exhibitions but first opened as a theatre on 18 March 1858. An advertisement to the effect that the evening service on 7 February 1858 would be supplemented by a selection from Handel's 'Messiah' can be found in *The history of the engagement of the Rev J.H. Rutherford of Newcastle, with the lessee of the Theatre-Royal, Drury-Lane, London, the inaugural sermon, and a full account of the performances at the Alhambra Palace*, John Bell, Newcastle-upon-Tyne 1858. This dates **2664**, preached on the previous Sunday evening, to 31 January 1858. I am grateful to Jane Pritchard of the Theatre Museum for providing a reference from *The Globe*, 6 April 1858, which reports that 'A week or two there was preaching, but the Nonconformist minister who undertook to conduct the special services, did not like his name being mixed up with applications for spirit licenses, dancing, and such secular affairs, and he withdrew his countenance and his oratory.'

2703: A footnote to this Thursday evening sermon (dated 1855) identifies **47**, preached 21 October 1855, as the sermon preached on the same text on a former occasion, thus placing **2703** towards the end of the year.

2815: In this sermon, preached at New Park Street Chapel on a Sunday evening early in 1861, Spurgeon remarks that he had lately been in Glasgow, which he had visited during a tour of the North and Scotland in March 1861. The only Sunday evening unaccounted for between this tour and the move to the Metropolitan Tabernacle at the end of March is 17 March 1861. **2811**, preached on Sunday evening 24 March 1861, was the final sermon at New Park Street Chapel (but see **3242** below); **368**, preached on Sunday morning 31 March 1861, was at Exeter Hall.

2836: This sermon is said to have been preached at the 100th anniversary of Amersham Baptist Chapel in November 1857. I am grateful to Sarah Charlton, Archivist at the Centre for Buckinghamshire Studies, for providing more specific details from *The Buckinghamshire Advertiser,* 28 November 1857. The history of the Baptist churches in Amersham is quite complex and 1857 does not seem to have been a centenary for any of them, but it is recorded that 'the Anniversary Sermons of "The Old Baptist Chapel" were to be preached by the Rev. C.H. Spurgeon, at two and six o'clock, on Tuesday, the 24th of November.' **2836** was the sermon preached in the evening; the description of the afternoon sermon on 1 Thessalonians 5:6 seems to indicate that it was a repetition of **163**, preached on 15 November 1857 at the Music Hall, Royal Surrey Gardens.

2850: A few nights before this sermon a cabman had produced a testament given to him by Spurgeon about fifteen years previously. In the second of Spurgeon's *Speeches at Home and Abroad* (delivered to The British and Foreign Bible Society on 5 May 1875) this is said to have happened about a month beforehand. The only vacant dates in April 1875 are Thursdays 1 and 15; **2850**, which first appeared in *Trumpet Calls to Christian energy* in 1875, was probably preached on the latter of these.

2875: This sermon is dated Sunday morning 27 August 1854 in *One hundred sermons on New Testament texts selected from 'The Penny-Pulpit' ...*, Charles Higham, 1886

2896: This sermon (dated August 1854) was originally the first of Spurgeon's sermons to be printed. G.H. Pike, *The life and work of Charles Haddon Spurgeon,* vol. 1, pp. 135–143, dates it to Sunday morning 20 August 1854 and describes the occasion at length.

2924: This sermon is dated 1862 and was preached on a Sunday evening. Spurgeon indicates that he had preached in the morning to the chief of sinners and notes that some of his congregation may have been in London to visit the Great Exhibition, which opened on 1 May 1862, or to attend the Handel Festival, which took place on 23, 25 and 27 June 1862 (see Michael Musgrave, *The musical life of the Crystal Palace* (C.U.P. 1995) pp. 215–6). **2924** would appear to be the evening sermon of 29 June 1862, the morning sermon on that day being **458**, entitled 'The friend of sinners'. I am grateful to the Gerald Coke Handel Collection (housed at the Foundling Museum, London) and to the curator of the Crystal Palace Museum for providing the dates of the 1862 Handel Festival.

2929: This sermon is dated 1862 and was preached on a Sunday evening. Spurgeon indicates that he had preached in the morning on 'Repent ye, and believe in the gospel', the text of **460**, preached on Sunday morning 13 July 1862.

3048: This sermon was preached on a Sunday morning in 1856 and entitled 'The Holy Spirit in the Covenant'. Spurgeon looks back to two earlier sermons, 'God in the Covenant' (**93**) and 'Christ in the Covenant' (**103**) preached on 3 and 31 August 1856 respectively. Only the evening sermons of Sundays 21 and 28 September are accounted for; **3048** may have been on the morning of either of these. No sermons are recorded for Sundays 5 and 12 October.

3050: This sermon is dated 1863, but Spurgeon's comment that he commenced his pastorate eleven years earlier would place it in 1865. The publishers inserted a footnote referring to those eleven years as 1854–1865. **3050** also appears in the 1865 volume of the *Baptist Messenger,* the periodical which seems to have been the source for many of the partly-dated posthumously-published sermons from Spurgeon's early years.

3114: *The Penny Pulpit,* 1855 commenced with this Sunday morning sermon, dated 15 October 1854. I am grateful to Paul Terry of the British Library's Rare Books & Music Reference Team for tracking down the original publication.

3120: This undated morning sermon was preached at New Park Street Chapel and entitled 'A view of God's glory'. G.H. Pike, *The life and work of Charles Haddon Spurgeon,* vol. 1 pp. 125–6 refers to it as one of the earliest published sermons and includes an excerpt derived from *The Penny Pulpit,* 1854. The sermon appears in the first volume of a representative collection of sermons from *The Penny Pulpit* published in 1886 and is there dated 17 September 1854.

3137: Spurgeon's call for a day of prayer and fasting in respect of 'this cattle disease' may relate to the cattle plague of 1865 which prompted J.C. Ryle to write his famous tract *The finger of God*. This sermon appears in *The Baptist Messenger* for 1866.

3155–3156: These were the first two sermons in an unfinished series on the Beatitudes in 1873. The third sermon (second Beatitude) is not represented in the published sermons, but the fourth to sixth (**3065, 3157, 3158** on the third to fifth Beatitudes) were preached on the evenings of Thursday 11, Sunday 14 and Sunday 21 December 1873 respectively. It is likely that **3155–6** were preached around the end of November 1873.

3167: This sermon is dated 1866 and was preached on a Sunday evening. Spurgeon indicates that in the morning he had spoken about 'the hope that salvation was possible', which seems to relate to **684,** entitled 'Hope, yet no hope. No hope, yet hope', preached on Sunday morning 8 April 1866.

3170: During this sermon Spurgeon relates that on the previous day, after months of prayer, he was talking with a friend when a letter arrived giving notification of an anonymous gift of £1,000 for the Stockwell Orphanage. The event is recorded in *C.H. Spurgeon's Autobiography*, vol. 3 p. 175 as having taken place on 20 November 1867, thus dating **3170** to Thursday 21 November 1867.

3181: This sermon, which originally appeared in *The Sword and the Trowel*, March 1876, is identified as having been preached on a Thursday evening in January 1876 by Pastor Henry Knee in *The Sword and the Trowel*, August 1900, pp.422–5. The only Thursday in the month for which there is no allocated sermon is 13 January 1876.

3185: This undated evening sermon, first published in the 1867 *Baptist Messenger*, refers to 'limpets clinging to the rocks.' In **3454**, preached on Thursday 6 September 1866, Spurgeon indicates that on the previous Sunday he had spoken of 'limpets at the seaside, sitting on the rocks.' Thus **3185** appears to have been preached on the evening of Sunday 2 September 1866.

3231/3283: Internal references indicate that both these Metropolitan Tabernacle sermons were preached on a New Year's Day. The only relevant Sunday and Thursday services not accounted for by dated sermons are Thursdays 1 January 1863 and 1874. **3231** also refers back to the building of the Orphanage, which was founded in 1867. Thus it would appear that **3231** was on Thursday 1 January

1874 (the previously published sermon was **3230**, preached on Sunday evening 28 December 1873); **3283** would have been on Thursday 1 January 1863.

3242: New Park Street Chapel is given as the location of this sermon, preached on Tuesday 17 November 1863, well over two years after the move to the Metropolitan Tabernacle. This is not a mistake! New Park Street Chapel continued to be used until the end of the summer of 1866, when the now small congregation 'finally took leave of the building' (see G.H. Pike, *The life and work of Charles Haddon Spurgeon,* vol. 3 pp. 179–80).

3283: See 3231 above.

3291: Extracts from this evening sermon on Psalm 95:5, preached at the Metropolitan Tabernacle on behalf of the British and Foreign Sailors' Society, are reproduced in *Sunday at Home,* 1880 pp. 738–41 and the date is given as 6 May 1880. A brief footnote at the end of **1539** reveals that this special sermon was also published separately at the time in May 1880. Other sermons preached on behalf of the society are **2206** and **3321**.

3294/3300: These Thursday evening sermons are wrongly dated 1886, but fit naturally into a chronological sequence of sermons from 1866 posthumously published in volume 58 of the *Metropolitan Tabernacle Pulpit* (see also **3369**).

3309: This is said to be the seventh sermon in a series on Christ's glorious achievements. In Spurgeon's book of the same title the fifth sermon is an addition to the original series, being **273** from the *New Park Street Pulpit* and listed in a footnote to **3309**, while the sixth sermon was originally presented by Spurgeon as the fifth in the series (**1325–1329**), preached on consecutive Sunday mornings from 19 November to 17 December 1876. **3309** would appear to have been originally the sixth and last sermon in the series, but to have been renumbered seventh posthumously to allow for the addition of **273**; the text of **3309** (Luke 19:10) would have been appropriate for the evening of Christmas Eve 1876, the morning sermon having been on a Christmas theme instead of the then current series.

3321: This sermon for the British and Foreign Sailors' Society would appear to be the forthcoming sermon on Thursday evening 6 June 1889, mentioned in a note in *The Sword and the Trowel* for June 1889. There are internal references to 'the last few weeks of spring' and to 'France and its exhibition,' no doubt meaning the Paris Exhibition of 1889.

3323: In this evening sermon Spurgeon refers back to the previous Sunday evening when his text had been Romans 13:11. This could be a reference to **857**, preached on Sunday evening 27 December 1868. Internal remarks such as 'during the past year' and 'Here is a blessed thing to think of all the year round' suggest that **3323** was preached at the turn of the year, either on Thursday 31 December 1868 or Sunday 3 January 1869. It appears in the 1869 *Baptist Messenger*.

3328: This evening sermon is the third of four sermons which make up Spurgeon's booklet *The Royal Wedding, the Banquet and the Guests*, issued to commemorate the marriage of Princess Louise on 21 March 1871. The second sermon does not seem to have been republished, but the first and fourth had already appeared as nos. **975** and **976**, preached on consecutive Sunday mornings 12 and 19 February 1871. At the start of **975** Spurgeon said 'If God grant me strength I hope to go through this parable'. To fit inside these dates, the middle two sermons would appear to have been preached on Sunday and Thursday evenings 12 and 16 February 1871 respectively, **3328** being on the latter of these.

3350: This was the inaugural address at the Annual Conference of the Pastors' College Association at Devonshire Square Chapel, Stoke Newington and dated 1887. G.H. Pike, *The life and work of Charles Haddon Spurgeon* vol.6 p. 285 indicates that the conference began on 18 April 1887. This inaugural address was given on the following day.

3360: This evening sermon was preached 15 years into Spurgeon's Ministry (1869) and refers to a recent fatal explosion at a fireworks factory in Bethnal Green. The incident was widely reported in the press on Saturday 2 January 1869 as having occurred 'on Thursday', which was New Year's Eve 1868. As the sermon originally appeared in *The Baptist Messenger* in April 1869, it would have been preached on a Sunday or Thursday evening sometime in January to March 1869.

3369: This sermon is confirmed as being on Thursday 4 October 1866, not 1886 as printed, by a reference to the forthcoming day of prayer and fasting on Monday 5 November 1866 (see G.H. Pike, *The life and work of Charles Haddon Spurgeon,* vol. 3 p. 187).

3370: A note in *The Sword and the Trowel*, August 1890 dates this address at the 1890 Mildmay Park Conference to the morning of Thursday 26 June.

3389: In this evening sermon on John 5:25 Spurgeon indicates that he had preached on the same chapter in the morning—'we saw in the chapter a three-fold gradation of life-giving in the person of Christ'. The three points involved the raising of the physically dead, the giving of life to the spiritually dead and the universal resurrection. This three-fold description can be found in **896**, preached on John 5:28–29 on Sunday morning 17 October 1869.

3397: This sermon was preached in June. The morning sermon had been on the subject of the Holy Spirit and could have been either **574** (Sunday 12 June 1864) or **754** (Whit Sunday 9 June 1867). The latter appears more likely as the publishers incorporated several sermons from 1867 at this time (e.g. **3373**, **3384**, **3392**, **3401**), but none from 1864.

3412: On the previous Sunday night Spurgeon had mentioned that a young person had attended the Tabernacle for two years without anybody ever speaking to her and he had said that he was ashamed of some of his congregation. The point is to be found in **790**, preached on Sunday evening 29 December 1867. **3412** was preached on Thursday 2 January 1868, said to be a wintry and snowy night.

3434: This sermon is said to have been preached at the Metropolitan Tabernacle on Sunday evening 21 February 1861. However, 21 February was a Thursday and services did not commence at the Metropolitan Tabernacle until the end of March 1861! (**886** is also described as being on a Sunday but carries a correct date for a Thursday, while **3398** and **3531** are described as being on Thursdays but carry correct dates for Sundays.)

3441: A footnote indicates that **512** (preached 31 May 1863) had been more than 8 years previously. The presence of **3441** at the end of the *Baptist Messenger* for 1871 places it late in that year.

3443: This Thursday evening sermon is dated 9 September 1896, an obvious misprint for 9 September 1869!

3446: This sermon appeared in advertisements in 1856.

3457: A footnote to this Sunday evening sermon indicates that the morning sermon on the day was **678**, preached on Sunday morning 25 February 1866. **3457** certainly refers back to **678**, but **3296** is also dated Sunday evening 25 February 1866! (Duplication of dates also occurs on 30 March 1856 (see **72–3** above), 22 April 1860, 29 July 1866, 16 January 1870 and 26 February 1871. **3415** and **3509** are double-booked for Sunday 27 June 1868, a totally incorrect date!)

3502: Part of the text of this sermon and some comments in it concerning the small degree in which believers actually know God are linked to 'Last Sunday night' in Spurgeon's 1874 College Conference address 'Forward', which is dated 14 April in *The Sword and the Trowel*, 1874, p. 219. **3502** was therefore the evening sermon on Sunday 12 April 1874 and also appeared in *The Baptist Messenger* later that year.

ATTU4: This is the only dateable sermon among the twenty undated evening sermons comprising Spurgeon's *Able to the Uttermost,* published in 1922 as a follow-up after publication of the *Metropolitan Tabernacle Pulpit* had ceased in 1917. Spurgeon says that the previous Friday was exactly 22 years after his baptism, which was on 3 May 1850, thus dating this communion sermon to Sunday evening 5 May 1872. The likelihood that **ATTU11** was the as yet unpublished sermon on Psalm 85:8 preached 'on a Thursday evening in June 1872' (see W. Williams, *Personal reminiscences of Charles Haddon Spurgeon*, p.24) raises the possibility that the publishers of *Able to the Uttermost* continued to use sermons from 1872, the year which accounts for 12 of the last 17 dated sermons in the final two volumes of the *Metropolitan Tabernacle Pulpit*.

BV63 no.43 (=S&T 1/02): This sermon was preached late in 1859 probably shortly after the laying of the first stone of the Metropolitan Tabernacle on 16 August. It contains a reference to a previous sermon concerning the Church being God's house and being built by him, probably **267** on Ephesians 2:22, which was preached on 14 August 1859. There is also a mention of a letter written to John Angell James, minister of Carr's Lane Congregational Church in Birmingham, in which Spurgeon invited him to the ceremony. John Angell James died on 1 October 1859.

BV63 no.44: This sermon, not published until 1870 and said to have been preached at the Metropolitan Tabernacle, contains an internal reference to being preached in the morning. However, the only Sunday morning dates of Spurgeon's ministry unaccounted for seem to be in 1854, 1855 and 1856, all during the New Park Street years and before the construction of the Metropolitan Tabernacle. It also contains a reference to a conversion at the same location the previous Sunday night, resulting from the words 'Jesu! Lover of my soul.' This happened to more than one person (see **201**, preached on 20 June 1858), the most notable being on a Sunday night at Exeter Hall, as recollected years later in **3476** and **3498**, both preached in 1871. The story is also told in **3081**, another undated Sunday morning sermon preached at New Park Street Chapel. Exeter Hall was used on every Sunday morning and evening for four months from 11 February to 27 May 1855 (see G. H. Pike, *The life and work of Charles Haddon Spurgeon* vol. 1, pp.159–160, 167) and on Sunday evenings from 8 June to at least 28 September 1856. This sermon may have been preached there on one of the following mornings for which there is no dated sermon: 6 May 1855; 21, 28 September or even 5 October 1856.

S&T 10/82: This communion address came at the close of a Pastors' College Conference; earlier notes concerning the Conference confirm it as having been given on Friday 21 April 1882.

S&T 7/95: G. H. Pike, *The Life and Work of Charles Haddon Spurgeon*, vol. 3.

P.114 dates this November sermon at Elgin Place Church, Glasgow to 25 November 1864.

S&T 9/95: This was the last of four sermons preached in Belfast in the weekdays between Sundays 15 and 22 August 1858, the sermon on the latter date being identified as **210** in the account given in *C. H. Spurgeon's Autobiography*, vol. 2 pp. 339–340 and *The Early Years*, pp. 511–513.

S&T 4/02: Various references made in this evening sermon would appear to date it to late February 1880. In the middle of the month Spurgeon returned from Mentone after a period of recuperation; in January, during his absence, special evangelistic services had been held at the Tabernacle. Two illustrations concerning a blacksmith's anvil outlasting many hammers and sheep outlasting wolves are also combined in **1533**, preached at Shoreditch Tabernacle on 9 March 1880.

S&T 9/04: This is probably the address 'upon the separateness of believers from the world' mentioned in a note in *The Sword and the Trowel*, December 1880, and delivered on Monday evening, 15 November 1880, at 'the annual communion in connection with the London Baptist Association'.

Annual analysis of numbered sermons (revised)

(a) New Park Street period

Year	Sun a.m.	p.m.	Mon	Tue	Wed	Thu	Fri	???	Error	TOTAL
1854	7	1	–	–	–	–	–	–	–	8
1855	46	12	2	2	1	2	–	–	–	65
1856	43	17	1	1	–	3	–	1	–	66
1857	51	13	–	1	2	2	–	2	–	71
1858	49	8	–	1	1	7	2	–	–	68
1858–9	–	–	–	–	–	1	–	–	–	1
1859	51	8	–	–	–	10	–	–	–	69
1859–60	–	1	–	–	–	–	–	–	–	1
1860	46	14	–	–	1	2	–	–	–	63
1860–1	–	2	–	–	–	–	–	–	–	2
1861	11	4	–	–	–	–	–	–	–	15
Unknown	3	2	–	–	–	–	–	8	–	13
TOTALS	**307**	**82**	**3**	**5**	**5**	**27**	**2**	**11**	**–**	**442**

(b) Metropolitan Tabernacle period

Year	Sun a.m.	p.m.	Mon	Tue	Wed	Thu	Fri	???	Error	TOTAL
1861	36	11	1	–	–	2	2	–	1	53
1861–2	–	5	–	–	–	1	–	–	–	6
1862	51	18	–	–	1	1	–	4	–	75
1863	49	19	–	1	–	4	–	10	–	83
1864	47	12	–	1	–	5	–	9	1	75
1865	45	9	–	–	1	1	–	4	–	60
1866	48	29	–	2	–	22	–	2	–	103
1867	43	13	–	1	–	18	–	–	–	75
1868	48	17	–	–	1	13	–	–	3	82
1868–9	–	–	–	–	–	–	–	1	–	1
1869	44	12	–	1	–	12	–	2	1	72
1870	49	26	–	–	–	15	–	–	1	91
1871	37	17	–	–	–	6	–	4	1	65
1872	44	18	–	–	–	15	–	1	–	78
1873	48	26	–	–	–	15	–	4	–	93
1874	44	25	–	–	–	15	–	1	–	85
1875	34	29	–	–	–	18	–	1	–	82
1876	45	39	–	–	–	23	1	–	–	108
1877	40	29	–	1	1	12	1	1	–	85
1878	33	20	–	–	–	9	–	–	1	63
1879	31	24	–	–	–	10	–	1	–	66
1880	36	23	–	1	–	11	–	5	–	76
1881	38	25	–	–	1	21	–	1	–	86
1882	41	39	–	–	–	23	–	1	–	104
1883	42	36	–	–	–	30	–	–	–	108
1884	38	30	–	–	2	24	–	4	1	99
1885	33	27	1	–	–	18	–	–	–	79
1886	37	29	–	–	–	22	–	–	–	88
1887	39	34	–	1	–	25	–	–	1	100
1888	37	31	–	–	–	26	–	1	–	95
1889	39	33	–	–	–	27	–	–	1	100
1890	40	32	–	–	1	28	1	–	–	102
1891	16	12	–	–	–	10	1	–	–	39
Unknown	1	6	–	–	–	18	–	492	–	517

Written	–	–	–	–	–	–	–	10	–	10
TOTALS	**1253**	**755**	**2**	**9**	**8**	**500**	**6**	**559**	**12**	**3104**
BOTH	**1560**	**837**	**5**	**14**	**13**	**527**	**8**	**570**	**12**	**3546**

N.B. The *New Park Street* and *Metropolitan Tabernacle Pulpits* consist of 3563 weekly numbers, but the total number of Spurgeon's sermons contained within them is only 3546 for the following reasons:-

(a) *The New Park Street Pulpit* includes 9 long sermons which take up double numbers plus 5 numbers reporting special meetings.

(b) *The Metropolitan Tabernacle Pulpit* includes 14 numbers containing reports of special meetings and sermons by other preachers marking the opening of the Metropolitan Tabernacle in 1861. However, there are also 11 numbers containing two sermons, 9 of which each include a short sermon written during Spurgeon's long absence at the start of 1879.

About Day One:

Day One's threefold commitment:

- TO BE FAITHFUL TO THE BIBLE, GOD'S INERRANT, INFALLIBLE WORD;

- TO BE RELEVANT TO OUR MODERN GENERATION;

- TO BE EXCELLENT IN OUR PUBLICATION STANDARDS.

I continue to be thankful for the publications of Day One. They are biblical; they have sound theology; and they are relative to the issues at hand. The material is condensed and manageable while, at the same time, being complete—a challenging balance to find. We are happy in our ministry to make use of these excellent publications.

JOHN MACARTHUR, PASTOR-TEACHER, GRACE COMMUNITY CHURCH, CALIFORNIA

It is a great encouragement to see Day One making such excellent progress. Their publications are always biblical, accessible and attractively produced, with no compromise on quality. Long may their progress continue and increase!

JOHN BLANCHARD, AUTHOR, EVANGELIST AND APOLOGIST

Visit our website for more information and to request a free catalogue of our books.

www.dayone.co.uk
www.dayonebookstore.com

TERENCE PETER CROSBY (EDITOR)

640 PAGES, HARDBACK

978-1-84625-145-0

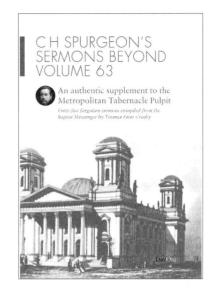

C H SPURGEON'S SERMONS BEYOND VOLUME 63

An authentic supplement to the Metropolitan Tabernacle Pulpit

Forty-five forgotten sermons compiled from the Baptist Messenger by Terence Peter Crosby

Here are 45 sermons which were awaiting publication in the Metropolitan Tabernacle Pulpit when it came to an abrupt end in 1917. The 63 volumes and 3563 sermons of Spurgeon's New Park Street and Metropolitan Tabernacle Pulpits were a remarkable achievement, and it was only on account of the shortage of paper and metal caused by the First World War that publication ceased on 10 May 1917.

Many hundreds of sermons were ready and waiting for their weekly publication and notices in the last two sermons indicated that it was the intention to resume publication once peace had been restored. However, only twenty hitherto unpublished sermons were to appear in 1922 in a volume entitled Able to the uttermost.

It is the purpose of this volume to bring to light the sermons which probably would have appeared in the remainder of Volume 63 and at the start of Volume 64 of the Metropolitan Tabernacle Pulpit, sermons which originally appeared only in magazine format from 1877 to 1881.

Terence Peter Crosby holds a PhD in Classics (Greek and Latin) from London University and was for some time Secretary of the Evangelical Library,

London. He is the compiler of Day One's volumes of daily readings 365 Days with Spurgeon, My book of hobbies and God's Book, the Bible, and the author of Greek to the Rescue.

Charles Haddon Spurgeon (1834–92) was England's best-known preacher for most of the second half of the nineteenth century. In 1854, just four years after his conversion, Spurgeon, then only 19, became pastor of London's famed New Park Street Church. The congregation quickly outgrew their building, moved to Exeter Hall, then to the Royal Surrey Gardens Music Hall. In these venues Spurgeon frequently preached to audiences numbering more than 10,000—all in the days before electronic amplification. In 1861 the congregation moved permanently to the newly constructed Metropolitan Tabernacle. Spurgeon's printed works are voluminous.

TERENCE PETER CROSBY (EDITOR)

ISBN: 978–1–84625–202–0

Lovers of Spurgeon's preaching have always had a special affection for the sermons of his New Park Street years, with their youthful vibrancy and freshness, but, when compared with their more numerous Metropolitan Tabernacle successors, a far lower percentage of these actually reached publication. Of the sermons preached mostly on Sundays and Thursdays an average of roughly 105 per year are extant for the 30 years of his Metropolitan Tabernacle ministry, but an average of only about 70 per year for his 7 New Park Street years. The purpose of this volume is to reintroduce some 28 of these early gems which appeared only in The Sword and the Trowel, all but one after his death.

This volume contains 28 of his early sermons ... Some of these items contain sermon notes rather than a fuller transcript of the messages, but the essence of his themes is clear. His topics inclue ones that are so often under challenge today: for example,the seriousness of sin (sermon 19). His style is down to earth and practical. Occasionally the language has a dated feel, but the majority of what he proclaimed could be uttered with profit in the pulpit today. This book is attractively laid out by its editor and reasonably priced by the publisher. It is recommended.'
Evangelicals Now, June 2011, Brian Talbot, pastor of Broughty Ferry Baptist Church, Dundee

TERENCE PETER CROSBY (EDITOR)

ISBN: 978-1-84625-238-9

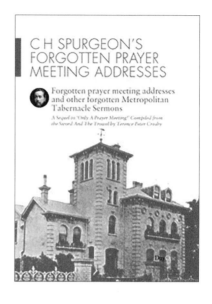

C H SPURGEON'S FORGOTTEN PRAYER MEETING ADDRESSES

Forgotten prayer meeting addresses and other forgotten Metropolitan Tabernacle Sermons

A Sequel to 'Only A Prayer Meeting' Compiled from the Sword And The Trowel by Terence Peter Crosby

Spurgeon's magazine, The Sword and the Trowel, provided the material for various collections of his addresses and writings compiled after his death in 1892. Among these was Only a Prayer Meeting, published in 1901 and containing forty prayer meeting addresses which appeared in the magazine up to and including that year. One other brief prayer meeting address from the 1901 volume ('Unequally yoked together' – 2 Corinthians 6:14-15) was included by Eric Hayden in his compilation C. H. Spurgeon's Sermons preached on Unusual Occasions. A further twenty two such addresses appeared in The Sword and the Trowel between 1904 and 1911, seventeen of these carrying dates for specific Monday evenings from 1866 to 1868. These are reproduced in the first part of this volume, which may be regarded as a sequel to Only a Prayer Meeting, together with several other forgotten sermons to be found in The Sword and the Trowel either on prayer or from roughly the same period of Spurgeon's ministry. May God's people be encouraged to regard individual prayer and the church prayer meeting as priorities in the Christian life.

Being of a firm conviction that the Prayer Meeting of the church is of immense importance to a believers walk with God, this volume had an immediate appeal. This book will not disappoint those who come with a heart that says, Lord, speak to me and help me to pray. There are 37 addresses. The topics are very wide in scope. They range from the subject of prayer to that of 'Are you saved?' Each message is pointed and instructive. Here is a book which will encourage, stir and strengthen faith. I hope it will give a flavour of what a prayer meeting address ought to be. How helpful this would be to ministers of God's word. The publishers desire that this book encourage God's people 'regard prayer and the church prayer meeting as priorities in the Christian life'—they have certainly helped to that end in publishing this volume.

Rev. David W Smith, Ardaragh Free Presbyterian Church of Ulster

TERENCE PETER CROSBY (EDITOR)

HARDBACK

VOLUME 1: 978–0–902548–84–8, 384PP

VOLUME 2: 978–1–903087–08–4, 384PP

VOLUME 3: 978–1–84625–006–4, 384PP

VOLUME 4: 978–1–84625–090–3, 448PP

VOLUME 5: 978–1–84625–230–3, 416PP

A unique collection of 365 daily readings from sermons preached by Charles Haddon Spurgeon from his New Park Street Pulpit

These excellent books will help if you are looking for something more challenging in your daily readings. From the archive of Charles Haddon Spurgeon's Park Street sermons and Metropolitan Tabernacle sermons we have true pearls of Biblical wisdom. What is particularly striking when reading these extracts is how appropriate they are to the ears of the modern Christian in need of genuine spiritual insight.

In this C H Spurgeon compilation, Charles Haddon Spurgeon—the 'Prince of Preachers'—needs little introduction! Terence Peter Crosby holds a PhD in Classics (Greek and Latin) from London University. He lives in south London with his wife, Daphne.

I recommend this without hesitation.
English Churchman

365 days with Calvin

JOEL R BEEKE

416PP, HARDBACK

ISBN 978–1–84625–114–6

A unique collection of 365 readings from the writings of John Calvin, selected and edited by Joel R. Beeke.

John Calvin exercised a profound ministry in Europe, and is probably one of the most seminal thinkers ever to have lived. A godly pastor, theologian and preacher, he led his flock by example and worked hard to establish consistent godliness in his city. A prolific writer, his sermons, letters, and, of course, his 'Christian Institutes' have been published again and again. His writings—once described as 'flowing prose'—are characterized by clarity, simplicity, and yet profoundness, too. In these heart-warming pieces, drawn from his commentaries and sermons, Calvin brings us to Christ, the glorious Savior of all his people.

Dr Joel R. Beeke is president and professor of systematic theology and homiletics at Puritan Reformed Theological Seminary, and a pastor of the Heritage Netherlands Reformed Congregation in Grand Rapids, Michigan.

Daily devotionals—spiritual aids to help us be accountable for a life of disciplined reading of Scripture and prayer—have been around for centuries and need a certain caliber of excellence and insight if they are to prove of lasting value through 365 days! Of those I'd like to spend a year with as my spiritual guide and mentor, John Calvin is most certainly one of them. Joel Beeke guides us through the Reformer's writings to help us discover the help and insight that every Christian needs to live a God-honoring life for Jesus Christ.

—Derek W. H. Thomas, John E. Richards Professor of Theology, Reformed Theological Seminary, Minister of Teaching, First Presbyterian Church, Jackson, MS, Editorial Director, Alliance of Confessing Evangelicals

365 Days with Newton

MARYLYNN ROUSE

384PP, HARDBACK

ISBN 978–1–903087–92–3

John Newton was a rich and princely teacher, a sensitive and caring Pastor, and a straight, outspoken guide. His whole ministry bore the marks so evident in his lovely hymns: it was consistently biblical (to share the Word of God), spiritual (to promote walking with God), simple (to make biblical truth and principles plain) and practical (to inculcate personal holiness and sound relationships in church and society). In this collection, every day bears these marks, so useful to every believer, so instructive for those called to minister.

Marylynn Rouse has for many years done extensive research into the life and work of John Newton. She is at present working on the publication of The Complete Works of John Newton through The John Newton Project, a charity of which she is executive researcher. She has published an annotated edition of the original biography of Newton and *The Searcher of Hearts*, Newton's sermon notes on Romans 8.

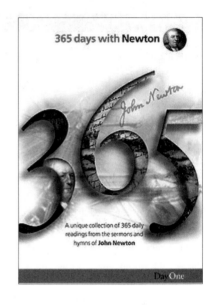

In Marylynn Rouse, Newton has found a true disciple and a skilled publicist. By enormous diligence, and self-sacrificing application, she has made herself a leading 'Newton expert', and in this sensitive compilation all that expertise is put at our disposal. Come, enjoy and profit!

From the Foreword, J Alec Motyer